T0016739

THE ROUGH GUIDE TO
USA: THE ROCKIES

This first edition was written by Stephen Keeling.

This book includes extractions from *The Rough Guide to the USA* written by Maria Edwards, Stephen Keeling, Todd Obolsky, Annelise Sorensen, Georgia Stephens and Greg Ward, updated and published in 2021 by Apa Publications Ltd. A big thank you to all the contributing authors of *The Rough Guide to the USA.*

ROUGH GUIDES

Contents

A NOTE TO READERS

At Rough Guides, we always strive to bring you the most up-to-date information. This book was produced during a period of continuing uncertainty caused by the Covid-19 pandemic, so please note that content is more subject to change than usual. We recommend checking the latest restrictions and official guidance.

Introduction to
USA: The Rockies

Few regions of the United States offer as many travel experiences as the Rocky Mountains. Sprawling across four states – Colorado, Montana, Idaho and Wyoming – and encompassing several booming cities, the Rockies present a remarkable panorama of sweeping, colourful vistas, towering peaks and ranches that stretch as far as the eye can see. Here are miles of trackless wilderness, a bounty of outdoor recreation and a surprisingly cosmopolitan urban scene. But though cities such as Denver, Colorado Springs and Boise are all intriguing destinations in their own right (relatively small towns and resorts like Telluride, Jackson, Sun Valley and Boulder also offer a surprising variety of shopping and dining), the Rockies is above all a region of stunningly diverse and achingly beautiful landscapes. Theodore Roosevelt called it "scenery that bankrupts the English language." In one region you have the mighty Bitterroot Mountains and spectacular Front Range, the otherworldly landscapes of the Craters of the Moon, the endless, rolling grasslands of Wyoming and eastern Montana, the trails of the Idaho Panhandle, isolated mountain springs and the old cowboy towns of Colorado. You can soak up the mesmerizing vistas in Yellowstone and Grand Teton national parks, stand in awe at the top of Pike's Peak, hike the Sawtooth Range, cruise Flathead Lake, paddle in the Missouri, and drive over 12,000ft passes on the Trail Ridge Road. Or you could easily plan a trip that focuses on the out-of-the-way hamlets, remote prairies, eerie ghost towns and forgotten byways that are every bit as iconic as the showpiece parks and monuments.

The Rockies also boast some of the best snow and most challenging slopes in the world. Ski resorts like Aspen and Vail in Colorado, Sun Valley in Idaho and Jackson in Wyoming are well-known for attracting a high-powered mix of Hollywood stars, corporate bigwigs and entrepreneurs.

GRIZZLY BEAR, YELLOWSTONE NATIONAL PARK

Today you'll find the Rockies as compelling as when Lewis and Clark first came this way early in the 19th century on their famous expedition to unlock the American West. Following them were the fabled mountain men, fur traders, prospectors in search of gold and silver, cattle barons and land barons, cowboys and ranchers, copper kings, prophets and visionaries of one sort or another. History buffs can still visit legendary sites like the Little Bighorn Battlefield, where George Armstrong Custer and the Seventh Cavalry made their famous "last stand" against the Sioux and Cheyenne; Fort Bridger in Wyoming, where thousands of pioneers bought supplies for their journey on the Oregon Trail; or Leadville in Colorado, where local miners saw Oscar Wilde perform at Tabor Opera House and sipped drinks at the Silver Dollar Saloon.

There are also the thrills of rodeo, ballooning over snowcapped mountains, and of whitewater rafting down a frothing river, not to mention abundant opportunities for trout fishing, sailing, camping and backpacking. You can ride mountain bikes over rocky passes, ski, hike, go rock climbing and kayaking. More relaxed activities include ice fishing, birdwatching, horseback riding, snowmobiling and golf – the point is to get outdoors, to enjoy the wilderness, the scenery, the crisp air and the blue skies. Indeed, the air really is fresher here, the water clearer, the sky bigger than just about any place else, at least in the USA. And while there is no such thing as a typical Rockies experience, there can be few places where strangers can feel so confident of a warm reception.

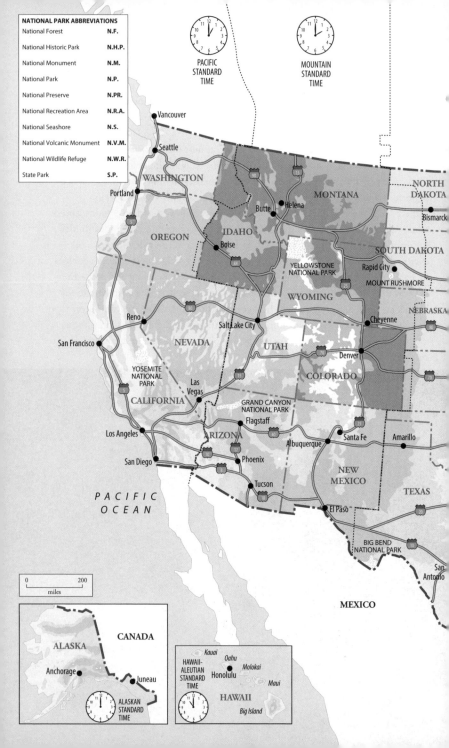

Where to go

You don't have to traverse the entire Rockies from north to south in order to appreciate its charms; it would take a long time to see the whole region, and you'll want to savour the small-town pleasures and backroad oddities that may well provide your strongest memories. You'll definitely need a car – that mandatory component of life in the USA.

The obvious place to start for most people is Denver, Colorado – the region's international gateway with a rich cultural scene, excellent museums, top restaurants and stellar microbreweries. From here the Front Range marks the eastern edge of the Rocky Mountains, running north to the inviting college town of Boulder, and south to Colorado Springs, where you can hike, ride the train or drive up one of America's most famous mountains, Pike's Peak. Heading west, I-70 cuts deep into the Rockies, passing the ski resorts, snow-smothered peaks, and crystal lakes of Summit County on route to Vail and Aspen, two of the most famous ski resorts in America. To the north lies Rocky Mountain National Park, where the Trail Ridge Road is one of the highest highways in the nation, cresting at 12,183ft. South of I-70, Leadville provides some historic allure, with its beautifully preserved Victorian architecture and old gold and silver mines. The lesser-visited Black Canyon of the Gunnison National Park is centered on an awe-inspiring one-mile deep chasm, while the pretty Victorian mining town of Crested Butte has re-invented itself as a skiing and mountain biking paradise. Further south, the steam trains of the Durango and Silverton Narrow Gauge Railroad make spectacular runs through the mountains.

Towards the western end of Colorado, the hot springs at Glenwood Springs and the bike trails of Grand Junction mark the transition to high desert with the Colorado National Monument, a mass of multi-colored rock spires, domes, arches and cliffs. Further south, the landscapes start to resemble the deserts of the American Southwest; the vast Great Sand Dunes National Park, and the mind-bending Ancestral Puebloan ruins at Mesa Verde National Park.

When it comes to Wyoming, all roads lead to Yellowstone National Park and Grand Teton National Park. Yellowstone is a tourism colossus, attracting millions of visitors annually, for good reason; its geysers, mud pools, pristine lakes, canyons, waterfalls and array of wildlife – seemingly oblivious to the crowds – is second to none. Accessed from the likeable Western (and ski resort) town of Jackson, the Grand Tetons are simply gasp-inducing, snow-capped pinnacles that seem to puncture the sky. But there's a lot more to Wyoming – and most of it sees a fraction of the Yellowstone/Teton tourist traffic. You can explore the state's well-warranted reputation as dinosaur graveyard at the Wyoming Dinosaur Center in Thermopolis, experience cowboy culture at Cheyenne Frontier Days and follow the Oregon Trail at Fort Laramie, Independence Rock and the Mormon Handcart Historic Site. A series of beautiful scenic byways traverse the Bighorn Mountains, home of the enigmatic Medicine Wheel, a site sacred to Native Americans. To the east of the Bighorns lies the remarkable Devils Tower National Monument. To the west there's Cody, forever linked to Old West showman Buffalo Bill. The Buffalo Bill Center of the West here comprises five absorbing museums.

SACAGAWEA

Of the many characters in the chronicles of the American West, few are as inspirational as Sacagawea (or Sacajawea), the young Shoshone woman who served as guide and interpreter for the Lewis and Clark expedition of 1804–6. Sacagawea was kidnapped by the Hidatsa tribe as a girl and later sold as a wife to French-Canadian fur trapper Toussaint Charbonneau. The couple encountered Lewis and Clark's Corps of Discovery at Fort Mandan in what is now North Dakota in the winter of 1804. Charbonneau was hired as a guide and interpreter, but it was his pregnant, 16-year-old wife who proved the most helpful. In February, Sacagawea gave birth to a son, Jean Baptiste, known to the other members of the party as "Little Pomp". She carried the child in a cradleboard on her back during the entire 3,000-mile adventure.

Sacagawea's ability to find food in the wilderness and make peace with suspicious Native Americans was vital to the group's survival, and her courage and even-tempered nature made her one of the most reliable and well-liked people on the expedition. She was particularly helpful when the party reached her native tribe, the Shoshone, in Montana. After a reunion with her brother, Chief Cameahwait, she helped procure 21 horses and two guides for the arduous trek over the Bitterroot Mountains. The expedition reached the Pacific in November of 1805, and Sacagawea and Charbonneau returned to Fort Mandan the following year.

Frustratingly little is known about her later life. In 1809 she travelled to St Louis, where William Clark educated and raised Little Pomp. Some accounts have Sacagawea dying as a young woman in Dakota Territory in 1812. Other reports say that she lived with the Comanche tribe, before finally settling with the Shoshone in Wyoming. A woman later identified as Sacagawea died on the Wind River Reservation in 1884 at nearly 100 years of age. She is buried in Fort Washakie (see page 78), where "she sleeps with her face towards the sunny side of the Rocky Mountains." Near her grave is a monument to Jean Baptiste who, after travelling in Europe, came back to the Rockies to work as a mountain man, dying in 1866.

The Big Sky Country of Montana is truly vast and again, sees surprisingly few tourists given the amount of natural beauty on offer. The must-see attraction is Glacier National Park in the state's northwest corner, which is a truly astounding blend of alpine lakes, snowy peaks and (fast retreating) glaciers. Not far away is Flathead Lake and Wild Horse Island State Park, and the charms of outdoorsy Whitefish. The rest of the state is laced with deep valleys, mountain ranges and rivers such as the Missouri, which provides another scenic wonder at the Gates of the Mountains. The Beartooth Scenic Highway makes a sensational run towards Yellowstone through rugged terrain, while the region around Missoula is rich in ski slopes, hiking paths and biking trails.

There's plenty of history here, too. The Little Bighorn Battlefield National Monument preserves the site of the legendary battle between Custer and Crazy Horse, remarkably unchanged from 1876, while Pompeys Pillar National Monument is home to the only physical evidence of the Corps of Discovery's 1804–06 expedition – the signature carved in rock of William Clark himself. The old Western town of Butte is rich in mining history but also the Victorian grand architecture of the "Copper Kings", Bozeman is home to the huge Museum of the Rockies, and the state's laid-back capital, Helena, features the enlightening Montana's Museum. Garnet Ghost Town is one of many atmospheric, once booming mining towns in the Rockies.

Finally, Idaho serves up some of the most spectacular scenery of all, best experienced on one of many scenic byways that crisscross the state. The Sawtooth Scenic Byway is one of the best, taking in serene Red Fish Lake, along with the Salmon River Scenic Byway, which cuts through wooded gorges and past old ghosts towns. You can go jet-boating in Hells Canyon, raft down the Salmon River, ski or mountain bike at Sun Valley Resort, go boating on Lake Coeur d'Alene and explore old cowboy towns like Wallace in the Idaho Panhandle. To the south, the Craters of the Moon National Monument is one of the weirdest sights in the region, fields of volcanic lava, frozen in time. The state capital, Boise, is also worth a look, a surprisingly urbane cultural centre, sporting Basque restaurants and a Shakespeare Festival.

When to go

The continental US is subject to dramatically shifting weather patterns, most notably produced by westerly winds sweeping across the continent from the Pacific. In the Rockies, between early June and early September you can expect temperatures in the high sixties all the way up to a hundred degrees Fahrenheit (20–37° Celsius), depending on whether you are in the high desert of Wyoming, the plains of Idaho or the mountains of Colorado.

Be prepared for wild variations in the mountains – and, of course, the higher you go the colder it gets, especially at night. The altitude is high enough to warrant a period of acclimatization, while the sun at these elevations can be uncomfortably fierce. In fact, parts of Wyoming and Colorado bask in more hours of sunshine per year than San Diego or Miami Beach.

Spring, when the snow melts, is the least attractive time to visit, and while the delicate golds and reds of aspen trees light up the mountainsides in early autumn, by October things are generally a bit cold for enjoyable hiking or sports. Most ski runs are open by late November and operate well into March – or even June, depending on snow conditions. The coldest month is January, when temperatures below 0°F (-17° Celsius) are common.

For visitors, one of the biggest factors to take into consideration when planning a Rockies trip is access to national parks – arguably the region's biggest attraction.

JENNY LAKE, GRAND TETON NATIONAL PARK, WY

AVERAGE TEMPERATURE (°F) AND RAINFALL

To convert °F to °C, subtract 32 and multiply by 5/9

	Jan	Feb	Mar	Apr	May	Jun	Jul	Aug	Sep	Oct	Nov	Dec
ASPEN, CO												
Max/min temp	36/9	39/12	46/20	53/27	63/35	73/42	78/48	76/47	69/40	58/30	44/19	35/10
Days of rain	8	9	10	10	8	4	8	8	7	7	8	8
BILLINGS, MT												
Max/min temp	39/14	43/18	53/25	62/34	71/43	81/51	89/56	88/54	78/45	64/35	49/24	39/16
Days of rain	3	3	3	6	7	6	3	3	4	4	3	3
BOISE, ID												
Max/min temp	39/22	46/27	56/32	65/37	74/44	84/51	93/58	92/57	68/39	82/72	51/30	40/23
Days of rain	8	8	9	7	6	4	1	1	2	6	5	9
DENVER, CO												
Max/min temp	49/20	49/21	58/29	65/35	73/45	86/55	92/61	90/59	82/50	68/37	57/27	47/19
Days of rain	2	3	3	6	6	5	5	5	3	3	3	4
GLACIER NP												
Max/min temp	30/11	33/13	39/18	48/25	58/33	66/39	75/44	75/42	64/36	51/29	37/21	29/12
Days of rain	9	7	9	8	7	8	5	4	6	6	8	8
JACKSON, WY												
Max/min temp	28/5	33/9	42/18	52/25	63/31	73/37	82/41	80/39	71/32	57/24	40/17	28/7
Days of rain	8	6	5	6	7	6	5	5	5	5	6	8
YELLOWSTONE NP												
Max/min temp	28/3	31/4	39/10	46/19	53/28	63/34	73/39	71/37	62/31	48/24	34/13	26/4
Days of rain	13	11	14	13	12	10	5	6	7	10	12	13

Unless you've come to ski (or snowmobile), most parks remain inaccessible to cars for large parts of year (typically Oct–April) because of heavy snowfall. All of Yellowstone's roads (apart from the Mammoth Springs entrance) start closing in October, and start opening again only on the third Friday in April – but don't expect everything to be open until the end of May.

Note that the Great Plains just to the east of the Rockies experience dramatically different weather conditions. Alternately exposed to seasonal icy Arctic winds and humid tropical airflows from the Gulf of Mexico, winters can be abjectly cold, and it can freeze or even snow in winter as far south as Texas (spring and fall get progressively longer and milder further south through the Plains, though). Unfortunately, Tornadoes (or "twisters") are a frequent local phenomenon, tending to cut a narrow swath of destruction in the wake of violent spring or summer thunderstorms. Eastern Montana is affected by tornadoes, however they are, for the most part, generally small and infrequent. Colorado typically sees a lot more tornadoes every year, but you'll mostly find them predominantly in the eastern plains region. Tornadoes in Idaho and Wyoming are very rare.

Author picks

Our hard-travelling authors have visited every corner of this vast, magnificent region and have picked out their personal highlights.

Most scenic highways Montana's Beartooth Highway blazes a mesmerizing path across the snow-tipped Beartooth Mountains (see page 94), while the Sawtooth Scenic Byway takes in the best of Idaho's peak-studded wilderness and churning Salmon River (see page 108). Going-to-the-Sun Road (see page 104) is an astonishing route through Glacier National Park.

Best microbreweries Since the 1990s, America has been experiencing a craft beer revolution, led by the likes of Great Divide Brewing Co and Wynkoop Brewing Co (see page 55) in Denver; and Breckenridge Brewery in the heart of Colorado (see page 62). Wyoming gets in on the action at Freedom's Edge Brewing (see page 76), while Überbrew in Montana (see page 94) and Wallace Brewing in Idaho (see page 113) are also worth seeking out.

Classic diners Few American icons are so beloved as the roadside diner, where burgers, apple pie and strong coffee are often served 24/7. The 1950s-style *Little Diner* in Vail is a buzzing spot with great daily specials (see page 68). Cheyenne's *Luxury Diner* is a 1920s converted railroad dining car (see page 76). *Red Box Car* in Red Lodge, MT, is a real classic, set inside a 100-year old railroad boxcar (see page 95), while *Red Light Garage* in Wallace, ID (see page 113) is a proper Old West throwback.

Top wildlife spots The Rockies are rich in wildlife, with national parks such as Yellowstone (see page 81) and Grand Teton (see page 86) especially good at preserving herds of elk and deer, moose and giant grizzlies, while reserves such as the National Bison Range in Montana (see page 102) protect herds of buffalo. Visit the the National Elk Refuge in Jackson, WY, in winter for a 11,000-strong herd of elk (see page 90). Pelicans, bald eagles, and occasionally mountain lions can be spotted off boats cruising the Gates of the Mountains (see page 100).

Our author recommendations don't end here. We've flagged up our favourite places – a perfectly sited hotel, an atmospheric café, a special restaurant – throughout the Guide, highlighted with the ★ symbol.

GOING-TO-THE-SUN ROAD, GLACIER NATIONAL PARK, MT

BULL MOOSE

15

things not to miss

It's obviously not possible to see everything that the Rockies has to offer in one trip. What follows is a selective and subjective taste of the region's highlights: unforgettable cities, spectacular drives, magnificent parks, spirited celebrations and stunning natural phenomena. All highlights have a page reference to take you straight into the Guide where you can find out more.

1

1 GRAND TETON NATIONAL PARK
See page 86
This spectacular chain of mountains is prime territory for hiking, biking and wildlife viewing.

2 GLACIER NATIONAL PARK, MT
See page 103
Montana's most spectacular park holds not only 25 glaciers, but also two thousand lakes, a thousand miles of rivers and the exhilarating Going-to-the-Sun highway.

3 DURANGO & SILVERTON NARROW GAUGE RAILROAD, CO
See page 73
This steam-train ride corkscrews through spectacular mountains to the mining town of Silverton.

4 MESA VERDE NATIONAL PARK, CO
See page 74
Explore the extraordinary cliffside dwellings, abandoned by the Ancestral Puebloans eight hundred years ago.

5 LITTLE BIGHORN, MT
See page 92
One of the most famous battlefields in America looks much as it did in 1876, when Custer faced off against Sitting Bull and Crazy Horse.

6 SAWTOOTH MOUNTAINS, ID
See page 108
Of all Idaho's 81 mountain ranges, the Sawtooth summits make for the most awe-inspiring scenic drive.

7 SKIING IN THE ROCKY MOUNTAINS
See pages 60, 62 and 64
The Rockies are ideal for skiing, with their glitzy resorts and atmospheric mining towns.

8 DENVER, CO
See pages 50 and 54
The de facto capital of the Rockies is crammed with world-class museums, restaurants and craft breweries.

9 YELLOWSTONE NATIONAL PARK, WY
See page 81
The national park that started it all has it all, from steaming fluorescent hot springs and spouting geysers to sheer canyons and meadows filled with wild flowers and assorted beasts.

10 PIKES PEAK, CO
See page 57
Hike, drive or take a train ride to the towering summit of Colorado's most famous mountain for mesmerizing views.

11 ROCKY MOUNTAIN NATIONAL PARK, CO

See page 59
Drive the Trail Ridge Road, across this pristine national park, home to elk, black bears and bighorn sheep.

12 BLACK CANYON OF THE GUNNISON, CO

See page 70
At the centrepiece of this national park lies an awe-inspiring gorge with rim roads and scenic trails.

13 BUFFALO BILL CENTER OF THE WEST, WY

See page 81
Home to five museums, covering Native American culture, the life of Buffalo Bill and more.

14 BUTTE, MT

See page 96
Fascinating Butte is crammed with remnants of its once flourishing copper industry.

15 CRATERS OF THE MOON, ID

See page 106
This volcanic landscape of craters and caverns really does look like an alien world.

Itineraries

The following itineraries span the entire length of this incredibly diverse region, from the oldest towns in the West to the greatest mountain ranges and the jaw-dropping Glacier National Park. Given the vast distances involved, you may not be able to cover everything, but even picking a few highlights will give you a deeper insight into the Rockies' natural and historic wonders.

CLASSIC ROCKIES

This three-week tour gives a taster of the Rockies' iconic landscapes and cities from the south to the north, travelling from Denver to the Idaho Panhandle.

❶ Denver, CO The Rockies' biggest city is home to Coors Field, the Denver Art Museum, the Clyfford Still Museum, the Molly Brown House, the Black American West Museum and a vast spread of microbreweries. See page 50

❷ Rocky Mountain National Park, CO Colorado's premier national park will provide your first sensational taster of the Rocky Mountains; snowy peaks and high passes, herds of elk and alpine lakes. See page 59

❸ Jackson, WY Cut through the grasslands of Wyoming to Jackson, the likeable Old West town that acts as a gateway to the Grand Tetons. See page 90

❹ Yellowstone National Park, WY Head north into America's most famous national park, home to Old Faithful and the Yellowstone Canyon, and crawling with wildlife. See page 81

❺ Bozeman, MT Travelling north into Montana along the Gallatin Valley you reach Bozeman, where the Museum of the Rockies provides a comprehensive overview of the region's natural history. See page 95

❻ Butte, MT As you continue west on I-90 across Montana, stop to explore the fascinating mining town of Butte, peppered with grand Victorian remnants of the nineteenth-century copper boom. See page 96

❼ Missoula, MT I-90 eventually reaches Missoula, the artsy capital of western Montana. Visit the Smokejumper Center to learn about the legendary forest firefighters. See page 100

❽ Glacier National Park, MT Around two-and-a-half hours' drive north of Missoula lies this phenomenal national park, containing 25 glaciers. See page 103

❾ Idaho Panhandle Drive across the Montana border into the Idaho Panhandle, where the atmospheric Old West town of Wallace, Lake Coeur d'Alene and Route of the Hiawatha Bike Trail await. See page 112

Create your own itinerary with Rough Guides. Whether you're after adventure or a family-friendly holiday, we have a trip for you, with all the activities you enjoy doing and the sights you want to see. All our trips are devised by local experts who get the most out of the destination. Visit **www.roughguides.com/trips** to chat with one of our travel agents.

THE NATIONAL PARKS LOOP

Only when you explore the national parks will you begin to grasp just how big – and rich in natural beauty – this region is. Come in summer to enjoy the sunshine and take three to four weeks to complete this trip.

❶ Colorado National Monument, CO
Around five hours west from Denver, you won't forget your first tantalizing glimpse of this rugged park of reddish sandstone spires, canyons and soaring cliffs. See page 69

❷ Craters of the Moon, ID Break the long journey up to Glacier with a stop at Idaho's Craters of the Moon, a stark landscape of lava fields and sagebrush steppe grasslands. See page 106

❸ Glacier, MT Soak up some of the most awe-inspiring scenery in America – snowy peaks, waterfalls, alpine lakes, and glaciers – on Going-to-the-Sun Road. See page 104

❹ Gates of the Mountains, MT It's not a national park, but a boat trip along the Missouri's stunning Gates of the Mountains is just as spectacular, and makes a worthy break on the long drive to Yellowstone. See page 100

❺ Yellowstone National Park, WY Yellowstone is the granddaddy of the national parks, crammed with wildlife, bubbling geysers, lakes and wild, wonderful scenery. See page 81

❻ Grand Teton National Park, WY
Yellowstone merges into Grand Teton to the south, with the jaw-dropping, jagged Teton ridge backing a series of picture-perfect lakes. See page 86

❼ Rocky Mountain National Park, CO
Break another long journey back to Denver with a visit to Colorado's high-altitude mountain wilderness, driving up to 12,000ft on Trail Ridge Road. See page 59

THE OLD WEST AND THE OREGON TRAIL

Explore the lesser travelled Old Western towns and landmarks in Wyoming whilst tracing the great nineteenth wagon trails across the grasslands.

❶ Cheyenne The capital of Wyoming, just over an hour-and-a-half north of Denver, hosts one of the biggest Western festivals, the Cheyenne Frontier Days. See page 75

❷ Fort Laramie National Historic Site Head north to Fort Laramie, an important fur trading post, military fort and stop on the Oregon, California and Mormon emigration trails. See page 77

❸ Casper Further northwest the trail passes through Casper, where the excellent National Historic Trails Interpretive Center provides an enlightening overview of trail history. See page 78

❹ Independence Rock In the heart of Wyoming, Independence Rock State Historic Site is covered in early pioneer graffiti. See page 92

❺ Mormon Handcart Historic Site This revered Mormon site commemorates the Mormon handcart pioneers and includes the Devil's Gate, an important trail landmark. See page 96

❻ Wind River Reservation Detour northwest into this Eastern Shoshone and Northern Arapaho reservation, the resting place of Sacagawea, the Shoshone guide of Lewis and Clark. See page 103

❼ Boise, ID The Oregon Trail cut through Idaho along the Snake River to Boise, where the Idaho State Museum and Old Idaho Penitentiary give a flavor of the pioneer days. See page 112

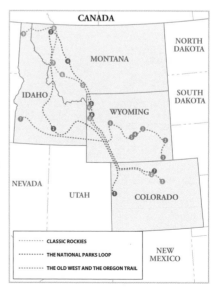

ENJOYING THE SLOPES

Basics

Getting there

Anyone travelling to the Rockies from abroad should start by deciding which area to explore first; the region is so vast that it makes a huge difference which airport you fly into. Once you've chosen whether to hit the peaks of Colorado, the wild ranges of Idaho, the national parks of Wyoming or the great plains and prairies of Montana, you can then buy a flight to the nearest hub city.

In general, ticket prices are highest from July to September, and around Easter, Thanksgiving and Christmas. Fares drop during the shoulder seasons – April to June, and October – and even more so in low season, from November to March (excluding Easter, Christmas and New Year). Prices depend more on when Americans want to head overseas than on the demand from foreign visitors. Flying at weekends usually costs significantly more.

Flights from the UK and Ireland

More than twenty US cities are accessible by nonstop flights from the UK, including the major Rockies hub of Denver. At these gateway cities, you can connect with onward domestic flights to smaller Rockies airports: Aspen/Pitkin County Airport, Colorado Springs Airport, Jackson Hole Airport, Yellowstone Airport-WYS, Missoula Montana Airport, Boise Airport and many others. Direct services (which may land once or twice on the way, but are called direct if they keep the same flight number throughout their journey) fly from Britain to nearly every other major US city.

Nonstop flights to Denver from London take around ten hours; the London to Chicago flight takes eight hours and 40 minutes; and flying time to New York is seven or so hours. Following winds ensure that return flights take an hour or two less. One-stop direct flights to destinations beyond the East Coast add time to the journey but can work out cheaper than nonstop flights.

Four airlines run nonstop scheduled services to the USA from Ireland. Flights depart from both Dublin and Shannon airports, and the journey times are very similar to those from London.

As for fares, Britain remains one of the best places in Europe to obtain flight bargains, though prices vary widely – high-season rates can more than double. These days the fares available on the airlines' own websites are often just as good as those you'll find on more general travel websites.

With an open-jaw ticket, you can fly into one city and out of another, though if you're renting a car remember that there's usually a high drop-off fee for returning a rental car in a different state than where you picked it up. An air pass can be a good idea if you want to see a lot of the country. These are available only to non-US residents, and must be bought before reaching the USA (see page 27).

Flights from Australia, New Zealand and South Africa

For passengers travelling from Australasia to the USA (when travel between the two regions has resumed in 2022), the most expensive time to fly has traditionally been during the northern summer (mid-May to end Aug) and over the Christmas period (Dec to mid-Jan), with shoulder seasons covering March to mid-May and September, and the rest of the year counting as low season. Fares no longer vary as much across the year as they used to, however.

Regular Air New Zealand, Qantas and United offer flights from eastern Australian cities to Los Angeles, the main US gateway airport. Flying from Western Australia can add around a little more to your ticket, while throughout the year, flying all the way through to Denver tends to cost a bit extra.

From New Zealand, the cheapest flights run from Auckland or Christchurch to LA or San Francisco, with onward connections to Denver or other Rockies destinations.

From South Africa (again, when travel restrictions are lifted), transatlantic flights from Cape Town or Johannesburg are not as expensive as they used to be

---

A BETTER KIND OF TRAVEL

At Rough Guides we are passionately committed to travel. We believe it helps us understand the world we live in and the people we share it with – and of course tourism is vital to many developing economies. But the scale of modern tourism has also damaged some places irreparably, and climate change is accelerated by most forms of transport, especially flying. We encourage all our authors to consider the carbon footprint of the journeys they make in the course of researching our guides.

PACKAGES AND TOURS

Although independent travel is usually cheaper, countless flight and accommodation packages allow you to bypass all the organizational hassles. A typical package from the UK might be a return flight plus mid-range hotel accommodation for three nights in Aspen/Yellowstone/Grand Teton.

Fly-drive deals, which give cut-rate car rental when a traveller buys a transatlantic ticket from an airline or tour operator, are always cheaper than renting on the spot, and give great value if you intend to do a lot of driving. They're readily available through general online booking agents such as Expedia and Travelocity, as well as through specific airlines. Several of the operators listed here also book accommodation for self-drive tours.

to New York or other East Coast cities and a bit more to Denver, depending on the time of year.

Various add-on fares and air passes valid in the continental US are available with your main ticket, allowing you to fly to destinations across the Rockies. These must be bought before you go.

AIRLINES

Aer Lingus Ⓦ aerlingus.com
Air Canada Ⓦ aircanada.com
Air India Ⓦ airindia.com
Air New Zealand Ⓦ airnewzealand.com
Alaska Airlines Ⓦ alaskaair.com
American Airlines Ⓦ aa.com
British Airways Ⓦ ba.com
Delta Air Lines Ⓦ delta.com
Emirates Ⓦ emirates.com
Frontier Airlines Ⓦ flyfrontier.com
Hawaiian Airlines Ⓦ hawaiianair.com
JAL (Japan Airlines) Ⓦ jal.com
JetBlue Ⓦ jetblue.com
KLM Ⓦ klm.com
Qantas Airways Ⓦ qantas.com.au
Singapore Airlines Ⓦ singaporeair.com
South African Airways Ⓦ flysaa.com
Southwest Ⓦ southwest.com
United Airlines Ⓦ united.com
Virgin Atlantic Ⓦ virgin-atlantic.com
WestJet Ⓦ westjet.com

AGENTS AND OPERATORS

Adventure World Australia Ⓦ adventureworld.com.au, New Zealand Ⓦ adventureworld.co.nz
American Holidays Ireland Ⓦ americanholidays.com
Wotif? Australia Ⓦ wotif.com

Getting around

Distances in the Rockies are so great that it's essential to plan in advance how you'll get from place to place. There are now a number of ways to get around and each method has different benefits. Amtrak provides a skeletal but often scenic rail service, and there are usually good bus links between the major cities. Even in rural areas, with advance planning, you can usually reach the main points of interest without too much trouble by using local buses and charter services.

That said, travel between cities is almost always easier if you have a car. Many worthwhile and memorable destinations in the Rockies are far from the cities: even if a bus or train can take you to the general vicinity of one of the great national parks, for example, it would be of little use when it comes to enjoying the great outdoors.

By rail

Travelling on the national Amtrak network (☎ 800 872 7245, Ⓦ amtrak.com) is rarely the fastest way to get around, though if you have the time it can be a pleasant and relaxing experience. The Amtrak system isn't comprehensive in the Rockies – there are two main routes: the California Zephyr from Chicago to Denver which cuts across central Colorado; and the Empire Builder from Chicago across the north of Montana to Glacier National Park and the Idaho Panhandle. What's more, these cross-country routes tend to be served by one or at most two trains per day, so in large areas of the region the only train of the day passes through at three or four in the morning. Amtrak also runs the coordinated, but still limited, Thruway bus service that connects some cities that their trains don't reach.

For any one specific journey, the train is usually more expensive than taking a Greyhound bus, or even a plane, though you can get better rates by booking online at least a month in advance – special deals, especially in the off-peak seasons (Sept–May,

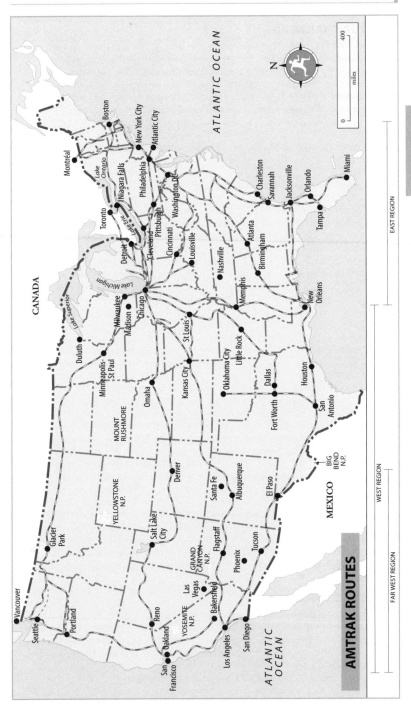

AMTRAK ROUTES

HISTORIC RAILROADS

While Amtrak has a monopoly on long-distance rail travel, a number of historic or scenic railways, some steam-powered or running along narrow-gauge mining tracks, bring back the glory days of train travel. Many are purely tourist attractions, doing a full circuit through beautiful countryside in two or three hours, though some can drop you off in otherwise hard-to-reach wilderness areas. Fares vary widely according to the length of your trip. We've covered the most appealing options in the relevant Guide chapters.

excluding Christmas), can bring the cost of a return trip down further. Money-saving passes are also available (see page 27).

Even with a pass, you should always reserve as far in advance as possible; all passengers must have seats, and some trains are booked solid. Sleeping compartment rates include three full meals. However, even standard Amtrak quarters are surprisingly spacious compared to aeroplane seats, and there are additional dining cars and lounge cars (with full bars and sometimes glass-domed 360° viewing compartments).

By bus

If you're travelling on your own and plan on making a lot of stops, buses are by far the cheapest way to get around. The main long-distance operator, Greyhound (☏ 800 231 2222, ⊕ greyhound.com, international customers without toll-free access can also call ☏ 214 849 8100 open 24/7), links all major cities and many towns. Out in the country, buses are fairly scarce, sometimes appearing only once a day, if at all. However, along the main highways, buses run around the clock to a full timetable, stopping only for meal breaks (almost always fast-food chains) and driver changeovers.

To avoid possible hassle, travellers should take care to sit as near to the driver as possible, and to arrive during daylight hours – many bus stations are in dodgy areas, at least in large cities. In many smaller places, the post office or a gas station doubles as the bus stop and ticket office. Reservations can be made in person at the station, online or on the toll-free number. Oddly they do not guarantee a seat, so it's

wise to join the queue early – if a bus is full, you may have to wait for the next one, although Greyhound claims it will lay on an extra bus if more than ten people are left behind. For long hauls there are plenty of savings available – check the website's discounts page.

Other operators include Trailways (☏ 877 908 9330, ⊕ trailways.com), whose regional divisions cover some parts of the country more comprehensively; Megabus (☏ 877 462 6342; ⊕ us.megabus.com), whose low-cost service covers the Northeast and Midwest; and the alternative Green Tortoise (see page 26).

By plane

Despite the presence of good-value discount airlines – most notably Southwest and JetBlue – air travel is a much less appealing way of getting around the country than it used to be. With air fuel costs escalating even faster than gas costs, and airlines cutting routes, demanding customers pay for routine services and jacking up prices across the board, the days of using jet travel as a spur to vacation adventuring are long gone. To get any kind of break on price, you'll have to reserve well ahead of time (at least three weeks), preferably not embark in the high season, and be firm enough in your plans to buy a "non-refundable" fare – which if changed can incur costs of $100 or more. Nonetheless, flying can still cost less than the train – though still more than the bus. In those examples where flying can make sense for short local hops, we mention such options wherever appropriate throughout this Guide. Otherwise, phone

GREEN TORTOISE

One alternative to long-distance bus torture is the fun, countercultural Green Tortoise, whose buses, complete with foam cushions, bunks, fridges and rock music, mostly ply the West and the Northwest of the country, but can go as far as New Orleans, Washington DC and New York. There are more than thirty seductive options, each allowing plenty of stops for hiking, river-rafting, bathing in hot springs and the like.

Green Tortoise's main office is in San Francisco (⊕ greentortoise.com).

PRE-TRIP PLANNING FOR OVERSEAS TRAVELLERS

AMTRAK PASSES

The USA Rail Pass (15-day/8 segments; 30-day/12 segments; 45-day/18 segments) covers the entire Amtrak network for the designated period, though you are restricted to a set number of individual journeys. The California Rail Pass buys you seven days' travel in a 21-day period within that state. Passes can be bought from the Amtrak website (ⓦamtrak.com).

AIR PASSES

The main American airlines offer air passes for visitors who plan to fly a lot within the USA. These must be bought in advance and are often sold with the proviso that you cross the Atlantic with the same airline or group of airlines (such as Star Alliance). Each deal will involve the purchase of a certain number of flights, air miles or coupons. Other plans entitle foreign travellers to discounts on regular US domestic fares, again with the proviso that you buy the ticket before you leave home. Check with the individual airlines to see what they offer and the overall range of prices.

the airlines or visit their websites to find out routes and schedules.

By car

For many, the concept of cruising down the highway, preferably in a convertible with the radio blasting, is one of the main reasons to set out on a tour of the Rockies. The romantic images of countless road movies are not far from the truth, though you don't have to embark on a wild spree of drinking, drugs and sex to enjoy driving across America. Apart from anything else, a car makes it possible to choose your own itinerary and to explore the astonishing wide-open landscapes that may well provide your most enduring memories of the country.

Driving in the cities, on the other hand, is not exactly fun, and can be hair-raising. Yet in larger places a car is by far the most convenient way to make your way around, especially as public transport tends to be spotty outside the major cities. Many urban areas, especially in the West, have grown up since cars were invented. As such, they sprawl for so many miles in all directions that your hotel may be fifteen or twenty miles from the sights you came to see, or perhaps simply on the other side of a freeway that can't be crossed on foot.

Renting a car

To rent a car, you must have held your licence for at least one year. Drivers under 25 may encounter problems and have to pay higher than normal insurance premiums. Rental companies expect customers to have a credit card; if you don't, they may let you leave a cash deposit (at least $500), but

don't count on it. All the major rental companies have outlets at the main airports but it can often be cheaper to rent from a city branch. Reservations are handled centrally, so the best way to shop around is either online, or by calling their national toll-free numbers. Potential variations are endless; certain cities and states are consistently cheaper than others, while individual travellers may be eligible for corporate, frequent-flier or AAA discounts. You can get some good deals from strictly local operators, though it can be risky as well. Make reading up on such inexpensive vendors part of your pre-trip planning.

Even between the major operators there can be a big difference in the quality of cars. Industry leaders like Alamo, Hertz and Avis tend to have newer, lower-mileage cars and more reliable breakdown services. Always be sure to get unlimited mileage and remember that leaving the car in a different city from the one where you rented it can incur a hefty drop-off charge.

Small print and insurance

When you rent a car, read the small print carefully for details on Collision Damage Waiver (CDW), sometimes called Liability Damage Waiver (LDW). This form of insurance specifically covers the car that you are driving yourself – you are in any case insured for damage to other vehicles. It can add substantially to the total cost, but without it you're liable for every scratch to the car – even those that aren't your fault. Increasing numbers of states are requiring that this insurance be included in the weekly rental rate and are regulating the amounts charged to cut down on rental-car company profiteering. Some credit card companies offer automatic CDW coverage to customers using their card; contact your issuing

---

DRIVING FOR FOREIGNERS

Foreign nationals from English-speaking countries can drive in the USA using their full domestic driving licences (International Driving Permits are not always regarded as sufficient). Fly-drive deals are good value if you want to rent a car (see above), though you can save up to fifty percent simply by booking in advance with a major firm. If you choose not to pay until you arrive, be sure you take a written confirmation of the price with you. Remember that it's safer not to drive right after a long transatlantic flight – and that most standard rental cars have automatic transmissions.

---

company for details. Alternatively, European residents can cover themselves against such costs with a reasonably priced annual policy from Insurance4Car-Hire (ⓦ insurance4carhire.com).

The American Automobile Association, or AAA (ⓣ 800 222 4357, ⓦ aaa.com), provides free maps and assistance to its members and to members of affiliated associations overseas, such as the British AA and RAC. If you break down in a rented car, call one of these services if you have towing coverage, or the emergency number pinned to the dashboard.

CAR RENTAL AGENCIES

Alamo USA ⓣ 800 462 5266, ⓦ alamo.com
Avis USA ⓣ 800 230 4898, ⓦ avis.com
Budget USA ⓣ 800 527 0700, ⓦ budget.com
Dollar USA ⓣ 800 800 3665, ⓦ dollar.com
Enterprise USA ⓣ 800 261 7331, ⓦ enterprise.com
Hertz USA ⓣ 800 654 3131, ⓦ hertz.com
Holiday Autos USA ⓣ 866 392 9288, ⓦ holidayautos.com
National USA ⓣ 800 227 7368, ⓦ nationalcar.com
Thrifty USA & Canada ⓣ 800 847 4389, ⓦ thrifty.com

Cycling

Cycling is another realistic mode of transport. An increasing number of big cities have cycle lanes and local buses equipped to carry bikes (strapped to the outside), while in country areas, roads have wide shoulders and fewer passing motorists. Unless you plan to cycle a lot and take your own bike, however, it's not especially cheap. Bikes can be rented per day, or at discounted weekly rates, from outlets that are usually found close to ski resorts in summer, university campuses and good cycling areas. Local visitor centres have details.

The national non-profit Adventure Cycling Association, based in Missoula Montana (ⓦ adventurecycling.org), publishes maps of several lengthy routes, detailing campgrounds, motels, restaurants, bike shops and places of interest. Many individual states issue their own cycling guides; contact the state tourist offices (see page 43). Before setting out on a long-distance cycling trip, you'll need a good-quality, multispeed bike, panniers, tools and spares, maps, padded shorts and a helmet (legally required in many states and localities). Plan a route that avoids interstate highways (on which cycling is unpleasant and usually illegal) and sticks to well-maintained, paved rural roads. Of problems you'll encounter, the main one is traffic: RVs, huge eighteen-wheelers and logging trucks can create intense backdraughts capable of pulling you out into the middle of the road.

Backroads Bicycle Tours (ⓦ backroads.com), and the HI-AYH hostelling group (see page 30) arrange multi-day cycle tours, with camping or stays in country inns; where appropriate we've also mentioned local firms that offer this.

Greyhound, Amtrak and major airlines will carry passengers' bikes – dismantled and packed into a box – for a small fee.

Accommodation

The cost of accommodation is significant for any traveller exploring the Rockies, especially in resorts and cities, but wherever

---

HITCHHIKING

Hitchhiking in the United States is generally a bad idea, making you a potential victim both inside (you never know who you're travelling with) and outside the car, as the odd fatality may occur from hitchers getting a little too close to the highway lanes. At a minimum, in the many states where the practice is illegal, you can expect a steep fine from the police and, on occasion, an overnight stay in the local jail. The practice is still fairly common, however, in more remote rural areas with little or no public transport.

---

you travel, you're almost certain to find a good-quality, reasonably priced motel or hotel. If you're prepared to pay a little extra, wonderful historic hotels and lodges can offer truly memorable experiences.

The four price codes we give in the Guide (see box) are based on a standard double room for one night, including breakfast, in peak season, though substantial discounts are available at slack times. Unsurprisingly, the sky's the limit for luxury hotels, where exclusive suites can easily run into four figures. Many hotels will set up a third single bed for a little extra, reducing costs for three people sharing. For lone travellers, on the other hand, a "single room" is usually a double at a slightly reduced rate at best. A dorm bed in a hostel usually costs $20–45 per night, but standards of cleanliness and security can be low, and for groups of two or more the saving compared to a motel is often minimal. In the Rockies, camping makes a cheap – and exhilarating – alternative. Alternative methods of finding a room online are through ⓦairbnb.com and the free hosting site ⓦcouchsurfing.org.

Wherever you stay, you'll be expected to pay in advance, at least for the first night and perhaps for further nights, too. Most hotels ask for a credit card imprint when you arrive, but many still accept cash for the actual payment. Reservations – essential in busy areas in summer – are held only until 6pm, unless you've said you'll be arriving late. Note that some cities and resorts – probably the ones you most want to visit – tack on a hotel tax that can raise the total tax for accommodation to as much as fifteen percent.

Note that as well as the local numbers we give in the Guide, many hotels have freephone numbers (found on their websites), which you can use within the USA.

Hotels and motels

The term "hotels" refers to most accommodation in the Guide. Motels, or "motor hotels", tend to be found beside the main roads away from city centres, and are thus much more accessible to drivers. Budget hotels or motels can be pretty basic, but in general standards of comfort are uniform – each room comes with a double bed (often two), a TV, phone and usually a portable coffeemaker, plus an attached bathroom. For places with higher rates, the room and its fittings simply get bigger and include more amenities, and there may be a swimming pool and added amenities such as irons and ironing boards, or premium cable TV (HBO, Showtime, etc). Almost all hotels and motels now offer wi-fi, albeit sometimes in the lobby only.

The least expensive properties tend to be family-run, independent "mom 'n' pop" motels, but these are rarer nowadays, in the big urban areas at least. When you're driving along the main interstates there's a lot to be said for paying a few dollars more to stay in motels belonging to the national chains. These range from the ever-reliable and cheap Super 8 and Motel 6 through to the mid-range Days Inn and La Quinta) up to the more commodious Holiday Inn Express and Hampton Inn.

During off-peak periods, many motels and hotels struggle to fill their rooms, so it's worth bargaining to get a few dollars off the asking price, especially at independent establishments. Staying in the same place for more than one night may bring further reductions. Also, look for discount coupons, especially in the free magazines distributed by local visitor centres and welcome centres near the borders between states. These can offer amazing value – but read the small print first. Online rates are also usually cheaper, sometimes considerably so.

Few budget hotels or motels bother to compete with the ubiquitous diners by offering full breakfasts, although most will provide free self-service coffee, pastries and if you are lucky, fruit or cereal, collectively referred to as "continental breakfast".

B&Bs

Staying in a B&B is a popular, often luxurious, alternative to conventional hotels. Some B&Bs consist of no more than a couple of furnished rooms in someone's home, and even the larger establishments tend to have fewer than ten rooms, sometimes without TV or phone, but often laden with potpourri, chintzy cushions and an assertively precious Victorian atmosphere. If this cosy, twee setting appeals to you, there's a range of choices throughout the region, but keep a few things in mind. For one, you may not be an anonymous guest, as you would in a chain hotel, but may be expected to chat with the host and other guests, especially during breakfast. Also, some B&Bs enforce curfews, and take

---

ACCOMMODATION PRICE CODES

$ under 75
$$ 75–149
$$ 150–200
$$$$ Over 200

Throughout the guide, accommodation is categorized according to a price code, which roughly corresponds to the following price ranges. Price categories reflect the cost of a double room, with breakfast, in peak season.

a dim view of guests stumbling in after midnight after an evening's partying. The only way to know the policy for certain is to check each B&B's policy online – there's often a lengthy list of do's and don'ts.

The price you pay for a B&B always includes breakfast (sometimes a buffet on a sideboard, but more often a full-blown cooked meal). The crucial determining factor is whether each room has an en suite bathroom; most B&Bs provide private bath facilities, although that can damage the authenticity of a fine old house. At the top end of the spectrum, the distinction between a "boutique hotel" and a "bed-and-breakfast inn" may amount to no more than that the B&B is owned by a private individual rather than a chain. In many areas, B&Bs have united to form central booking agencies, making it much easier to find a room at short notice; we've given contact information for these where appropriate.

Historic hotels and lodges

Throughout the country, but especially out West, many towns still hold historic hotels, whether dating from the arrival of the railroads or from the heyday of Route 66 in the 1940s and 1950s. So long as you accept that not all will have up-to-date facilities to match their period charm, these can make wonderfully ambient places to spend a night or two.

In addition, several national parks feature long-established and architecturally distinguished hotels, traditionally known as lodges, that can be real bargains thanks to their federally controlled rates. The only drawback is that all rooms tend to be reserved far in advance. Among the best are the Jackson Lake Lodge in Grand Teton; the Old Faithful Inn in Yellowstone; and Glacier Park Lodge and Many Glacier Hotel in Glacier National Park.

Hostels

Hostel-type accommodation is not as plentiful in the USA as it is in Europe, but provision for backpackers and low-budget travellers does exist. Unless you're travelling alone, most hostels cost about the same as motels; stay in them only if you prefer their youthful ambience, energy and sociability. Many are not accessible on public transport, or convenient for sightseeing in the towns and cities, let alone in rural areas.

These days, most hostels are independent, with no affiliation to the HI-AYH (Hostelling-International-American Youth Hostels; ⓦ http://hiusa.org) network. Many are no more than converted motels, where the "dorms" consist of a couple of sets of bunk beds in a musty room, which is also let out as a private unit on demand. Most expect guests to bring sheets or sleeping bags. Those few hostels that do belong to HI-AYH tend to impose curfews and limit daytime access hours, and segregate dormitories by sex.

Food and drink

The USA is not all fast food. Every state offers its own specialities, and regional cuisines are distinctive and delicious. In addition, international food turns up regularly – not only in the big cities, but also in more unexpected places. Many farming and ranching regions – Idaho in particular – have a number of Basque restaurants; mountain pizza, invented in Colorado, enlivens ski resorts; and bison, elk and other wild game-based dishes can be found in towns all over the Rockies.

Eating

In the Guide restaurants are given one of four price codes, based on a two-course meal for one including a glass of wine (see box). In the big cities, you can pretty much eat whatever you want, whenever you want, thanks to the ubiquity of restaurants, 24-hour diners, and bars and street carts selling food well into the night. Also, along all the highways and on virtually every town's main street, restaurants, fast-food joints and cafés try to outdo one another with bargains and special offers. Whatever you eat and wherever you eat it, service is usually prompt, friendly and attentive – thanks in large part to the institution of tipping. Waiters depend on tips for the bulk of their earnings; fifteen to twenty percent is the standard rate, with anything less sure to be seen as an insult.

Regional cuisine

Many US regions have developed their own cuisines, combining available ingredients with dishes and techniques of local ethnic groups. Broadly, steaks and other cuts of beef are prominent in the Rockies, over items such as fresh seafood (with the exception of Denver), though local trout and salmon are ubiquitous throughout the mountains. Wild game, including bison and elk, is also popular (often served as burgers).

There are some local differences. In Colorado, lamb is also very popular, with some critics claiming it produces the best in the world, usually served as lamb chops (often with a warm cheese fondue). Mexican food (or at least the Tex-Mex version) is also popular, with even small towns serving up nachos,

VEGETARIAN AND VEGAN EATING

In the big US cities at least, being a vegetarian – or even a vegan – presents few problems. However, don't be too surprised in rural areas if you find yourself restricted to a diet of eggs, grilled-cheese sandwiches and limp salads. Note however, that baked beans nationwide, and the nutritious-sounding red beans and rice dished up the West, usually contain bits of diced pork.

tacos, cheese enchiladas and burritos from one or two holes-in-the-wall. Other more exotic Colorado dishes include "Rocky Mountain oysters", otherwise known as the testes of a bull or bison, served breaded and fried.

Wyoming is serious cowboy country, and chuckwagon-style dinners are wildly popular here – communal meals of baked beans, steak, chicken and buffalo sausages cooked on a pitchfork, with deep-fried onions and homemade brownies. Other popular meaty dishes include chicken-fried steaks, prime rib, buffalo steaks, elk sausage and biscuits and gravy for breakfast.

In Montana, desserts made from local huckleberries appear on menus everywhere, while "Beans and Sheepherders" is a legendary pinto bean and ham soup invented in Ingomar's Jersey Lilly Saloon in 1948. Ice cream (especially Wilcoxson's and Big Dipper), flathead cherries, chokecherries, Hutterite chicken, lentils, morels and even Cornish pasties are other Montana specialties.

Idaho, in addition to the Basque food served up in Boise, the capital, is of course known for potatoes (best served with local "fry sauce"; there's even ice cream potatoes), but also Idaho white sturgeon caviar, habanero pizza, fresh trout and lamb.

Finally, there are also regional variations on American staples. You can get plain old burgers and hot dogs anywhere, but for a truly American experience, grab a green chili burger, or a piping-hot "Double Johnny Burger", gooey with cheese and thin-sliced beef from My Brother's Bar in Denver, or one of the city's signature "Elk-Jalapeno Dogs" at Biker Jim's Gourmet Dogs. Mountain pie pizzas were invented in Idaho Springs, Colorado. Almost every state has at least one spot

claiming to have invented the hamburger, and regardless of where you go, you can find a good range of authentic diners where the buns are fresh, the patties are large, handcrafted and tasty, and the dressings and condiments are inspired.

Other cuisines

In the cities, in particular, where centuries of settlement have created distinctive local neighbourhoods, each community offers its own take on the cuisine of its homeland. Mexican food is so common it might as well be an indigenous cuisine, especially in Colorado. The food is different from that found south of the border, focusing more on frying and on a standard set of staples. The essentials, however, are the same: lots of rice and black or pinto beans, often served refried (boiled, mashed and fried), with variations on the tortilla, a thin corn or flour pancake that can be wrapped around fillings and eaten by hand (a burrito); folded and filled (a taco); rolled, filled and baked in sauce (an enchilada); or fried flat and topped with a stack of filling (a tostada).

Italian food is widely available, too; the top-shelf restaurants in cities tend to focus on the northern end of the boot, while the tomato-heavy, gut-busting portions associated with southern Italian cooking are usually confined to lower-end, chequered-table-cloth diners with pictures of Frank and Dino on the walls. Pizza restaurants occupy a similar range from high-end gourmet places to cheap and tasty dives.

When it comes to Asian eating, Indian cuisine is usually better in the cities, though there are increasing exceptions as the resident population grows. When found in the Chinatown neighbourhoods of major cities Chinese cooking can be top-notch – beware, though, of the dismal-tasting "chop suey" and "chow mein" joints in the suburbs and small towns. Japanese, once the preserve of the coasts and sophisticated cities, has become widely popular, with sushi restaurants in all price ranges and chain teriyaki joints out on the freeways. Thai and Vietnamese restaurants, meanwhile, provide some of the best and cheapest food available, sometimes in diners mixing the two, and occasionally in the form of "fusion" cooking with other Asian cuisines (or "pan-Asian", as it's widely known).

EATING PRICE CODES

$̄ under 25
$̄$̄ 25–49
$̄$̄$̄ 50–75
$̄$̄$̄$̄ Over 75

Throughout the guide, eating out listings are categorized according to a price code, which roughly corresponds to the following price ranges. Price categories reflect the cost of a two-course meal for one with alcohol.

Drink

Denver is a consummate booze town – filled with tales of famous, plastered authors indulging in famously bad behaviour – but you shouldn't have to search very hard for a comfortable place to drink, as even the smallest Western towns have at least one aging saloon. You need to be 21 years old to buy and consume alcohol in the USA, and it's likely you'll be asked for ID if you look under 30.

"Blue laws" – archaic statutes that restrict when, where and under what conditions alcohol can be purchased – are held by many states, and prohibit the sale of alcohol on Sundays; Colorado restricts the alcohol content in beer sold in grocery stores to just 3.2 percent, almost half the usual strength, though there are plenty of unrestricted liquor stores. In Wyoming, you can only buy alcohol in liquor stores; in Idaho liquor cannot be sold on Sundays.

Note that if a bar is advertising a happy hour on "rail drinks" or "well drinks", these are cocktails made from the liquors and mixers the bar has to hand (as opposed to top-shelf, higher-quality brands).

Beer

The most popular American beers may be the fizzy, insipid lagers from national brands, but there is no lack of alternatives. The craze for microbreweries started in northern California several decades ago, and today Colorado especially, is at the vanguard of the microbrewing movement – even the smaller towns in the Rockies have their own share of decent handcrafted beers. Denver and other western cities rank at the top, and you can even find excellent brews in tiny spots such as Whitefish, Montana, where the beers of Great Northern Brewing are well worth seeking out. Indeed, microbreweries have undergone an explosion in most parts of the country in recent years and brewpubs can now be found in virtually every sizeable US city and college town. Almost all serve a wide range of good-value, hearty food to help soak up the drink. For more on craft beers, see Ⓦ craftbeer.com.

Wine

Wine isn't as big here as in California, say, but there are local producers, typically of varying quality, though there are always a few standouts in each state that may merit a taste while you're on your journey. Colorado has a relatively developed wine industry with well over 150 producers (as well as cider makers). Idaho has a burgeoning ice wine scene, with producers such as Koenig Vineyards & Distillery and Ste. Chapelle. You'll find details of tours and tastings throughout the Guide.

Festivals

In addition to the main US public holidays – on July 4, Independence Day, the entire country takes time out to picnic, drink, salute the flag, and watch or participate in fireworks displays, marches, beauty pageants, eating contests and more, to commemorate the signing of the Declaration of Independence in 1776. There is a diverse multitude of engaging local events in the Rockies: arts-and-crafts shows, county fairs, music festivals, rodeos, sandcastle-building competitions, chilli cookoffs and countless others.

Certain festivities, such as Cheyenne Frontier Days in Wyoming, are well worth planning your holiday around but obviously other people will have the same idea, so visiting during these times requires an extra amount of advance effort, not to mention money. Halloween (Oct 31) is also immensely popular. No longer just the domain of masked kids running around the streets banging on doors and demanding "trick or treat", in some bigger cities Halloween has evolved into a massive celebration. Thanksgiving Day, on the fourth Thursday in November, is more sedate. Relatives return to the nest to share a meal (traditionally, roast turkey and stuffing, cranberry sauce, and all manner of delicious pies) and give thanks for family and friends. Ostensibly, the holiday recalls the first harvest of the Pilgrims in Massachusetts, though Thanksgiving was a national holiday before anyone thought to make that connection.

Annual festivals and events

For further details of the festivals and events listed below, including more precise dates, see the relevant page of the Guide (where covered) or access their websites. The state tourist boards (see page 43) can provide more complete calendars for each area.

JANUARY

X Games Aspen Aspen, CO Ⓦ aspensnowmass.com.

FEBRUARY

Lionel Hampton Jazz Festival Moscow, ID Ⓦ uidaho.edu/class/jazzfest.
Whitefish Winter Carnival Whitefish, MT Ⓦ explorewhitefish.com.
Winter Carnival Steamboat Springs, CO Ⓦ steamboatchamber.com.

MAY

Old West Days Jackson, WY Ⓦ jacksonholewy.com.
Denver Arts Festival Denver, CO Ⓦ denverartsfestival.com.

JUNE

Bluegrass Festival Telluride, CO Ⓦ bluegrass.com.
Colorado Shakespeare Festival Boulder, CO Ⓦ cupresents.org/series/shakespeare-festival.
Eastern Shoshone Indian Days Powwow Fort Washakie, WY Ⓦ windriver.org.
Idaho Shakespeare Festival Boise, ID Ⓦ idahoshakespeare.org.
Jackson Hole Rodeo Jackson, WY Ⓦ jhrodeo.com.
Wyoming Brewers Festival Cheyenne, WY Ⓦ wyobrewfest.com.
Little Bighorn Days Hardin, MT Ⓦ littlebighornreenactment.com.

JULY

Aspen Music Festival Aspen, CO Ⓦ aspenmusicfestival.com.
Cheyenne Frontier Days Cheyenne, WY Ⓦ cfdrodeo.com. See page 77.
Cody Stampede Rodeo Cody, WY Ⓦ codystampederodeo.com.
Montana Folk Festival Butte, MT Ⓦ montanafolkfestival.com.
Montana State Fair Great Falls, MT (into Aug) Ⓦ cascadecountymt.gov.

AUGUST

Colorado State Fair Pueblo, CO (into Sept) Ⓦ coloradostatefair.com.
Crow Fair Crow Agency, MT Ⓦ crow-nsn.gov/crow-fair.html.
North Idaho State Fair Coeur d'Alene, ID Ⓦ nisfair.fun.
Rocky Mountains Folk Festival Lyons, CO Ⓦ bluegrass.com/folks.
Wyoming State Fair Douglas, WY Ⓦ wystatefair.com.
Western Idaho Fair Boise, ID Ⓦ idahofair.com.

SEPTEMBER

Eastern Idaho State Fair Blackfoot, ID Ⓦ funatthefair.com.
Telluride Film Festival Telluride, CO Ⓦ telluridefilmfestival.org.

OCTOBER

Great American Beer Festival Denver, CO Ⓦ greatamericanbeerfestival.com.

NOVEMBER

Sandpoint Film Festival Sandpoint, ID Ⓦ sandpointfilmfestival.com.

DECEMBER

Vail Snow Days Vail, CO Ⓦ vailsnowdays.com.

The outdoors

Coated by dense forests, cut by deep canyons and capped by great mountains, the Rockies are blessed with fabulous backcountry and wilderness areas. Here you can experience the full breathtaking sweep of America's wide-open stretches.

National parks and monuments

The National Park Service administers both national parks and national monuments. Its rangers do a superb job of providing information and advice to visitors, maintaining trails and organizing such activities as free guided hikes and campfire talks.

In principle, a national park preserves an area of outstanding natural beauty, encompassing a wide range of terrain and prime examples of particular landforms and wildlife. Thus Yellowstone has boiling geysers and herds of elk and bison, while Rocky Mountain National Park offers towering peaks and cascading waterfalls. A national monument is usually much smaller, focusing perhaps on just one archeological site or geological phenomenon, such as Devil's Tower in Wyoming. Altogether, the national park system comprises around four hundred units, including national seashores, lakeshores, battlefields and other historic sites.

While national parks tend to be perfect places to hike – almost all have extensive trail networks – all are far too large to tour entirely on foot (Yellowstone, for example, is bigger than Delaware and Rhode Island combined). Even in those rare cases where you can use public transport to reach a park, you'll almost certainly need some sort of vehicle to explore it once you're there.

Most parks and monuments charge admission fees, which cover a vehicle and all its occupants for up to a week. For anyone on a touring vacation, it may well make more sense to buy the Inter-agency Annual Pass, also known as the "America the Beautiful Pass". Sold at all federal parks and monuments, or online at Ⓦ store.usgs.gov, this grants unrestricted access for a year to the bearer, and any accompanying passengers in the same vehicle, to all national parks and monuments, as well as sites managed by such agencies as the US Fish and Wildlife Service, the Forest Service and the BLM (Bureau of Land Management). It does not, however, cover or reduce additional fees like charges for camping in official park campgrounds, or permits for backcountry hiking or rafting.

Two further passes, obtainable at any park or online, grant free access for life to all national parks

---

MAIN ATTRACTIONS IN NATIONAL PARKS

The Park Service website, Ⓦ nps.gov, details the main attractions of the national parks, plus opening hours, the best times to visit, admission fees, hiking trails and visitor facilities.

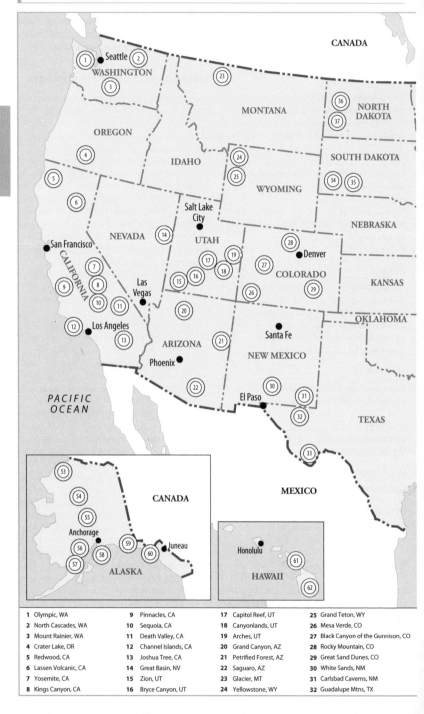

1	Olympic, WA	9	Pinnacles, CA	17	Capitol Reef, UT	25	Grand Teton, WY
2	North Cascades, WA	10	Sequoia, CA	18	Canyonlands, UT	26	Mesa Verde, CO
3	Mount Rainier, WA	11	Death Valley, CA	19	Arches, UT	27	Black Canyon of the Gunnison, CO
4	Crater Lake, OR	12	Channel Islands, CA	20	Grand Canyon, AZ	28	Rocky Mountain, CO
5	Redwood, CA	13	Joshua Tree, CA	21	Petrified Forest, AZ	29	Great Sand Dunes, CO
6	Lassen Volcanic, CA	14	Great Basin, NV	22	Saguaro, AZ	30	White Sands, NM
7	Yosemite, CA	15	Zion, UT	23	Glacier, MT	31	Carlsbad Caverns, NM
8	Kings Canyon, CA	16	Bryce Canyon, UT	24	Yellowstone, WY	32	Guadalupe Mtns, TX

US NATIONAL PARKS

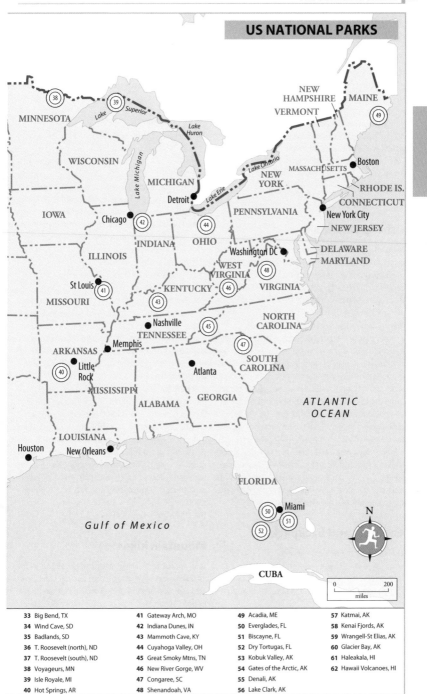

33 Big Bend, TX	**41** Gateway Arch, MO	**49** Acadia, ME	**57** Katmai, AK
34 Wind Cave, SD	**42** Indiana Dunes, IN	**50** Everglades, FL	**58** Kenai Fjords, AK
35 Badlands, SD	**43** Mammoth Cave, KY	**51** Biscayne, FL	**59** Wrangell-St Elias, AK
36 T. Roosevelt (north), ND	**44** Cuyahoga Valley, OH	**52** Dry Tortugas, FL	**60** Glacier Bay, AK
37 T. Roosevelt (south), ND	**45** Great Smoky Mtns, TN	**53** Kobuk Valley, AK	**61** Haleakala, HI
38 Voyageurs, MN	**46** New River Gorge, WV	**54** Gates of the Arctic, AK	**62** Hawaii Volcanoes, HI
39 Isle Royale, MI	**47** Congaree, SC	**55** Denali, AK	
40 Hot Springs, AR	**48** Shenandoah, VA	**56** Lake Clark, AK	

and monuments, again to the holder and any accompanying passengers, and also provide a fifty-percent discount on camping fees. The Senior Pass is available to any US citizen or permanent resident aged 62 or older for a one-time fee, while the Access Pass is issued free to blind or permanently disabled US citizens or permanent residents, with a small processing fee. While hotel-style lodges are found only in major parks, every park or monument tends to have at least one well-organized campground. Often, a cluster of motels can be found not far outside the park boundaries. With appropriate permits – subject to restrictions in popular parks – backpackers can also usually camp in the backcountry (a general term for areas inaccessible by road).

Other public lands

National parks and monuments are often surrounded by tracts of national forest – also federally administered but much less protected. These too usually hold appealing rural campgrounds but, in the words of the slogan, each is a "Land Of Many Uses", and usually allows logging and other land-based industry (thankfully, more often ski resorts than strip mines).

Other government departments administer wildlife refuges, national scenic rivers, recreation areas and the like. The Bureau of Land Management (BLM) has the largest holdings of all, most of it open rangeland, such as in Montana and Idaho, but also including some enticingly out-of-the-way reaches. Environmentalist groups engage in endless running battles with developers, ranchers and the extracting industries over uses – or alleged misuses – of federal lands.

While state parks and state monuments, administered by individual states, preserve sites of more limited, local significance, many are explicitly intended for recreational use, and thus hold better campgrounds than their federal equivalents.

Camping and backpacking

The ideal way to see the great outdoors – especially if you're on a low budget – is to tour by car and camp in state and federal campgrounds. If you're camping in high season, either reserve in advance or avoid the most popular areas.

Backcountry camping in the national parks is usually free, by permit only. Before you set off on anything more than a half-day hike, and whenever you're headed for anywhere at all isolated, be sure to inform a ranger of your plans, and ask about weather conditions and specific local tips. Carry sufficient food and drink to cover emergencies, as well as all the necessary equipment and maps. Check whether fires are permitted; even if they are, try to use a camp stove in preference to local materials. In wilderness areas, try to camp on previously used sites. Where there are no toilets, bury human waste at least six inches into the ground and 100ft from the nearest water supply and campground.

Health issues

Backpackers should never drink from rivers and streams; you never know what acts people – or animals – have performed further upstream. Giardia – a water-borne bacteria that causes an intestinal disease characterized by chronic diarrhoea, abdominal cramps, fatigue and weight loss – is a serious problem. Water that doesn't come from a tap should be boiled for at least five minutes or cleansed with an iodine-based purifier or a giardia-rated filter.

Hiking at lower elevations should present few problems, though near water mosquitoes can drive you crazy; Avon Skin-so-Soft or anything containing DEET are fairly reliable repellents. Ticks – tiny beetles that plunge their heads into your skin and swell up – are another hazard. They sometimes leave their heads inside, causing blood clots or infections, so get advice from a ranger if you've been bitten. One species of tick causes Lyme Disease, a serious condition that can even affect the brain. Nightly inspections of your skin are strongly recommended.

Beware, too, of poison oak, which grows throughout the west, usually among oak trees. Its leaves come in groups of three (the middle one on a short stem) and are distinguished by prominent veins and shiny surfaces. If you come into contact with it, wash your skin (with soap and cold water) and clothes as soon as possible – and don't scratch. In serious cases, hospital emergency rooms can give antihistamine or adrenaline shots. A comparable curse is poison ivy, found throughout the country. For both plants, remember the sage advice, "Leaves of three, let it be".

Mountain hikes

Take special care hiking at higher elevations, in the 14,000ft peaks of the Rockies for example. Late snows are common, and in spring avalanches are a real danger, while meltwaters make otherwise simple stream crossings hazardous. Weather conditions can also change at the blink of an eye so remember to stay aware of your surroundings. Altitude sickness can affect even the fittest of athletes. Remember to take it easy for your first few days above 7000ft. Drink lots of water, avoid alcohol, eat plenty of carbohydrates and always protect yourself from the sun.

Desert hikes

If you intend to hike in the desert, carry plentiful extra food and water, and never go anywhere without a map. Cover most of your ground in early morning: the midday heat is too debilitating. If you get lost, find some shade and wait. So long as you've registered, the rangers will eventually come looking for you.

At any time of year, you'll stay cooler during the day if you wear full-length sleeves and trousers, while a wide-brimmed hat and good sunglasses will spare you the blinding headaches that can result from the desert light. You may also have to contend with flash floods, which can appear from nowhere. Never camp in a dry wash, and don't attempt to cross flooded areas until the water has receded.

It's essential to carry – and drink – large quantities of water in the desert. In particular, hiking in typical summer temperatures requires drinking a phenomenal amount. Loss of the desire to eat or drink is an early symptom of heat exhaustion, so it's possible to become seriously dehydrated without feeling thirsty. Watch out for signs of dizziness or nausea; if you start to feel weak and stop sweating, it's time to get to the doctor. As a precaution check whether water is available on your trail; ask a ranger, and carry plenty with you even if it is.

When driving in the desert, remember to carry ample water in the car, take along an emergency pack with flares, a first-aid kit and snakebite kit, matches and a compass. A shovel, tyre pump and extra gas are always a good idea. If the engine overheats, don't turn it off; instead, try to cool it quickly by turning the front end of the car towards the wind. Carefully pour some water on the front of the radiator, and turn the air conditioning off and the heat up full blast. In an emergency, never panic and leave the car: you'll be harder to find wandering around alone.

Adventure travel

The opportunities for adventure travel in the Rockies are all but endless, whether your tastes run towards whitewater rafting down the Colorado River, mountain biking in Crested Butte, canoeing down the Yellowstone River, horseback riding in Grand Teton or rock climbing on the sheer granite monoliths of the Sawtooth Range.

While an exhaustive listing of the possibilities could fill a huge volume, certain places have an especially high concentration of adventure opportunities, such as Missoula, Montana (see page 100) or Wyoming's Grand Tetons (see page 87). Throughout the text we recommend guides, outfitters and local adventure-tour operators.

Skiing

Downhill ski resorts can be found all over the Rockies, notably Vail and Aspen in Colorado. A cheaper alternative is cross-country skiing, or ski touring. Backcountry ski lodges dot mountainous areas in the Rockies. They offer a range of rustic accommodation, equipment rental and lessons.

Wildlife

Watch out for bears, deer, moose, mountain lions and rattlesnakes in the backcountry, and consider the effect your presence can have on their environment.

Other than in a national park, you're highly unlikely to encounter a bear. Even there, it's rare to stumble across one in the wilderness. If you do, don't run, just back away slowly. Most fundamentally, it will be after your food, which should be stored in airtight containers when camping. Ideally, hang both food and garbage from a high but slender branch some distance from your camp. Never attempt to feed bears, and never get between a mother and her young. Young animals are cute; their irate mothers are not.

Snakes and creepy-crawlies

Though the deserts in particular are home to a wide assortment of poisonous creatures, these are rarely aggressive towards humans. To avoid trouble, observe obvious precautions. Don't attempt to handle wildlife; keep your eyes open as you walk, and watch where you put your hands when scrambling over obstacles; shake out shoes, clothing and bedding before use; and back off if you do spot a creature, giving it room to escape.

If you are bitten or stung, current medical thinking rejects the concept of cutting yourself open and attempting to suck out the venom. Whether snake, scorpion or spider is responsible, apply a cold compress to the wound, constrict the area with a tourniquet to prevent the spread of venom, drink lots of water and bring your temperature down by resting in a shady area. Stay as calm as possible and seek medical help immediately.

Sports

As well as being good fun, catching a baseball game at Denver's Coors Field on a summer afternoon or joining the screaming throngs at a Broncos football game Empower Field at Mile High can give visitors an unforgettable insight into Denver and its people. Professional teams almost always put on the most spectac-

ular shows, but big games between college rivals – a very big deal in the Rocky Mountain states – Minor League baseball games and even Friday night high-school football games provide an easy and enjoyable way to get on intimate terms with a place. Denver is the only city in the region with pro sports teams. In addition to the the Broncos (football) and Colorado Rockies (baseball), there's the Colorado Avalanche (ice hockey), Colorado Rapids (soccer) and Denver Nuggets (basketball).

Specific details for the most important teams in all the sports are given in the various city accounts in this Guide. They can also be found through the Major League websites: Wmlb.com (baseball); Ⓦnba. com (basketball); Ⓦnfl.com (football); Ⓦnhl.com (ice hockey); and Ⓦmlssoccer.com (soccer). ·

Other sports

Soccer remains much more popular as a participant sport, especially for kids, than a spectator one, and those Americans who are interested in it usually follow foreign matches like England's Premier League, rather than their home-grown talent. The good news for international travellers who are avid football fans is that any decent-sized city will have one or two pubs where you can catch games from England, various European countries or Latin America; check out Ⓦlivesoccertv.com for a list of such establishments and match schedules.

Golf, once the province of moneyed businessmen, has attracted a wider following in recent decades due to the rise of celebrity golfers such as Tiger Woods and Jack Nicklaus, as well as the construction of numerous municipal and public courses. You'll have your best access at these, while private golf courses have varying standards for allowing non-members to play (check their websites), steeper fees and often a more formal dress code.

Travel essentials

Costs

When it comes to average costs for travelling expenses, much depends on where you've chosen to go. A road trip around the backroads of Montana and Wyoming won't cost you much in accommodation, dining or souvenir-buying, although the amount spent on gas will add up – this varies from state to state, but at the time of writing the average price was between $3.30 and $3.60 per gallon. By contrast, getting around a city such as Denver will be relatively cheap, but you'll pay much more for your hotel, meals, sightseeing and shopping. Most items you buy will be subject to some form of state – not federal – sales tax, from six percent in Idaho and four percent to Wyoming, to less than three percent (in Colorado) and zero percent (in Montana). In addition, varying from state to state, some counties and cities may add on another point or two to that rate. Though Montana has no state sales tax, goods may be liable to some other form of tax from county to county (and in certain resorts).

Unless you're camping or staying in a hostel, accommodation will be your greatest expense while in the Rockies. A detailed breakdown is given in the Accommodation section, but you can reckon on at least $50–80 per day, based on sharing, more or less double that if travelling solo. Unlike accommodation, prices for good food don't automatically take a bite out of your wallet, and you can indulge anywhere from the lowliest (but still scrumptious) burger shack to the choicest restaurant helmed by a celebrity chef. You can get by on as little as $25 a day, but realistically you should aim for more like $50.

Where it exists, and where it is useful (which tends to be only in the larger cities), public transport is usually affordable, with many cities offering good-value travel passes. Renting a car, at $175–250 per week, is a far

---

ROUGH GUIDES TRAVEL INSURANCE

Rough Guides has teamed up with WorldNomads.com to offer great travel insurance deals. Policies are available to residents of over 150 countries, with cover for a wide range of adventure sports, 24hr emergency assistance, high levels of medical and evacuation cover and a stream of travel safety information. Roughguides.com users can take advantage of their policies online 24/7, from anywhere in the world – even if you're already travelling. And since plans often change when you're on the road, you can extend your policy and even claim online. Roughguides.com users who buy travel insurance with WorldNomads.com can also leave a positive footprint and donate to a community development project. For more information go to Ⓦroughguides.com/travel-insurance.

more efficient way to explore the broader part of the region, and, for a group of two or more, it could well work out cheaper. Drivers staying in larger hotels in the cities should factor in the increasing trend towards charging even for self-parking; this daily fee may well be just a few dollars less than that for valet parking.

For attractions in the Guide, prices are quoted for adults, with children's rates listed if they are significantly lower or when the attraction is aimed primarily at youngsters; at some spots, kids get in for half-price, or for free if they're under six.

Tipping

In the USA, waiters earn most of their income from tips, and not leaving a fair amount is seen as an insult. Waiting staff expect tips of at least fifteen percent, and up to twenty percent for very good service. When sitting at a bar, you should leave at least a dollar per round for the barkeeper; more if the round is more than two drinks. Hotel porters and bellhops should receive at least $2 per piece of luggage, more if it has been lugged up several flights of stairs. About fifteen percent should be added to taxi fares, rounded up to the nearest 50¢ or dollar.

Crime and personal safety

No one could pretend that America is crime-free, although away from the urban centres crime is often remarkably low. All the major tourist areas and the main nightlife zones in cities are invariably brightly lit and well policed. By planning carefully and taking good care of your possessions, you should, generally speaking, have few problems.

Car crime

Crimes committed against tourists driving rented cars aren't as common as they once were, but it still pays to be cautious. In major urban areas such as Denver, any car you rent should have nothing on it – such as a particular licence plate – that makes it easy to spot as a rental car. When driving, under no circumstances should you stop in any unlit or seemingly deserted urban area – and especially not if someone is waving you down and suggesting that there is something wrong with your car. Similarly, if you are accidentally rammed by the driver behind you, do not stop immediately, but proceed on to the nearest well-lit, busy area and call ☎911 for assistance. Hide any valuables out of sight, preferably locked in the trunk or in the glove compartment.

Electricity

Electricity runs on 110V AC. All plugs are two-pronged and rather insubstantial. Some travel plug adapters don't fit American sockets.

Entry requirements

At the time of writing, proof of a vaccination as well as testing or proof of a negative Covid test is required due to measures to limit the spread of Covid-19. For the latest information, consult ⓦtravel.state.gov/content/ travel/en/international-travel.html.

Temporary restrictions aside, citizens of 35 countries – including the UK, Ireland, Australia, New Zealand and most Western European countries – can enter under the Visa Waiver Program if visiting the United States for a period of less than ninety days. To obtain authorization,

---

MARIJUANA AND OTHER DRUGS

Over recent years, the legalization of marijuana for recreational purposes has been introduced in a number of states. The first to pass the measure in the Rockies was Colorado; it is now legal in Montana, but still illegal in Idaho and Wyoming, where even being under the influence of marijuana is a misdemeanor that can land you in jail. As of 2022, the recreational use of marijuana had been legalized in eighteen states. Pot, as it is commonly referred to in America, is now on sale at licensed shops in these states, though there are no Amsterdam-style coffeeshops anywhere as of yet. Rules as to whether only local residents can buy it and how much vary from state to state; smoking in public is usually still illegal.

Paradoxically, the substance is still illegal at the federal level but this has not been creating problems in the above states. Many other states allow the usage of medical marijuana but only with a licence. Note that in states where pot is still illegal like Idaho and Wyoming, you can be prosecuted even if you have bought it legally elsewhere, so it's wise not to take it across state lines in such cases. Also note that all other recreational drugs remain illegal at both state and federal level, so even simple possession can get you into serious trouble.

you must apply online for ESTA (Electronic System for Travel Authorization) approval before setting off. This is a straightforward process – simply go to the ESTA website (Ⓦesta.cbp.dhs.gov), fill in your info and wait a very short while (sometimes just minutes, but it's best to leave at least 72hr before travelling to make sure) for them to provide you with an authorization number. You will not generally be asked to produce that number at your port of entry, but it is as well to keep a copy just in case, especially in times of high-security alerts – you will be denied entry if you don't have one. This ESTA authorization is valid for up to two years (or until your passport expires, whichever comes first) and costs $14, payable by credit card when applying. When you arrive at your port of entry you will be asked to confirm that your trip has an end date, that you have an onward ticket and that you have adequate funds to cover your stay. The customs official may also ask you for your address while in the USA; the hotel you are staying at on your first night will suffice. Each traveller must also undergo the US-VISIT process at immigration, where both index fingers are digitally scanned and a digital head shot is also taken for file.

Prospective visitors from parts of the world not mentioned above require a valid passport and a non-immigrant visitor's visa for a maximum ninety-day stay. How you'll obtain a visa depends on what country you're in and your status when you apply; check Ⓦtravel.state.gov. Whatever your nationality, visas are not issued to convicted felons and anybody who owns up to being a communist, fascist, drug dealer or guilty of genocide (fair enough, perhaps). On arrival, the date stamped on your passport is the latest you're legally allowed to stay. The Department of Homeland Security (DHS) has toughened its stance on anyone violating this rule, so even overstaying by a few days can result in a protracted interrogation from officials. Overstaying may also cause you to be turned away next time you try to enter the USA. To get an extension before your time is up, apply at the nearest Department of Homeland Security office, whose address will be under the Federal Government Offices listings at the front of the phone book. INS officials will assume that you're working in the USA illegally, and it's up to you to convince them otherwise by providing evidence of ample finances. If you can, bring along an upstanding American citizen to vouch for you. You'll also have to explain why you didn't plan for the extra time initially.

FOREIGN EMBASSIES IN THE USA

Australia 1601 Massachusetts Ave NW, Washington DC 20036, ☎ 202 797 3000, Ⓦusa.embassy.gov.au
Canada 501 Pennsylvania Ave NW, Washington DC 20001, ☎ 202 682 1740, Ⓦinternational.gc.ca

Ireland 2234 Massachusetts Ave NW, Washington DC 20008, ☎ 202 462 3939, Ⓦdfa.ie/irish-embassy/usa
New Zealand 37 Observatory Circle NW, Washington DC 20008, ☎ 202 328 4800, Ⓦmfat.govt.nz
South Africa 3051 Massachusetts Ave NW, Washington DC 20008, ☎ 202 232 4400, Ⓦsaembassy.org
UK 3100 Massachusetts Ave NW, Washington DC 20008, ☎ 202 588 6500, Ⓦukinusa.fco.gov.uk

Health

If you have a serious accident while in the USA, emergency medical services will get to you quickly and charge you later. For emergencies or ambulances, dial ☎911, the nationwide emergency number.

Should you need to see a doctor, look online, or ask your accommodation for a local recommendation. The basic consultation fee is $150–200, payable in advance. Tests, X-rays etc are much more. Medications aren't cheap either – keep all your receipts for later claims on your insurance policy.

Foreign visitors should bear in mind that many pills available over the counter at home – most codeine-based painkillers, for example – require a prescription in the USA. Local brand names can be confusing; ask for advice at the pharmacy in any drugstore.

In general, inoculations aren't required for entry to the USA, though check the latest Covid-19 regulations.

Covid-19

The global Covid-19 pandemic impacted the US from early 2020 well into 2022, claiming the lives of over 860,000 Americans, the highest number in the world by some margin, and a total that was still climbing at time of writing. More positively, the US's vaccination programme to protect citizens from future infections was well underway, with 200 million vaccine shots given before President Biden's 100th day in office, doubling his original pledge made.

Starting in November 2021, the US has required all non-citizen air travellers to the United States to be fully vaccinated before boarding a plane to the country – check the latest at Ⓦtravel.state.gov, or Ⓦcdc.gov.

MEDICAL RESOURCES FOR TRAVELLERS

CDC Ⓦcdc.gov/travel. Official US government travel health site.
International Society for Travel Medicine Ⓦistm.org. Full listing of travel health clinics.

Insurance

In view of the high cost of medical care in the USA, all travellers visiting from overseas should be sure to buy some form of travel insurance. American and Canadian citizens should check whether they are already covered – some homeowners' or renters' policies are valid on holiday, and credit cards such as American Express often include some medical or other insurance, while most Canadians are covered for medical mishaps overseas by their provincial health plans. If you only need trip cancellation/interruption coverage (to supplement your existing plan), this is generally available at a cost of about six percent of the trip value.

Internet

Almost all hotels and many coffeeshops and restaurants offer free wi-fi for guests, though some upmarket hotels charge for access. As a result, cybercafés, where you can use a terminal in the establishment for an hourly charge, are increasingly uncommon. Nearly all public libraries provide free internet access, but often there's a wait and machine time is limited.

LGBTQ travellers

The LGBTQ scene in America is huge, albeit heavily concentrated in the major cities. San Francisco, where between a quarter and a third of the voting population is reckoned to be gay or lesbian, is arguably the world's premier LGBTQ city. New York runs a close second, and up and down both coasts LGBTQ people enjoy the kind of visibility and influence those in other places can only dream about. LGBTQ public officials and police officers are no longer a novelty. Resources, facilities and organizations are endless.

In the rural heartland of some parts of the Rockies, however, life can look more like the Fifties – homosexuals are still oppressed and can be subjected to discrimination or harassment.

National publications are available from any good bookstore. Bob Damron in San Francisco (Ⓦ damron.com) produces the best and sells them at a discount online. These include the Men's Travel Guide, a pocket-sized yearbook listing hotels, bars, clubs and resources for gay men; the Women's Traveller, which provides similar listings for lesbians; the Damron City Guide, which details lodging and entertainment in major cities; and Damron Accommodations, with 1000 accommodation listings for LGBTQ travellers worldwide.

Gayellow Pages in New York (Ⓦ gayellowpages.com) publishes a useful directory of businesses in the USA and Canada, plus regional directories for New England, New York and the South. The Advocate, based in Los Angeles (Ⓦ advocate.com) is a bimonthly national LGBTQ news magazine, with features, general info and classified ads. Finally, the International Gay & Lesbian Travel Association in Fort Lauderdale, FL (Ⓦ iglta.org), is a comprehensive, invaluable source for LGBTQ travellers.

Mail

Post offices are usually open Monday to Friday from 8.30am to 5.30pm, and Saturday from 9am to 12.30pm, and there are blue mailboxes on many street corners. Airmail between the USA and Europe may take a week.

In the USA, the last line of the address includes the city or town and an abbreviation denoting the state ("CA" for California; "TX" for Texas, for example). The last line also includes a five-digit number – the zip code – denoting the local post office. It is very important to include this, though the additional four digits that you will sometimes see appended are not essential. You can check zip codes on the US Postal Service website, at Ⓦ usps.com.

Rules on sending parcels are very rigid: packages must be in special containers bought from post offices and sealed according to their instructions. To send anything out of the country, you'll need a green customs declaration form, available from a post office.

OPENING HOURS AND PUBLIC HOLIDAYS

The traditional summer holiday period runs between the weekends of Memorial Day, the last Monday in May, and Labor Day, the first Monday in September. Many parks, attractions and visitor centres operate longer hours or only open during this period and we denote such cases as "summer" throughout the Guide. Otherwise, specific months of opening are given.

Government offices (including post offices) and banks will be closed on the following national public holidays:
Jan 1 New Year's Day
Third Mon in Jan Martin Luther King, Jr's Birthday
Third Mon in Feb Presidents' Day
Last Mon in May Memorial Day
July 4 Independence Day
First Mon in Sept Labor Day
Second Mon in Oct Columbus Day
Nov 11 Veterans' Day
Fourth Thurs in Nov Thanksgiving Day
Dec 25 Christmas Day

Maps

The free road maps distributed by each state through its tourist offices and welcome centres are usually fine for general driving and route planning.

Though most travellers now use GPS (SatNav) – which are available at all car rental offices – Rand McNally still produces maps for each state, bound together in the Rand McNally Road Atlas, and you're apt to find even cheaper state and regional maps at practically any gas station along the major highways. Britain's best source for maps is Stanfords, at 7 Mercer Walk, London WC2H 9FA (Ⓦstanfords.co.uk), and 29 Corn St, Bristol BS1 1HT; it also has a mail-order service.

The American Automobile Association, or AAA ("Triple A"; ☎800 222 4357, Ⓦaaa.com) provides free maps and assistance to its members, as well as to British members of the AA and RAC. Call the main number to get the location of a branch near you; bring your membership card or at least a copy of your membership number.

If you're after really detailed maps that go far beyond the usual fold-out, try Thomas Guides (Ⓦmapbooks4u. com). Highly detailed park, wilderness and topographical maps are available through the Bureau of Land Management for the West (Ⓦblm.gov) and for the entire country through the Forest Service (Ⓦfs.fed.us/maps). The best supplier of detailed, large-format map books for travel through the American backcountry is Benchmark Maps (Ⓦbenchmarkmaps.com), whose elegantly designed depictions are easy to follow and make even the most remote dirt roads look appealing.

Money

The US dollar comes in $1, $2, $5, $10, $20, $50 and $100 denominations. One dollar comprises one hundred cents, made up of combinations of one-cent pennies, five-cent nickels, ten-cent dimes and 25-cent quarters. You can check current exchange rates at Ⓦx-rates.com.

Bank hours generally run from 9am to 5pm Monday to Thursday, and until 6pm on Friday; the big bank names are Capital One, Chase, Bank of America, Citibank, Wells Fargo and US Bank. With an ATM card, you'll be able to withdraw cash just about anywhere, though you'll be charged $2–5 per transaction for using a different bank's network. Foreign cash-dispensing cards linked to international networks, such as Plus or Cirrus, are also widely accepted – ask your home bank or credit card company which branches you can use. To find the location of the nearest ATM, check with AmEx (Ⓦnetwork.americanexpress.com); Mastercard (Ⓦmastercard.us); Accel (Ⓦaccelnetwork. com); or Plus (Ⓦusa.visa.com).

Credit and debit cards are the most widely accepted form of payment at major hotels, restaurants and retailers, even though a few smaller merchants still do not accept them. You'll be asked to show some plastic when renting a car, bike or other such item, or to start a "tab" at hotels for incidental charges; in any case, you can always pay the bill in cash when you return the item or check out of your room.

Phones

The USA currently has well over one hundred area codes – three-digit numbers that must precede the seven-figure number if you're calling from abroad (following the 001 international access code) or from a different area code, in which case you prefix the ten digits with a 1. It can get confusing, especially as certain cities have several different area codes within their boundaries; for clarity, in this Guide, we've included the local area codes in all telephone numbers. Note that some cities require you to dial all ten digits, even when calling within the same code. Numbers that start with the digits 800 – or increasingly commonly 888, 877 and 866 – are toll-free, but these can only be called from within the USA itself; most hotels and many companies have a toll-free number that can easily be found on their websites.

Unless you can organize to do all your calling online via Skype (Ⓦskype.com), the cheapest way to make long-distance and international calls is to buy a prepaid phonecard, commonly found in newsagents or grocery stores, especially in urban areas. These are cheaper than the similar cards issued by the big phone companies, such as AT&T, that are usually on sale in pharmacy outlets and chain stores, and will charge only a few cents per minute to call from the USA to most European and other western countries. Such cards can be used from any touchpad phone but there is usually a surcharge for using them from a payphone (which, in any case, are increasingly rare).

CALLING HOME FROM THE USA

For country codes not listed below, dial 0 for the operator, consult any phone directory or log onto Ⓦcountrycallingcodes.com.
Australia 011 + 61 + area code minus its initial zero.
New Zealand 011 + 64 + area code minus its initial zero.
Republic of Ireland 011 + 353 + area code minus its initial zero.
South Africa 011 + 27 + area code.
UK 011 + 44 + area code minus its initial zero.

You can also usually arrange with your local telecom provider to have a chargecard account with free phone access in the USA, so that any calls you make are billed to your home. This may be convenient, but it's more expensive than using prepaid cards.

If you are planning to take your mobile phone (more often called a cell phone in America) from outside the USA, you'll need to check with your service provider whether it will work in the country: you will need a tri-band or quad-band phone that is enabled for international calls. Using your phone from home will probably incur hefty roaming charges for making calls and charge you extra for incoming calls, as the people calling you will be paying the usual rate. Depending on the length of your stay, it might make sense to rent a phone or buy a compatible prepaid SIM card from a US provider; check Ⓦ triptel.com or Ⓦ telestial.com. Alternatively, you could pick up an inexpensive pay-as-you-go phone from one of the major electrical shops.

Senior travellers

Anyone aged over 62 (with appropriate ID) can enjoy a vast range of discounts in the USA. Both Amtrak and Greyhound offer (smallish) percentage reductions on fares to older passengers, and any US citizen or permanent resident aged 62 or over is entitled to free admission for life to all national parks, monuments and historic sites using a Senior Pass. This free admission applies to all accompanying travellers in the same vehicle and also gives a fifty-percent reduction on park user fees, such as camping charges.

For discounts on accommodation, group tours and vehicle rental, US residents aged 50 or over should consider joining the AARP (American Association of Retired Persons; Ⓦ aarp.org) for an annual fee, or a multi-year deal; the website also offers lots of good travel tips and features. Road Scholar (☎ 800 454 5768, Ⓦ roadscholar.org) runs an extensive network of educational and activity programmes for people over 60 throughout the USA, at prices in line with those of commercial tours.

Shopping

The Rockies offers plenty of shopping opportunities – from the malls and boutiques of Denver and Aspen, to the arts and crafts stalls of small towns across the plains and mountains.

CLOTHING AND SHOE SIZES

WOMEN'S CLOTHING

American	4	6	8	10	12	14	16	18
British	6	8	10	12	14	16	18	20
Continental	34	36	38	40	42	44	46	48

WOMEN'S SHOES

American	5	6	7	8	9	10	11
British	3	4	5	6	7	8	9
Continental	36	37	38	39	40	41	42

MEN'S SHIRTS

American	14	15	15.5	16	16.5	17	17.5	18
British	14	15	15.5	16	16.5	17	17.5	18
Continental	36	38	39	41	42	43	44	45

MEN'S SHOES

American	7	7.5	8	8.5	9	9.5	10	10.5	11	11.5
British	6	7	7.5	8	8.5	9	9.5	10	11	12
Continental	39	40	41	42	42.5	43	44	44	45	46

MEN'S SUITS

American	34	36	38	40	42	44	46	48
British	34	36	38	40	42	44	46	48
Continental	44	46	48	50	52	54	56	58

When buying clothing and accessories, international visitors will need to convert their sizes into American equivalents (see page 43). For almost all purchases, state taxes will be applied (see page 38).

Time

The continental US covers four time zones, and there's one each for Alaska and Hawaii as well. Most of the Rockies fall within the Mountain Time Zone (MT), two hours behind the East Coast (10am in New York is 8am in Denver). However, the Idaho Panhandle in northern Idaho observes Pacific Time (north of the Salmon River); the Pacific zone also includes the three coastal states and Nevada, and is three hours behind New York (10am in the Big Apple is 7am in the Idaho Panhandle). The Eastern zone is a further five hours behind Greenwich Mean Time (GMT), so 3pm London time is 8am in Denver. The USA puts its clocks forward one hour to daylight saving time on the second Sunday in March and turns them back on the first Sunday in November.

Tourist information

Each state has its own tourist office (see box). These offer prospective visitors a colossal range of free maps, leaflets and brochures on attractions from overlooked wonders to the usual tourist traps. You can either contact the offices before you set off, or, as you travel around the country, look for the state-run "welcome centres", usually along main highways close to the state borders. In heavily visited states, these often have piles of discount coupons for cut-price accommodation and food. In addition, visitor centres in most towns and cities – often known as the "Convention and Visitors Bureau", or CVB, and listed throughout this Guide – provide details on the area, as do local Chambers of Commerce in almost any town of any size.

Travelling with children

Children under two years old go free on domestic flights (assuming they sit on your lap; seats are charged full price) and for ten percent of the adult fare on international flights – though that also doesn't mean they get a seat, let alone frequent-flier miles. Most airlines now charge kids aged between two and fourteen full-price tickets, though some country-specific discounts may apply for international flights. Discounts for Amtrak trains are better: children under two years go free (sharing a seat with an adult), but kids aged 2–12 also get 50 percent off. Bus travel is broadly similar to air travel – children (over two) and adults pay the same full fare.

Car-rental companies usually provide kids' car seats – which are required by law for children under the age of four – for around a daily charge. You would, however, be advised to check, or bring your own; they are not always available. Recreational vehicles (RVs) are a particularly good option for families. Even the cheapest motel will offer inexpensive two-double bed rooms as a matter of course, which is a relief for non-US travellers used to paying a premium for a "family room", or having to pay for two rooms.

Virtually all tourist attractions offer reduced rates for kids. Most large cities have natural history museums or aquariums, and quite a few also have hands-on children's museums; in addition most state and national parks organize children's activities. All the national restaurant chains provide highchairs and special kids' menus; and the trend for more upmarket family-friendly restaurants to provide crayons with which to draw on paper tablecloths is still going strong.

For a database of kids' attractions, events and activities all over the USA, check the useful site Ⓦ nickelodeonparents.com.

Travellers with disabilities

By international standards, the USA is exceptionally accommodating for travellers with mobility concerns or other physical disabilities. By law, all public buildings, including hotels and restaurants, must be wheelchair accessible and provide suitable toilet facilities. Most street corners have dropped curbs (less so in rural areas), and most public transport systems include subway stations with elevators and buses that "kneel" to let passengers in wheelchairs board.

Getting around

The Americans with Disabilities Act (1990) obliges all air carriers to make the majority of their services accessible to travellers with disabilities, and airlines will usually let attendants of more severely disabled people accompany them at no extra charge.

Almost every Amtrak train includes one or more coaches with accommodation for handicapped passengers. Guide dogs travel free and may accompany blind, deaf or disabled passengers. Be sure

---

STATE TOURISM INFORMATION

Colorado Ⓣ 800 265 6723, Ⓦ colorado.com
Idaho Ⓣ 800 847 4843, Ⓦ visitidaho.org
Montana Ⓣ 800 847 4868, Ⓦ visitmt.com
Wyoming Ⓣ 800 225 5996,
Ⓦ travelwyoming.com

to give 24 hours' notice. Hearing-impaired passengers can get information on ☎ 800 523 6590 (TTY/TDD).

Greyhound, however, has its challenges. Buses are not equipped with lifts for wheelchairs, though staff will assist with boarding (intercity carriers are required by law to do this), and the "Helping Hand" policy offers two-for-the-price-of-one tickets to passengers unable to travel alone (carry a doctor's certificate). The American Public Transportation Association, in Washington DC (Ⓦ apta.com), provides information about the accessibility of public transport in cities.

The American Automobile Association (contact Waaa.com for phone number access for each state) produces the Handicapped Driver's Mobility Guide, while the larger car-rental companies provide cars with hand controls at no extra charge, though only on their full-sized (ie most expensive) models; reserve well in advance.

Resources

Most state tourism offices provide information for disabled travellers (see page 43). In addition, SATH, the Society for Accessible Travel and Hospitality, in New York (Ⓦ sath.org), is a not-for-profit travel-industry group of travel agents, tour operators, hotel and airline management, and people with disabilities. They pass on any enquiry to the appropriate member, though you should allow plenty of time for a response. Mobility International USA, in Eugene, OR (Ⓦ miusa.org), offers travel tips and operates exchange programmes for disabled people; it also serves as a national information centre on disability.

The "America the Beautiful Access Pass", issued without charge to permanently disabled or blind US citizens, gives free lifetime admission to all national parks. It can only be obtained in person at a federal area where an entrance fee is charged; you'll have to show proof of permanent disability, or that you are eligible for receiving benefits under federal law.

Women travellers

A woman travelling alone in America is not usually made to feel conspicuous, or liable to attract unwelcome attention. Cities can feel a lot safer than you might expect, though particular care must be taken at night: walking through unlit, empty streets is never a good idea, and, if there's no bus service, take a taxi. Avoid travelling at night by public transport – deserted bus stations, if not actually threatening, will do little to make you feel secure.

Hitchhiking in the USA is never a good idea. Similarly, you should never pick up anyone who's trying to hitchhike. If someone is waving you down on the road,

ostensibly to get help with a broken-down vehicle, just drive on by or call the highway patrol to help them.

If you have been sexually assaulted the local sheriff's office will arrange for you to get help and counselling. The National Organization for Women (☎ 202 628 8669, Ⓦ now.org) has branches listed in local phone directories and on its website, and can provide information on rape crisis centres and counselling services.

RESOURCES AND SPECIALISTS

Gutsy Women Travel Anaheim, CA, Ⓦ gutsywomentravel.com. International agency that provides practical support and organizes trips for lone female travellers.

Her Ladyship Tavernier, FL, Ⓦ ladyshipsailing.com. Live-aboard, learn-to-sail cruises for women of all ages. Destinations may include Chesapeake Bay, Florida, the Pacific Northwest and the Virgin Islands.

The Women's Travel Group Bloomfield, NJ, Ⓦ thewomenstravelgroup.com. Arranges luxury and unusual vacations, itineraries, room-sharing and various activities for women.

Working in the USA

Permission to work in the USA can only be granted by the Immigration and Naturalization Service in the USA itself. Contact your local embassy or consulate for advice on current regulations, but be warned that unless you have relatives or a prospective employer in the USA to sponsor you, your chances are at best slim. Students have the best chance of prolonging their stay, while a number of volunteer and work programmes allow you to experience the country less like a tourist and more like a resident.

STUDY, VOLUNTEER AND WORK PROGRAMMES

American Field Service Intercultural Programs Ⓦ afs.org, Ⓦ afs.org.au, Ⓦ afs.org.nz, Ⓦ afs.org.za. Global UN-recognized organization running summer student exchange programmes to foster international understanding.

Camp America Ⓦ campamerica.co.uk. Well-known company that places young people as counsellors or support staff in US summer camps, for a minimum of nine weeks.

Council on International Educational Exchange (CIEE) Ⓦ ciee.org. Leading NGO offering study programmes and volunteer projects around the world.

Earthwatch Institute Ⓦ earthwatch.org. Long-established international charity with environmental and archeological research projects worldwide.

Frontier Ⓦ frontier.ac.uk. Global educational and conservation volunteering programmes at affordable prices, including some in the USA.

Go Overseas Ⓦ gooverseas.com. Specializes in gap year programmes and internships around the world, including a good number of opportunities in the USA.

The Rockies

WINTER TRAILS IN IDAHO

1 The Rockies

Only when you traverse the Rocky Mountain states of Colorado, Wyoming, Montana and Idaho does the immense size of the American West really hit home. Stretching over one thousand miles from the virgin forests on the Canadian border to the deserts of New Mexico, America's rugged spine encompasses an astonishing array of landscapes – geyser basins, lava flows, arid valleys and huge sand dunes – each in its own way as dramatic as the region's magnificent snow-capped peaks. All that geological grandeur is enhanced by wildlife such as bison, bear, moose and elk, and the conspicuous legacy of the miners, cowboys, outlaws and Native Americans who struggled over the area's rich resources during the nineteenth century.

Each of the four states has its own distinct character. **Colorado**, with fifty peaks over 14,000ft, is the most mountainous and populated, as well as the economic leader of the region with a liberal, progressive reputation. Friendly, sophisticated **Denver**, the Rockies' only major metropolis, is also the most visited city, in part because it serves as gateway to some of the best ski resorts in the country. Less touched by the tourist circus is vast, brawny **Montana**, where the "Big Sky" looks down on a glorious verdant manuscript scribbled over with gushing streams, lakes and tiny communities.

Vast stretches of scrubland fill **Wyoming**, the country's least populous state, its most conservative and traditionally Western, best known for gurgling, spitting **Yellowstone**, adjacent **Grand Teton National Park** and the nearby **Bighorn Mountains**. Rugged, remote whitewater-rafting hub **Idaho** holds some of the Rocky Mountains' last unexplored wildernesses, most notably the mighty **Sawtooth** range.

Colorado

Progressive and increasingly multicultural, **COLORADO** is the snowboarding, outdoorsy mountain state that produces more beer than any other, gave us *South Park* in 1997, and in 2012, legalized marijuana – its culture is often more Californian than cowboy, albeit without the ocean. Yet Colorado remains proud of its traditional Western roots, and it's not all mountains; a third of the state is covered by plains as flat as Nebraska, and in the south the dry, desert terrain resembles New Mexico. And it's only liberal to a point; parts are still very conservative, and it was here that horrific mass shootings took place in Columbine (1999) and Aurora (2012).

GREAT REGIONAL DRIVES

Beartooth Hwy, MT The most dramatic and scenic entry to Yellowstone, following US-212 from Red Lodge in Montana high across the snow-capped Beartooth Mountains.

I-70, CO The most spectacular interstate in the country begins to climb immediately beyond Denver, rising high into the Rockies, passing alpine ski villages and frozen lakes.

Hwy-24 to Pikes Peak, CO A staggeringly beautiful 19-mile drive up Pikes Peak, just west of Colorado Springs, with mountain views up to seventy miles distant.

Lariat Loop, CO Tour the rugged mountain scenery just west of Denver on this stunning 40-mile loop, passing the Buffalo Bill Museum & Grave.

Sawtooth Scenic Byway, ID Drive into the heart of pristine Idaho wilderness on meandering Hwy-75, 115 miles beside the Salmon River toward jagged, snowy peaks.

YELLOWSTONE NATIONAL PARK, WY

Highlights

❶ Durango & Silverton Narrow Gauge Railroad, CO This steam train ride corkscrews through spectacular mountains to the mining town of Silverton. See page 73

❷ Mesa Verde National Park, CO Explore the extraordinary cliffside dwellings, abandoned by the Ancestral Puebloans eight hundred years ago. See page 74

❸ Yellowstone National Park, WY A thermal wonderland, where wolves and bears prowl, and shaggy bison wander past towering geysers. See page 81

❹ Grand Teton National Park, WY This spectacular chain of mountains is prime territory for hiking, biking and wildlife viewing. See page 86

❺ Little Bighorn, MT One of the most famous battlefields in America looks much as it did in 1876, when Custer faced off against Sitting Bull and Crazy Horse. See page 92

❻ Going-to-the-Sun Road, Glacier National Park, MT The hairpin turns along this fifty-mile stretch offer staggering views near the Continental Divide. See page 104

❼ Sawtooth Mountains, ID Of all Idaho's 81 mountain ranges, the Sawtooth summits make for the most awe-inspiring scenic drive. See page 108

HIGHLIGHTS ARE MARKED ON THE MAP ON PAGE 4

1

Beyond the trendy capital **Denver**, the obvious attraction for travellers are the Rocky Mountains, littered with ski resorts such as **Aspen** that double as hiking and biking nirvanas in the summer, and with old silver towns like **Leadville** and **Crested Butte**. The most spectacular terrain and wildlife is protected within **Rocky Mountain National Park** and around **Pikes Peak**, which towers over the state's second largest city, **Colorado Springs**. The far west of the state stretches onto the red-rock deserts of the Colorado Plateau, where the dry climate has preserved the extraordinary natural sculptures of **Colorado National Monument**, while the southwest boasts **Mesa Verde National Park**, home to remarkable cliff cities left by the ancient Ancestral Puebloans.

Denver

Its substantial ensemble of glittering skyscrapers marking the final transition between the Great Plains and the American West, **DENVER** stands at the threshold of the **Rocky Mountains**. Though clearly visible from downtown, the majestic peaks of the Front

HIGHLIGHTS

1. Durango & Silverton Narrow Gauge Railroad, CO
2. Mesa Verde National Park, CO
3. Yellowstone National Park, WY
4. Grand Teton National Park, WY
5. Little Bighorn, MT
6. Going-to-the-Sun Road, Glacier National Park, MT
7. Sawtooth Mountains, ID

THE ROCKIES

1

Range start to rise roughly fifteen miles west, and the "**Mile High City**" (at an elevation of 5280ft) is itself uniformly flat.

Denver was founded in 1858, near turgid Cherry Creek and the location of Colorado's first **gold** strike. Prospectors swiftly moved on, but Denver has remained the state's most important commercial and transport nexus and today's artsy, liberal population coexists happily with a dynamic business community.

16th Street Mall

Denver is highly unusual among the cities of the West in having a lively **downtown** core, its regeneration sparked by the opening of **Coors Field** (home of Major League baseball's Colorado Rockies) in 1995. At its heart lie the shops and restaurants of **LoDo** (Lower Downtown) and of **16th Street Mall** (ⓦ16thstreetmalldenver.com), a pedestrianized strip more than a mile in length. Sprinkled with shady trees, food carts and painted pianos (summer daily 8am–10pm), free for anyone to play, the street is also served by **free MallRide buses** (Mon–Fri 5am–1.30am, Sat 5.30am–1.30am, Sun 6.30am–1.30am; every 1.5–15min) and on summer evenings in particular it's bursting with activity. It can also boast one of the best independent **bookstores** in the US: the **Tattered Cover** (ⓦtatteredcover.com), at 1991 Wazee St, and inside the venerable Union Street train station at 1701 Wynkoop St. Further south along the mall, the 1910 **D&F Clocktower** (325ft), modelled on the Campanile in Piazza San Marco, Venice, is all that remains of a department store demolished in the 1970s. A few blocks southwest, a 40ft **blue bear** peers hopefully in through the windows of the Denver Convention Center on 14th Street, officially titled *I See What You Mean*, it has rapidly established itself as an iconic landmark.

Colorado State Capitol

200 E Colfax Ave • Mon–Fri 7.30am–5pm; free tours (45min) hourly, or every 30min June & July (Mon–Fri 10am–3pm) • ⓦ leg.colorado.gov/agencies/legislative-council-staff/tour-information

Three blocks from the southeastern end of 16th Street, the **Colorado State Capitol** offers a commanding view of the Rockies swelling on the western horizon; the thirteenth step up to its entrance is exactly one mile above sea level. The building itself is an elegant but fairly subdued Neoclassical pile compared to other state capitols, completed in 1908 as a rather predictable copy of the Capitol in Washington DC, replete with giant murals and ornate stained glass. Climb the 99 steps up the dome for an even better view (on guided tours only).

Denver Art Museum

100 W 14th Ave Pkwy • Daily 10am–5pm, Tues until 9pm • Charge • ⓦ denverartmuseum.org

The splendidly eclectic collections of the **Denver Art Museum** spread through two separate modern buildings, either side of 13th Avenue. The Hamilton Building holds contemporary artworks, including Sandy Skoglund's spooky installation *Fox Games*, as well as galleries of African and Pacific island works, while the North Building has a spectacular array of Native American and pre-Columbian artefacts of all kinds – its Olmec miniatures are truly extraordinary.

Clyfford Still Museum

1250 Bannock St • Tues–Sun, 10am–5pm • Charge • ⓦ clyffordstillmuseum.org

When abstract painting pioneer **Clyfford Still** died in Maryland in 1980, his will stipulated that his estate be given to any American city willing to establish a museum dedicated solely to his work. It wasn't until 2004 that Denver stepped up, and seven years later the **Clyfford Still Museum** opened next to the art museum, a wonderful space for a rotating collection of 825 paintings and 1575 works on paper. Still's abstract expressionism can be heavy going, but the giant canvases and jagged swirls of colour are incredibly absorbing.

1

History Colorado Center

1200 Broadway • Daily 10am–5pm • Charge • ⓦ historycolorado.org

The history of the state is artfully explored at the **History Colorado Center**, not a typical museum experience: exhibits are enhanced with videos and interactive displays throughout, with permanent galleries organized by theme rather than chronology. One section recreates life in the plains town of Keota in the 1920s, while "Colorado Stories" features everything from the exploits of Kit Carson to the advent of leisure skiing.

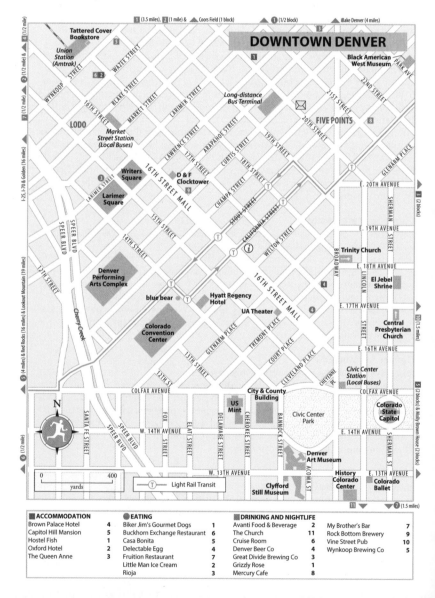

DOWNTOWN DENVER

1

Molly Brown House Museum

1340 Pennsylvania St • Tues–Sat 10am–4.30pm (also Mon June–Aug), Sun noon–4.30pm (tour every 30min till 3.30pm) • Charge • ⓦ mollybrown.org

The "**unsinkable Molly Brown**" has been an American icon since her survival of the *Titanic* disaster in 1912, her myth cemented by the eponymous musical and the Debbie Reynolds movie of 1964. The gorgeously preserved **Molly Brown House Museum**, purchased by Margaret Tobin Brown's rich husband in 1894, explodes many of the myths (not least the fact Margaret was never "Molly"), but tours (the only way to get inside the house) also emphasize just how remarkable and generous a life the real woman led, working tirelessly for causes such as women's suffrage and social justice. The house has been restored to its 1910 grandeur, loaded with period pieces, many of which belonged to the Browns.

Black American West Museum

3091 California St • Fri & Sat 10am–2pm • Charge • ⓦ bawmhc.org

Denver's black community is most prominent in the old **Five Points** district, northeast of LoDo, created to house black railroad workers in the 1870s. The **Black American West Museum** has intriguing details on black pioneers and outlaws, and debunks Western myths: one third of all nineteenth-century cowboys were black, and many were former slaves who left the South after the Civil War. The museum is housed in the former home and clinic of Colorado's first black female doctor, Justina Ford (1871–1952), who purchased this property in 1911.

Coors Brewery Tour

1221 Ford St, at 13th, Golden • Mon & Thurs–Sat, 10am–4pm (June–Aug also Tues & Wed), Sun noon–4pm • Charge • ⓦ millercoors.com/breweries/coors-brewing-company/tours

Ever since 1873 the town of **Golden**, fifteen miles west of downtown but essentially a Denver suburb, has been virtually synonymous with beer giant **Coors** and the world's largest single brewery facility (known since 2007 as MillerCoors). The brewery is three blocks east of Golden's main thoroughfare, Washington Avenue, served by regular buses from Market Street Station in Denver. Self-guided tours highlight the malting, brewing and packaging processes, ending with a tasting session of such products as the much-maligned low-cal Coors Light, and the wildly successful **Blue Moon Belgian White**.

Lookout Mountain

987½ Lookout Mountain Rd, Golden • **Buffalo Bill Museum** May–Oct daily, 9am–5pm; Nov–April, Tues–Sun, 10am–5pm • Charge • ⓦ buffalobill.org

Among the peaks that rise sharply behind downtown Golden is **Lookout Mountain**, the final (and highly photogenic) resting place of **Buffalo Bill Cody**, the famed frontiersman and showman who died in Denver in 1917. Despite protests from Cody, Wyoming, the town Bill had co-founded (see page 80), Cody's wife insisted that Lookout Mountain was always his first choice (folks in Cody have argued for the body's "return" ever since). The views of Denver, framed by the two Table mountains, are spectacular, and the modest gravesite itself is free – you'll have to pay to see the gruesome artefacts in the adjacent **Buffalo Bill Museum**, which include a pistol with a handle fashioned from human bone. The mountain lies on the **Lariat Loop** (ⓦ lariatloop.org), a forty-mile National Scenic Byway that takes in the grandest mountain scenery in a half-day's drive from Denver.

Red Rocks Park

18300 W Alameda Pkwy, Morrison • Visitor Center, April–Oct, 7am–7pm; Nov–March, 8am–4pm; Center and Amphitheatre close at 2pm on event days • Free • ⓦ redrocksonline.com

Some fifteen miles west of downtown Denver, the remarkable sandstone outcrops of **Red Rocks Park** are best known for the **Red Rocks Amphitheatre** (open 1hr before

1

COLORADO MARIJUANA – THE RULES

Since 2012, **adults 21 or older** in Colorado can **legally buy and possess one ounce** (28 grams) of **marijuana** – this also applies to tourists and foreigners, but you will need an official picture ID to prove your age (passport should do). Most marijuana stores operate from 8am until midnight (Denver stores are required to close by 7pm, however). Consumption is a bit of a problem for visitors; officially, it's still illegal to smoke/ingest marijuana "openly and publicly", and so far there are no Amsterdam-style coffeeshops here. Your best bet is to ask at your hotel/hostel about the latest places where you can consume the drug legally. **The Coffee Joint**, 1130 Yuma Court (Ⓦthecoffeejointco.com) allows electronic vaping and the consumption of edibles, as long as you bring your own. Otherwise your only other (legal) options are "private" clubs such as **iBake Denver** (Ⓦibakedenver.com), where you pay a small fee to enter ($3/day). Note also that in the states surrounding Colorado – Nebraska, New Mexico, Kansas, Utah and Wyoming – smoking or possession of any amount of marijuana is illegal, regardless of where you purchased it, and will result in a hefty fine or even jail time. For other states where marijuana is legal, see page 39.

sunrise to 1hr after sunset). This spectacular 9000-capacity venue, squeezed between two glowing 400ft red-sandstone rocks, has been the setting for thousands of rock and classical concerts since completion in 1941 (though the location itself has hosted concerts since 1906); U2 filmed *Under a Blood Red Sky* here in 1983. The surrounding park features several trails and viewpoints, while the Visitor Center contains displays on the history of the site and the Performers' Hall Of Fame. Just down the road, the Trading Post (the original park store completed in 1931) contains the **Colorado Music Hall of Fame** (daily: March & Oct 9am–5pm; April & Sept 9am–6pm; May–Aug 9am–7pm; Nov–Feb 9am–4pm; free; Ⓦcmhof.org).

ARRIVAL AND DEPARTURE   DENVER

By plane Denver International Airport (Ⓦflydenver.com) is 24 miles northeast of downtown. Taxis charge a flat rate to downtown and to Boulder (elsewhere is on the meter). The University of Colorado A Line (light rail) links the airport with Union Station, downtown (37min), every 15–30min (daily 3am–1am). RTD buses (Ⓦrtd-denver.com) serve various locations downtown every 15–30min (daily 3.30am–midnight). Shared-ride shuttles, such as Denver Best Rides (Ⓦdenverbestrides.com), drop passengers at downtown hotels, and also serve the ski resorts further afield.

By train Amtrak trains arrive on the northwest edge of downtown at Union Station, 1701 Wynkoop St.
Destinations Chicago (1 daily; 18hr 40min); Glenwood Springs (1 daily; 5hr 40min); Grand Junction (1 daily; 7hr 52min); Omaha (1 daily; 8hr 50min); Salt Lake City (1 daily; 15hr).

By bus The Greyhound terminal (☎303 293 6555) is close to downtown at 1055 19th St.
Destinations Colorado Springs (4 daily; 1hr 30min–1hr 45min); Glenwood Springs (2 daily; 3hr 35min); Grand Junction (3 daily; 5hr 5min–5hr 45min); Omaha (2 daily; 9hr 5min–10hr 20min); Vail (5 daily; 2hr 20min–3hr).

GETTING AROUND AND INFORMATION

By bus Free buses run up and down 16th Street Mall (see page 51), while RTD also run pay-to-ride buses throughout the city (Ⓦrtd-denver.com); frequent services to local sports venues and the airport leave from the Market Street Station at Market and 16th. Buy a MyRide reloadable fare card to get up to $0.20 off each ride (accepted on light rail also).

By bike The Denver Bike Sharing Program (Ⓦdenverbcycle. com) requires a minimum access pass of $9/24hr, and charges

$5/30min after the first 30min (unlimited 30min trips free).

By light rail Denver's multi-line light rail system (daily, 24hr; Ⓦrtd-denver.com) links downtown, the 16th Street Mall, the Denver Broncos stadium, the Pepsi Center and the airport.

Visitor centre Downtown at 1575 California St, near 16th Street Mall (May–Oct Mon–Fri 9am–5.30pm, Sat 9am–5pm, Sun 10am–2pm; Nov–April Mon–Fri 9am–5pm, Sat 9am–2pm, Sun 10am–2pm; ☎303 892 1505, Ⓦdenver.org).

ACCOMMODATION   SEE MAP PAGE 52

Brown Palace Hotel 321 17th St, Ⓦbrownpalace.com. Beautiful downtown landmark dating from 1892, with elegant dining rooms and public areas, as well as impeccable rooms. The eight-storey cast-iron atrium is stunning. $̲$̲$̲$̲

Capitol Hill Mansion 1207 Pennsylvania St, ⓦcapitolhillmansion.com. Luxurious, LGBT-friendly B&B in a turreted 1891 Richardson Romanesque sandstone mansion on a leafy street near the State Capitol. Each of its eight antique-furnished rooms is delightful, and several include large whirlpool tubs. $$$

Hostel Fish 1217 20th St, ⓦhostelfish.com. Solid budget option near downtown, with modern dorms (triple bunks), all with different themes and compact but comfy doubles. Free iPad use, charging stations at every bed and strong wi-fi. Dorms $̄; doubles $$$

Oxford Hotel 1600 17th St, ⓦtheoxfordhotel.com. In LoDo since 1891, this historic hotel oozes charm and offers stylish rooms featuring European antiques and Bose stereo systems. $$$$

★**The Queen Anne** 2147 Tremont Place, ⓦqueenannebnb.com. Central, eco-friendly and very hospitable 1879 B&B near a peaceful park where you can catch a carriage ride; each of the fourteen rooms and suites is tastefully and individually decorated. $$$

EATING   SEE MAP PAGE 52

★**Biker Jim's Gourmet Dogs** 2148 Larimer St, ⓦbikerjimsdogs.com. Originally a street vendor, Jim Pittinger knocks out superb hot dogs from this bricks-and-mortar venue near Coors Field, with everything from reindeer or wild boar brats (bratwurst sausages) to spicy elk and buffalo, all perfectly charred and served with caramelized onions. $̄

Buckhorn Exchange Restaurant 1000 Osage St, ⓦbuckhorn.com. Denver's (and one of America's) oldest restaurants since 1893, an old-school saloon that specializes in huge beef steaks, buffalo steaks, lamb and game like elk and quail. $$$$

Casa Bonita 6715 W Colfax Ave, Lakewood, ⓦcasabonitadenver.com. This Denver institution (lampooned in *South Park*) has been serving up Mexican food and kitsch family fun since 1974, aided by its 85ft pink tower, puppet shows and Tex-Mex paraphernalia. Try the "all-you-can-eat deluxe dinners" (beef or chicken). $$

Delectable Egg 1625 Court Place, ⓦdelectableegg. com. Local mini-chain knocking out the extra fluffy Denver omelette (filled with ham, green peppers and onions), "Delectable" Burgers and a vast range of specials, wraps and burritos. $̄

★**Fruition Restaurant** 1313 E 6th Ave ⓦfruitionrestaurant.com. Gourmet trend-setter on Denver's dynamic farm-to-table scene, with seasonal menus that might include pan-roasted scallops, walleye pike with roast fennel and roasted lamb loin with lentils and apricots. $$$

Little Man Ice Cream 2620 16th St ⓦlittlemanicecream.com. Purveyors of hugely addictive ice cream, with scoops of hand-made flavours such as nutmeg, gingerbread and bourbon-spiked buttercream. $̄

Rioja 1431 Larimer St ⓦriojadenver.com. Creative and hugely enjoyable Mediterranean cuisine, with robust meat, fish and pasta mains, and some tables outside. $$

DRINKING AND NIGHTLIFE   SEE MAP PAGE 52

Denver's liveliest nightlife is concentrated in the LoDo district, which runs the gamut from brewpubs and sports bars to upmarket cocktail bars, while SoCo (South of Colfax) boasts several nightclubs within four blocks (see ⓦcoclubs. com). For events listings, see the free weekly *Denver Westword* (ⓦwestword.com).

Avanti Food & Beverage 1962 Market St, ⓦavantifandb.com. This "collective eatery" features four bars serving twenty draft beers, cocktails and affordably priced wines, with stellar views from the rooftop deck.

The Church 1160 Lincoln St, ⓦcoclubs.com/the-church. A dance club inside a gutted 1865 church that combines a downtown nightlife landmark, wine bar, sushi bar and three invariably busy dancefloors. Programming varies from Latin (Sat) to garage to hip-hop, and the crowd can be equally eclectic. Cover charged.

Cruise Room Oxford Hotel, 1600 17th St, ⓦtheoxfordhotel.com. This 1933 replica of the Art Deco martini bar on the *Queen Mary* ocean liner boasts a free jukebox and excellent cocktails.

DENVER'S TOP FIVE BREWPUBS

Denver Beer Co 1695 Platte St, ⓦdenverbeerco. com. Seasonal, small-batch producer, with German-style beer garden. Sample the Graham Cracker Porter, a robust stout.

Great Divide Brewing Co 2201 Arapahoe St ⓦgreatdivide.com. Pioneer since 1994, home of Denver Pale Ale and Titan IPA.

Rock Bottom Brewery 1001 16th St, ⓦrockbottom.

com. Craft brewing chain founded in Denver. Best brew: Molly's Titanic Brown Ale.

Vine Street Pub 1700 Vine St, ⓦmountainsunpub. com. Best neighbourhood brewpub, home of the ultra-hoppy Colorado Kind Ale.

Wynkoop Brewing Co 1634 18th St, ⓦwynkoop. com. The state's oldest brewpub; try the Railyard Ale, a smooth amber beer.

1

Grizzly Rose 5450 N Valley Hwy, ⓦgrizzlyrose.com. Huge, legendary country-music venue, 10min drive north of downtown on I-25, where nightly bands include some famous names, and there's even a mechanical bull. Cover charged.

★ **Mercury Cafe** 2199 California St, ⓦmercurycafe. com. When the *Merc*'s not hosting jazz, you'll find tango dance classes, poetry readings or some other form of entertainment. A good-value restaurant serves healthy choices (many vegetarian) as well as high tea.

My Brother's Bar 2376 15th St, ⓦmybrothersbar.com. Legendary dive bar with appropriately crabby staff, superb burgers and loyal regulars. Open since 1873, this is where Jack Kerouac hung out when visiting regular Neal Cassady in the 1950s.

ENTERTAINMENT

Denver Performing Arts Complex 1400 Curtis St, ⓦartscomplex.com. Home to the Denver Center for the Performing Arts, Colorado Symphony Orchestra, Opera Colorado and the Colorado Ballet. Facilities include eight theatres, as well as the acoustically superb, in-the-round Symphony Hall.

Colorado Springs and around

Sprawling for ten miles alongside I-25, **COLORADO SPRINGS** was founded as a holiday resort in 1871 by railroad tycoon William Jackson Palmer. He attracted so many English gentry to the town that it earned the nickname "Little London". Today the city of more than half a million remains a tourist magnet, peppered with family-friendly attractions under the shadow of **Pikes Peak**, and happily coexisting with some major defence industry contractors and a high military presence (most notably Fort Carson, Peterson Air Force Base and the US Air Force Academy).

Colorado Springs is also home to the **United States Olympic Training Center** and the **World Figure Skating Museum** (20 First St; ⓦworldskatingmuseum.org). There's otherwise not much to see downtown, but **Historic Old Colorado City** (west of downtown along Colorado Avenue, between 23rd and 27th streets) is a great place to shop and eat, and the stretch of Hwy-24 further west is especially fun for families.

Garden of the Gods

I-25 exit 146 • **Garden of the Gods** Daily: May–Oct 5am–10pm; Nov–April 5am–9pm • Free • **Visitor & Nature Center** 1805 N 30th St • Daily: summer 8am–7pm; rest of year 9am–5pm • Free • ⓦ gardenofgods.com

Maintained as a city park, the **Garden of the Gods** is a bizarre ensemble of gnarled and warped red sandstone that looks more like arid Arizona than the Rocky Mountains that frame it. Loop roads and hiking trails lace the park (which is just over five square miles), passing finely balanced overhangs, jagged pinnacles, massive pedestals and mushroom formations; you'll find maps and exhibits on the area's geology and history at the **visitor centre** at the eastern border. Avoid summer weekends when the place is packed.

Manitou Springs

Small **Manitou Springs**, five miles west of Colorado Springs on Hwy-24, is an attractive if touristy town of stately Victorian buildings, shops, restaurants and eleven natural springs – carbonated (and cool) mineral waters that made the resort famous in the 1880s. You can still safely sip the water for free; each spring has a subtly different taste, but the **Twin Spring** on Ruxton Avenue is the sweetest.

Manitou Cliff Dwellings

10 Cliff Rd (5 miles west of I-25 on Hwy-24) • Daily: May–Aug 9am–6pm; March, April, Sept & Oct 9am–5pm; Nov 9am–4pm; Dec–Feb 10am–4pm • Charge • ⓦ cliffdwellingsmuseum.com

If you don't have time to visit Mesa Verde (see page 74) or any of the ancient pueblos further south, the **Manitou Cliff Dwellings** will provide a decent if slightly incongruous introduction to the great **Anasazi culture** of the southwest. The small on-site **museum** contains artefacts, pottery and descriptions of Anasazi life, but the centrepiece is the strip of impressive dwellings themselves, set enigmatically into the red sandstone cliffside – you can wander through them via narrow passageways. What isn't made especially clear, however, is that these dwellings are actually reconstructions, using original Anasazi bricks and stones salvaged from ruins in McElmo Canyon (close to Mesa Verde), but opened here specifically as a tourist attraction in 1907.

Pikes Peak

Toll road 5069 Pikes Peak Hwy, Cascade • Daily: Late May to early Sept 7.30am–6pm; rest of Sept 7.30am–5pm; Oct to late May 9am–3pm • Charge • ⓦ pikespeak.us.com • **Railway** 515 Ruxton Ave, Manitou Springs • Charge • ⓦ cograilway.com

The mind-bending, nineteen-mile drive up **Pikes Peak**, ten miles west of Colorado Springs on Hwy-24, is one of the most spectacular roads in the country, affording (on a clear day) jaw-dropping panoramas of snow-capped Rockies to the north and west, and the immense vastness of the Great Plains to the eastern horizon; it's even possible to see Denver seventy miles north.

Though not the tallest mountain in the Rockies (or even Colorado), Pikes Peak (14,115ft) is the best known – largely because the view from its crest inspired songwriter **Katharine Lee Bates** to write the words to "*America The Beautiful*" after a visit in 1893. It's named after American army general and explorer Zebulon Pike, who mapped the summit in 1806, but failed to climb it himself.

Most visitors drive up the mountain; the **toll road** is paved all the way, with plenty of pull-outs to admire the views. An easy alternative is the thrilling **Pikes Peak Cog Railway**, which grinds its way up an average of 847ft per mile on its ninety-minute journey to the summit. Hardier souls can hike to the top via the 11.8-mile **Barr Trail**, which gains 7900ft elevation from a trailhead just beyond the cog railway depot; this is an extremely tough climb, and most hikers spend one night in Barr Camp (ⓦ barrcamp.com).

However you reach it, be prepared for freezing winds and snow on the bleak and windswept peak; a gift shop and café provide welcome relief.

ARRIVAL AND DEPARTURE   **COLORADO SPRINGS AND AROUND**

By bus Greyhound stops at 120 S Weber St downtown (ⓦ greyhound.com). Groome Transportation runs direct to Denver Airport (☎ 719 687 3456, ⓦ groometransportation. com). Destinations Albuquerque (1 daily; 7hr); Denver (4 daily; 1hr 10min–1hr 50min).

Visitor centre 515 S Cascade Ave, I-25 exit 141 (summer daily 8.30am–5pm; rest of year Mon–Fri 8.30am–5pm; ☎ 719 635 7506, ⓦ visitcos.com).

ACCOMMODATION AND EATING

Airplane Restaurant 1665 N Newport Rd, ⓦ theairplanerestaurant.com. Not the best food in town (think baby back ribs), but hey, this restaurant is actually inside an old military aeroplane (a Boeing KC-97, built in 1953). The cockpit is open for kids to play in. $$

Marigold Café 4605 Centennial Blvd, ⓦ marigoldcoloradosprings.com. Good lunchtime sandwiches, patisserie (Mon–Sat 8am–9pm) and, in the evenings, delicious French-inspired bistro food that belies the drab exterior. $$

★ **The Mining Exchange** 8 S Nevada Ave, ⓦ wyndhamhotels.com. Well worth the splurge, with spacious, luxurious rooms, excellent staff and beautifully restored premises dating from 1901 (it was once a stock exchange for mining companies). $$$

Phantom Canyon Brewing Co 2 E Pikes Peak Ave, ⓦ phantomcanyon.com. Great place for craft-brewed beer and filling pub food such as loaded chile fries, beer pretzels and beer-battered fish and chips. Includes great vegetarian options too. $$

Pikes Peak Chocolate and Ice Cream 805 Manitou Ave, Manitou Springs, ⓦ pikespeakchocolate.com. Sweet treat central, selling chocolates, fudge and exquisite ice cream. $

Great Sand Dunes National Park

11500 Hwy-150, Mosca • Open daily 24hr • Charge

Your first sight of **GREAT SAND DUNES NATIONAL PARK** comes as a shock; far from being tucked away in crevices or sheltered in a valley, the dunes are simply a colossal pile of sand that appears to have been dumped alongside the craggy Sangre de Cristo

1

Mountains, 170 miles southwest of Colorado Springs. Over millions of years, these fine glacial grains have eroded from the San Juan Mountains and blown east until they could drift no further; the result is an eerie and deeply incongruous fifty-square-mile area of silky, shifting trackless desert, visible from miles around.

The park's **visitor centre** is three miles beyond the park entrance. Shortly beyond that lies the goal for most visitors, the "**beach**" beside Medano Creek, which flows along the eastern and southern side of the dune mass, often mobbed by local families frolicking in the water in summer. To reach the dunes themselves, you'll have to wade across the shallow creek, but be sure to take shoes – the sand can get incredibly hot. The dunes loom very large from the moment you start walking, but depending on current drifting it may take ten minutes or just to reach the base, which can be hugely tiring, especially when the often-high winds swirl grit into your eyes at every step. Your reward is the sheer fun of climbing up the actual dunes, and, especially, sliding back down again (bring your own dune board). The scenery is spectacular; climb the 750ft peak of **Star Dune**, the tallest, for views across the whole park, but start early and take plenty of water.

INFORMATION   GREAT SAND DUNES NATIONAL PARK

Visitor centre Daily: summer 8.30am–5pm, rest of year   9am–4.30pm; ☎ 719 378 6399, ⓦ nps.gov/grsa.

ACCOMMODATION AND EATING

Great Sand Dunes Lodge 7900 Hwy-150, Mosca, ⓦ gsdlodge.com. The only hotel in the area is just outside the park entrance, with pleasant rooms (satellite TV included), views of the dunes, an indoor pool and outdoor gas grills. Open mid-March to late Oct. $$$

Great Sand Dunes Oasis 7800 Hwy-150, Mosca, ⓦ greatdunes.com. In front of the lodge, this is the only restaurant for miles around, serving burgers, frybread and Mexican specialities, and also offers showers, laundry and tent sites (some with hook-ups), as well as a small number of basic cabins and more comfortable motel-like doubles (April to mid-Oct). Camping from $, cabins $, doubles $$$

Boulder

The lively college town of **BOULDER**, just 27 miles northwest of Denver on US-36, was founded in 1858 by a prospecting party who felt that the nearby Flatiron Mountains "looked right for gold"; they found little, but the community grew anyway. Today it's an affluent, liberal and outdoorsy place, dominated by the **University of Colorado** (CU) and surrounded by miles of hiking trails and parks. Downtown centres on the leafy pedestrian mall of **Pearl Street**, lined with bustling cafés, buskers, galleries and stores (including several places where you can rent **mountain bikes**). The most obvious short excursion by bike (or on foot) is the 5.5-mile **Boulder Creek Path**, which runs through the centre to Boulder Canyon, along the lush riverbank. The **Boulder Museum of Contemporary Art**, 1750 13th St (Tues–Sun 11am–5pm; charge; ⓦ bmoca.org), across the creek from the exceptional *Dushanbe Teahouse* (see page 59), holds high-quality temporary exhibits from a global roster of artists. The manicured campus of **University of Colorado** (CU), founded in 1876, lies two miles southeast of Pearl Street mall, home of the beloved Colorado Buffaloes sports teams and marked by distinctive sandstone red-tiled buildings and a handful of museums (ⓦ colorado.edu). The well-respected **Colorado Shakespeare Festival** (ⓦ coloradoshakes.org) is held here each summer.

ARRIVAL, GETTING AROUND AND INFORMATION   BOULDER

By bus Denver's RTD (ⓦ rtd-denver.com) runs the regular FF1 and FF2 buses (45–50min) from downtown Denver to the Downtown Boulder Station, at 1800 14th St (☎ 303 299 6000). **By bike** The Boulder Bike Sharing Program (ⓦ boulder.bcycle. com) requires a minimum access pass of $8/24hr, and charges

$3/30min after first 30min (unlimited 30min trips free). **Visitor centres** 1301 Pearl St (daily 10am–8pm, hours vary seasonally; ☎ 303 417 1365, ⓦ bouldercoloradousa. com); Boulder Convention & Visitors Bureau, 2440 Pearl St (Mon–Fri 8.30am–5pm; ☎ 303 442 2911).

1

ACCOMMODATION

Foot of the Mountain Motel 200 W Arapahoe Ave, ⓦfootofthemountainmotel.com. Friendly, log-cabin-style motel redolent of the 1950s, nine blocks west of downtown beside Boulder Creek. $$

★ **Hotel Boulderado** 2115 13th St, ⓦboulderado.com. Gorgeous historic hotel opened in 1909, with its famous stained-glass canopy ceiling, cherry-wood staircase and balcony overlooking the lobby. Rooms are decked out in Victorian grandeur, with period furniture and wallpaper. Worth a visit even if you're not staying here. $$$$

EATING, DRINKING AND NIGHTLIFE

★ **Boulder Dushanbe Teahouse** 1770 13th St, ⓦboulderteahouse.com. Gorgeous teahouse and restaurant decorated by artisans from Tajikistan (Dushanbe is Boulder's sister city); choose from over 100 kinds of tea, but also from a menu of Basque, Persian, Japanese and Indian dishes. $

★ **Flagstaff House** 1138 Flagstaff Rd, ⓦflagstaffhouse.com. The undisputed five-star champ of Boulder restaurants, with spectacular views and specializing in French cuisine with Asian influences; the soft-shell crab season is justly legendary. $$$$

★ **Fox Theatre** 1135 13th St, ⓦfoxtheatre.com. Excellent live venue in the "Hill" CU district, built in 1926, but with a sensational sound system and a high-quality line-up of bands.

Laughing Goat 1709 Pearl St, ⓦthelaughinggoat.com. Classic Boulder boho café, with tasty coffee, wacky art, music, poetry and even local beer. $

West End Tavern 926 Pearl St, ⓦthewestendtavern.com. Nice spot for roots music, locally brewed beer, tasty barbecue and spectacular views of the Flatirons from the roof terrace. $$

Rocky Mountain National Park

Open daily 24hr • Charge • There is no public transport to the park nor its gateway towns, the nearest of which is Estes Park, 65 miles northwest of Denver

To experience the full, pristine grandeur of the Rockies, and especially its wildlife, a visit to the **ROCKY MOUNTAIN NATIONAL PARK** is essential. The park straddles the Continental Divide at elevations often well in excess of 10,000ft, with large sections inhabited by elk herds, moose, black bears and bighorn sheep. A full third of the park is above the tree line, and large areas of snow never melt; the name of the **Never Summer Mountains** speaks volumes about the long, empty expanses of arctic-style tundra. The park's lower reaches, among the rich forests, hold patches of lush greenery; you never know when you may stumble upon a sheltered mountain meadow flecked with flowers. Parallels with the European Alps spring to mind – helped, of course, by the heavy-handed Swiss and Bavarian themes of so many local motels and restaurants. Note however, that at a tenth of the size of Yellowstone, the park attracts a similar number of visitors – more than three million per year, the bulk of whom come in high summer, meaning that the one main road through the mountains can get incredibly congested.

Trail Ridge Road

The showpiece of the park is **Trail Ridge Road** (open late May to mid-Oct), the 45-mile stretch of US-34 that connects the small gateway towns of **Estes Park** and **Grand Lake** (on the west side of the park). The highest-elevation paved road in any US national park (cresting at 12,183ft) it affords a succession of tremendous views, and several short trails

---

HIKING THE ROCKY MOUNTAIN NATIONAL PARK

As ever, the best way to appreciate the Rocky Mountain National Park is on foot. The obvious launching point for numerous day and overnight hikes is **Bear Lake**, a pretty spot at the end of a spur road from Estes Park where the mountains are framed to perfection in its cool, still waters. A favourite is the one-way hike from Bear Lake to the Fern Lake Trailhead (9.2 miles) in the Moraine Park area (taking the shuttle back), though the hike to Emerald Lake (3.5 miles) is also recommended. Experienced hikers tackle the hard but spectacular 9.6-mile round-trip climb up Mt Ida (12,865ft).

1

start from car parks along the way. Majestic peaks and alpine tundra are at their most breathtaking to either side of the **Alpine Visitor Center** (see page 61), halfway along at Fall River Pass at 11,796ft. If you're generally happy to admire the scenery from your car, the visitor centre is really the only requisite stop along the way, for its **exhibits** explaining the flora and fauna of the tundra and also its simple, good-value **cafeteria**. Good areas for wildlife viewing (especially elk) lie a little further east around Timber Creek.

Old Fall River Road

An alternative scenic drive through the park follows the unpaved, summer-only **Old Fall River Road**, completed in 1920. Running east–west (one-way) along the bed of a U-shaped glacial valley, it doesn't have open mountain vistas, but it's much quieter than its paved counterpart, and there's far more chance of spotting **wildlife**: roaming the area are moose, coyote, mountain lions and black bears.

GETTING AROUND AND INFORMATION   ROCKY MOUNTAIN NATIONAL PARK

By shuttle bus Free shuttle buses (late May to early Oct, daily 7am–7pm) run through the park; between Moraine Park Discovery Center and Sprague Lake (every 20min), and between Sprague Lake and Bear Lake (every 15min).
Visitor centres The park HQ and Beaver Meadows

Visitor Center is 3 miles west of Estes Park on US-36 (daily 8am–5pm; ☏970 586 1206, ⓦnps.gov/romo). The Fall River Visitor Center is 5 miles west of Estes Park on US-34 (late May to mid-Oct daily 9am–4pm). The Kawuneeche Visitor Center is a mile north of Grand Lake on US-34 (daily

---

COLORADO'S HISTORIC SKI RESORTS

The historic ski resorts northwest of Denver may not be Colorado's trendiest, but they still offer plenty of entertainment in winter and increasingly during the summer months.

STEAMBOAT SPRINGS

Surrounded by wide, snowy valleys, **Steamboat Springs**, 65 miles north of I-70 via Hwy-131, is where Colorado's skiing industry was born. When Norwegian ski-jump champion Karl Hovelsen moved here in 1914, it was still a ranching town, but after he designed his own ski jump locals soon caught on and today the town is home to more Winter Olympic champions than any other resort, while each February, the town's **Winter Carnival** celebrates the season with a range of fun events. Steamboat's top-notch **ski resort** (ⓦsteamboat. com), snuggled into Mount Werner four miles south of downtown, is enhanced by night skiing and the Mavericks Superpipe, one of the nation's top snowboard and skiing half-pipes. The town also benefits from its hot springs: you can soak year-round in the secluded 105°F Strawberry Park Hot Springs (Mon–Thurs & Sun 10am–10.30pm, Fri & Sat 10am–midnight; charge; ⓦstrawberryhotsprings.com), seven miles north of town and only accessible by 4WD in winter; various shuttles, detailed on the website, make the trip from town. The Old Town Hot Springs at 136 Lincoln Ave (Mon–Fri 5.30am–10pm, Sat & Sun 7am–10pm; charge; ⓦoldtownhotsprings.org) has more of a water-park feel.

WINTER PARK

Winter Park, 67 miles northwest of Denver, was established in 1938 and its wide, ever-expanding variety of ski and bike terrain, friendly atmosphere, family attractions and good-value lodgings draw more than a million visitors a year. The **ski resort** (mid-Nov to mid-April; ⓦwinterparkresort.com) also has exceptional facilities for kids and disabled skiers, and comprises three interconnected mountain peaks – Winter Park itself, Mary Jane and the Vasquez Ridge (they all share a single lift pass). Experienced skiers relish the mogul runs on Mary Jane Mountain and the backcountry idyll of Vasquez Cirque. Summer visitors enjoy six hundred miles of excellent **mountain-biking** trails, the best of which are accessible from the chairlift, in addition to the exhilarating 1.5-mile-long Alpine Slide sled ride and several contemporary music festivals.

8am–4.30pm; reduced hours Nov to late May). The Alpine Visitor Center (late May to early Oct daily 9.30am–5pm) is on Trail Ridge Rd, while the Moraine Park Discovery Center is open daily 9am–4.30pm on Bear Lake Rd, 1.5 miles from the Beaver Meadows Entrance.

ACCOMMODATION AND EATING

ESTES PARK

Alpine Trail Ridge Inn 927 Moraine Ave (US-36), Ⓦ alpinetrailridgeinn.com. Comfortable, standard motel accommodation, a short drive from the park entrance, with outdoor heated pool and spacious rooms. Open year-round. $$$

Baldpate Inn 4900 S Hwy-7, Ⓦ baldpateinn.com. Local restaurants are generally poor, though the excellent buffet at this 1917 inn includes hearty soups, freshly baked gourmet breads and a range of salads (make sure you check out the "Key Room" before you leave). Homemade pies are extra. $$

Stanley Hotel 333 Wonderview Ave, Ⓦ stanleyhotel. com. Historic inn, occupying a fantastic mountainside location since 1909. It's perhaps best known for inspiring Stephen King's *The Shining*, but don't let that put you off – the rooms and condos are ultra-luxurious and demon free. $$$$

GRAND LAKE

Blue Water Bakery 928 Grand Ave, Ⓦ bluewaterbakery. com. Serves fine coffee, pastries and sandwiches, as well as more exotic items like mango coconut scones. $

Fat Cat Café 185 E Agate Ave, Granby, ☎ 970 887 8987. A little further south in Granby, this small café (decorated with cat figurines) knocks out a tasty breakfast buffet at weekends (including dessert bar), excellent coffee and cinnamon rolls. $

★ **Shadowcliff Lodge** 105 County Road 663, Ⓦ shadowcliff.org. Gorgeous, log-built youth hostel, perched high in the woods, which has dorm rooms and clean, comfortable lodge doubles (with shared bathrooms), larger en suite cabins (4 people and up) and also hosts residential workshops on environmental themes. Open late May–Sept. Dorms $, doubles $$, cabins $$$

Western Riviera Lakeside Lodging 419 Garfield St, Ⓦ westernriv.com. Sixteen old-fashioned but clean rooms overlooking the lake, with microwaves and cable TV. $$$

CAMPING

Campgrounds Five official campgrounds provide the only accommodation within the park; all fill early each day in summer, when reservations are essential for Moraine Park, Glacier Basin and Aspenglen (☎ 877 444 6777, Ⓦ recreation. gov), while Longs Peak and Timber Creek remain first-come, first-served. Late May to Sept. $

Backcountry camping You'll need a permit (☎ 970 586 1242), valid for up to seven days and available from either Beaver Meadows or the Kawuneeche visitor centres (see page 60).

Summit County

The purpose-built ski resorts, old mining towns, snow-covered peaks, alpine meadows and crystal lakes that make up **SUMMIT COUNTY** lie alongside I-70, roughly seventy miles west of Denver. This section of the interstate was one of the last in the national system to be completed, and is justly regarded as an engineering marvel: it crosses the Continental Divide via the Eisenhower Tunnel, at 11,158ft, before snaking high above Vail Pass. Beyond the simple pleasure of driving I-70, the most enticing target is the mountain town of **BRECKENRIDGE** (eleven miles south of the highway at a mere 9603ft). This is the liveliest of Summit County's four towns; born in 1859 as a Gold Rush camp, it boasts a large historic district (with homes from the 1890s and early 1900s), touristy but tasteful stores, art galleries and excellent restaurants.

ARRIVAL, GETTING AROUND AND INFORMATION · SUMMIT COUNTY

By bus Greyhound buses stop at the Frisco Transfer Center, 1010 Meadow Drive, just off I-70 exit 203 (10 miles north of Breckenridge), from where free buses radiate to the surrounding ski resorts. Shuttles from Denver airport include Epic Mountain Express, which runs to the Transfer Center and Keystone, Copper Mountain and Breckenridge for $59 (☎ 970 754 7433, Ⓦ epicmountainexpress.com). Summit Express serves the same destinations (☎ 970 668 6000, Ⓦ summitexpress.com).

Destinations (Frisco) Denver (5 daily; 1hr 45min–2hr 10min); Glenwood Springs (2 daily; 1hr 50min); Grand Junction (3 daily; 3hr 30min); Vail (5 daily; 30–40min).

By local transport Summit Stage (daily 6.30am–1.30am; ☎ 970 668 0999, Ⓦ co.summit.co.us) provides free local transport from the Frisco Transfer Center to Breckenridge, Copper Mountain and Keystone. In Breckenridge itself, the

1

Free Ride bus system (☎970 547 3140, ⓦbreckfreeride. com) connects the town and its Summit Stage bus station with various ski slopes (daily 6.15am–11.15pm).

Breckenbridge Welcome Center & Museum 203 S Main St (daily 9am–5pm, longer hours in summer; ☎877 864 0868, ⓦgobreck.com). Supplies all sorts of information and maps, and also contains an excellent movie and museum on the history of the town. Ask here about local hiking and biking trails.

ACCOMMODATION

Lodging rates in Summit County double in winter. Frisco, near I-70, generally has the best-priced inns and motels, while Breckenridge holds a few downtown B&Bs and a large number of expensive slopeside condos. Resort accommodation at both Copper Mountain and Keystone is first class, and so too are the prices. For something with a little more character, the Summit Huts Association manages five backcountry huts in the area (July–Sept & Nov–May; ⓦsummithuts.org).

★ **The Bivvi Hostel** 9511 Hwy-9, at River Park Drive, Breckenridge, ⓦthebivvi.com. Sleek hostel aimed at the snowboarding set, offering comfy private rooms and four dorms, plus decent breakfast, outdoor hot tub and a cool sunken bar with craft beers on tap. No kids under 12. Dorms $̲$̲, doubles $̲$̲$̲

Fireside Inn 114 N French St, Breckenridge, ⓦfiresideinn.com. Homely little B&B with floral, antique-filled bedrooms (all with private bath), plus several cramped dorm rooms that share a TV lounge, showers and kitchenette. Dorms $̲$̲, doubles $̲$̲$̲

Frisco Lodge 321 Main St, Frisco, ⓦfriscolodge.com. Creaky B&B that oozes character, built back in 1885 in a vaguely Austrian style. Units have kitchenettes and access to an outdoor hot tub, and cooked buffet breakfast and teatime snacks are served in the cluttered lounge. $̲$̲$̲

Skiway Lodge 275 Ski Hill Rd, Breckenridge ⓦskiwaylodge.com. Friendly, good-value motel a short walk from Main St, with spacious rooms sporting gas fireplaces, LCD TVs and balconies. Guests have access to two outdoor hot tubs and a fire pit. $̲$̲

EATING

★ **Alpenglow Stube** Keystone Resort, ⓦkeystoneresort.com. The best dining experience in Summit County – take the free gondola ride to the top of 11,444ft North Peak, don Austrian slippers and feast in beautiful surroundings on New American cuisine with a Bavarian edge. Reservations required for dinner. $̲$̲$̲$̲

Breckenridge Brewery 600 S Main St, Breckenridge, ⓦbreckbrew.com. This huge brewpub, a landmark at the southern edge of town since 1990, serves good-quality microbrews and hearty local food. $̲$̲

Gold Pan Saloon 103 N Main St, ⓦthegoldpansaloon. com. The local dive bar since 1879, with real swinging doors, cheap breakfasts and decent burgers, live music (Thurs) and DJs (Fri & Sat). Happy hour 4–7pm. $̲

Hearthstone 130 S Ridge St, ⓦhearthstonebreck.com. Restaurant in the gorgeous 1886 Kaiser House featuring local produce and seasonal menus, with mains such as blackberry elk and Alaskan black cod. $̲$̲$̲$̲

SKIING AND SUMMERS IN SUMMIT COUNTY

Winter is the busiest time in Summit County. **Breckenridge Ski Resort** (ⓦbreckenridge. com), the oldest of the area's four top-class resorts, spans five peaks and offers ideal terrain as does the plush **Keystone Resort** (ⓦkeystoneresort.com), where the biggest night-ski operation in the US permits skiing until 9pm. The smallest resort in the county, **Arapahoe Basin** ("A-Basin"; ⓦarapahoebasin.com), usually offers skiing from mid-October right through to June thanks to its high elevation. The slopes at **Copper Mountain** (ⓦcoppercolorado. com) are divided into four clear ability sections.

In **summer**, mountain bikers and road-racers alike especially relish **cycling** the stretch of Hwy-9 between Frisco and Breckenridge; **Alpine Sports** at 435 N Park Ave in Breckenridge (ⓦalpinesportsrental.com) rents mountain bikes (its **Vail Pass Bike Shuttle** takes you to the top of Vail Pass so you can cruise fourteen miles downhill on a paved bike path all the way back). Each resort runs a chairlift or **gondola** to the top of the mountains for access to great **hiking** and cycling trails. Keystone is particularly outstanding for its mountain-bike trails with world-class downhill and cross-country trails accessed by its lifts (mid-June to early Sept, Mon–Thurs & Sun 10am–5pm, Fri & Sat 10am–7pm). Breckenridge offers its Summer Fun Park (mid-June to early Sept daily 9.30am–5.30pm; charge), featuring toboggan rides down the dry Alpine Slide, as well as trampolining, mini-golf and a giant maze.

Mountain Top Cookie Shop 128 S Main St, cookies loaded with fudge, oatmeal, M&Ms, chocolate and ⓦ breckenridgecookies.com. Knocking out delicious, hot macadamia nuts. §

Leadville

Ringed by snow-capped mountains at an elevation of more than 10,000ft, 24 miles south of I-70 and Summit County, the atmospheric old mining town of **LEADVILLE** enjoys a magnificent vista of mounts Elbert (14,440ft) and Massive (14,421ft), Colorado's two highest peaks. Leadville is rich in character and history, its old red-brick streets abounding with tales of gunfights (Doc Holliday fought his last here), miners dying of exposure and graveyards being excavated to get at the seams. Gold was discovered in 1860, but silver took over in the 1870s and later copper and zinc; by 1880 Leadville was the second largest town in Colorado. After a seventeen-year shutdown, the Climax molybdenum mine reopened in 2012, resuming Leadville's longest tradition.

National Mining Hall of Fame & Museum

120 W 9th St • Daily 9am–4.45pm • Charge • ⓦ mininghalloffame.org

Leadville's rich history and the story of gold mining is chronicled at the **National Mining Hall of Fame & Museum**, which also owns and operates the Matchless Mine (see page 63), through exhibits, nuggets of real gold and a walk-through replica of an underground mine shaft.

Matchless Mine

E 7th St (1.25 miles east of town) • Late May to late Sept daily 11am–4.45pm (1hr guided tours 1pm, 2pm & 3pm Fri–Sun) • Charge; cash only • ⓦ mininghalloffame.org

In 1878, **Horace Tabor**, a storekeeper and one-time mayor who grubstaked prospectors in exchange for potential profits, hit the jackpot when two of his clients developed a silver mine that produced $20 million within a year. Collecting his one-third share, Tabor left his wife to marry waitress "**Baby Doe**" McCourt and purchased the profitable **Matchless Mine**. However, by the time of his death in 1899, Tabor was financially ruined. Baby Doe survived him by 36 years, living a hermit-like existence in the godforsaken wooden shacks above the Matchless Mine. The buildings still stand, two miles out of town, and in the crude wooden shack in which she died, emaciated and frostbitten, guides recount Baby Doe's bizarre saga in full, fascinating detail.

Tabor Opera House

308 Harrison Ave • Late May to mid-Oct Tues–Sun noon–5pm (tours on the hour; 30–45min) • Charge • ⓦ taboroperahouse.net

Silver king Horace Tabor funded construction of the stately red-brick **Tabor Opera House** in 1879, its old stage, ranks of red velvet-and-gilt seats and eerie, dusty old dressing rooms mostly unchanged since then. In 1882, garbed in black velvet knee britches and diamonds, **Oscar Wilde** addressed a host of dozing miners here on

---

TOP OF THE ROCKIES

By far the most spectacular way to reach Aspen from Leadville is to drive over Independence Pass via the **Top of the Rockies National Scenic Byway** (aka Hwy-82), a scintillating route that passes the pretty village of Twin Lakes and crosses the Continental Divide at 12,095ft. On the western side the road winds along the Roaring Fork River, past **Independence Ghost Town** (late June to late Aug daily 10am–6pm; suggested donation), into Aspen. The pass is generally closed between November and late May; the alternate route via I-70 and Glenwood Springs adds an extra seventy miles to the trip from Denver.

1

the "Practical Application of the Aesthetic Theory to Exterior and Interior House Decoration with Observations on Dress and Personal Ornament".

ACCOMMODATION, EATING AND DRINKING   LEADVILLE

Delaware Hotel 700 Harrison Ave, ⓦdelawarehotel. com. Old-fashioned, quirky Victorian hotel opened in 1886, with comfy, antique-filled rooms that you'll either find charming or creepy (Room 316 is supposed to be haunted by Doc Holliday). No elevators – be prepared for a stiff climb at this altitude. Open May–Oct. $\overline{\underline{\$\$}}$

★ **Golden Burro Café** 710 Harrison Ave, ⓦgoldenburro.com. Classic diner since 1938, with cosy booths and friendly local ladies serving hefty breakfasts, fried chicken and a meatloaf dinner – it's one of those places where the menu is fun to read. $\overline{\underline{\$}}$

Governor's Mansion 129 W 8th St, ⓦgovernorsmansion.net. Built in 1881 and once the home of former governor Jesse McDonald, this wonderful property now sports three spacious and tastefully decorated guest units, all with full kitchens. $\overline{\underline{\$\$}}$

Silver Dollar Saloon 315 Harrison Ave, ⓦlegendarysilverdollarsaloon.com. Leadville's oldest bar (1879) is a wood-panelled and welcoming dive filled, rather incongruously given the Wild West exterior, with Irish memorabilia (it's been owned by an Irish American family since 1943). $\overline{\underline{\$\$}}$

Aspen

While there's more than a grain of truth to the image of **ASPEN**, sixty miles west of Leadville (and 160 miles west of Denver), as a celebrity hangout, it's a perfectly accessible and appealing place for ordinary folks to visit, and in summer at least the room rates are affordable for all but those on shoestring budgets. Indeed, unlike in resorts like Vail, which are often deserted out of season, affordable housing and local development have made this a real working town where ski bums really do mingle with millionaires. While spending too much time in Aspen itself is something of a waste given the virtually limitless recreation opportunities in the neighbouring mountains, hanging out around the town's leafy pedestrianized streets or browsing in the chichi stores and galleries makes a pleasant way to spend a couple of hours. Visiting in winter

SKIING AND SUMMERS IN ASPEN

The mogul-packed monster of **Aspen Mountain**, looming over downtown, is for experienced skiers only. On the other hand, **Buttermilk** is great for beginners, with an excellent ski school managed by **Aspen Skiing Co** (ⓦaspensnowmass.com) that offers a three-day guaranteed "Learn to Snowboard" programme; the wide-open runs of **Snowmass**, though mostly for intermediate skiers, feature some testing routes. **Aspen Highlands** has high-speed lifts and offers excellent extreme skiing terrain. The town's best value has to be its fifty miles of groomed **Nordic ski trails** – one of the most extensive free cross-country trail networks in the US. **Lift passes** are expensive (and feature a complicated pricing matrix); serious skiers will get better deals by buying a package with their accommodation. You can rent skis and snowboards at any Four Mountain Sports stores at all four mountains.

Cycling is the main **summer** pursuit around Aspen; the Four Mountain Sports outlets offer cruiser and mountain bikes to rent, including one-way bike rentals between each of their four locations. The Roaring Fork River, surging out of the Sawatch Range, is excellent for **kayaking** and **rafting** during a short season that's typically over by early to mid-July. Beware, though, as sections of Class V rapids here are dangerous and every summer sees fatalities. Aspen Whitewater Rafting, 520 Durant St (ⓦaspenwhitewater.com), offers guided trips.

If you fancy **hiking** in the mountains, an easy way to get your bearings and enjoy great valley views is to take the **Silver Queen Gondola** from 601 Dean St to the summit of Aspen Mountain (mid-June to early Sept daily 10am–4pm; charge; ☏970 925 1220). **Elk Camp Gondola** (same times) runs up Snowmass.

does require more cash, though you can save money by commuting to the slopes from Glenwood Springs (see page 68), less than fifty miles away.

Brief history

From inauspicious beginnings in 1879, this pristine, remote and mountain-locked town established itself as one of the world's top **silver** producers. By the time the silver market crashed fourteen years later, it had acquired tasteful residential palaces, grand hotels and an opera house. Ironically enough, during the 1930s, when Aspen's population had slumped below seven hundred, the anti-poverty WPA programme gave the struggling community the cash to build its first crude ski lift. Entrepreneurs seized the opportunity presented by the varied terrain and plentiful snow, and the first chairlift was dedicated on **Aspen Mountain** in 1947. In 1950, inspired by its great natural beauty, Chicago businessman Walter Paepcke created what is now the **Aspen Institute**, a respected think-tank, and also helped found the **Aspen Music Festival** (see page 67). Skiing really drove Aspen's growth, however, and it has since spread to three more mountains – **Aspen Highlands**, **Snowmass** and **Buttermilk**, with the jet set arriving in force during the 1960s. All four mountains are now operated by **Aspen Skiing Company** (Ⓦaspensnowmass.com), with Highlands and especially Snowmass (on Brush Creek Rd, off Hwy-82) featuring their own "villages" of condos, shops and restaurants.

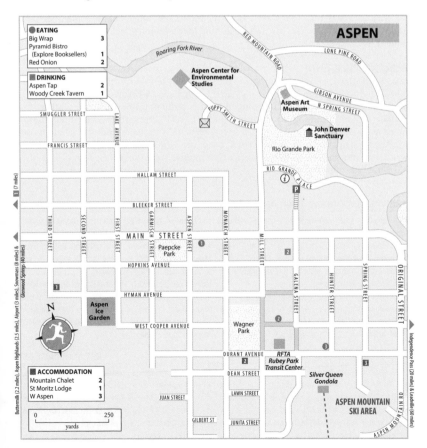

1

John Denver Sanctuary
Rio Grande Park (near the visitor centre) • Daily 24hr • Free

Beloved folk singer **John Denver** moved to Aspen in 1971 and was inspired to write many of his biggest hits, such as *Rocky Mountain High*, by the surrounding countryside. Denver was killed in an air crash in 1997, and the tranquil **John Denver Sanctuary** commemorates the singer with many of his songs etched into granite rocks – fans still gather at the memorial every year, on the anniversary of Denver's death (Oct 12).

Maroon Bells Recreation Area
Maroon Creek Rd • Daily 24hr • Vehicle charge (pedestrians/bikes free) • ☎ 970 925 3445 • From early June to early Oct, from 8am to 5pm, access is by bike, skates, on foot and public bus only (Castle/Maroon bus from downtown, transfer to Maroon Bells Bus at Aspen Highlands; charge; every 20min); the road normally closes completely once it snows heavily, generally mid-Nov to mid-May (open to cross-country skiers or snowmobile tours)

An essential excursion from Aspen, the alluring landscapes of the **Maroon Bells Recreation Area** are centred on the twin purple-grey peaks of the Maroon Bells peaks themselves (14,014ft and 14,156ft), protected within the White River National Forest. Hiking trails lead from the car park around dark blue Maroon Lake, where mesmerizing views of the Bells blend with the equally jaw-dropping Pyramid Peak (14,018ft) and the reddish crags of the Sievers Mountains. Longer trails lead up to Crater Lake (10,076ft), nearer the base of the mountains, where moose sometimes graze. The Bells are reached via the eleven-mile-long Maroon Creek Road, but **access is limited** (see above).

Ashcroft Ghost Town
Castle Creek Rd • Daily 24hr; tours mid-June to Aug daily 9am–5pm (open-access rest of year) • Charge • ⓦ aspenhistory.org

Some eleven miles south of Aspen on Castle Creek Road, **Ashcroft Ghost Town** is an enigmatic site surrounded by mountains, its handful of timber buildings all that remains of a silver mining community founded in 1880. Ashcroft and its mines were never really sustainable, and though a few hardy settlers stayed on into the 1920s, most inhabitants had gone after just five years. Even when the site is officially closed you can wander around the old buildings for free (interpretive signs explain the history of the old jail, blacksmith shop, Blue Mirror Saloon and infamous Hotel View), set along one main strip. You'll need to drive or cycle to get here.

ARRIVAL, GETTING AROUND AND INFORMATION   ASPEN

By plane Tiny Aspen/Pitkin County Airport (ⓦaspenairport.com) lies 4 miles north of town; free buses run into Aspen and Snowmass. If you fly into Denver, connecting flights may only cost the same as a shuttle from Denver airport with Epic Mountain Express (☎970 926 9800, ⓦepicmountainexpress.com).

By bus and train The nearest Amtrak and Greyhound stations are in Glenwood Springs (see page 68), 40 miles from Aspen. RFTA buses (see page 68) run to Aspen (1hr 40min).

Local buses Free RFTA buses (☎970 925 8484, ⓦrfta.

com), centred on the Rubey Park transit station on Durant St in the heart of town, connect the four mountains with each other in winter, plus the airport and outlying areas (Aspen to Snowmass Village is free and runs all year). Access to Maroon Bells is limited (see above).

Visitor centres 590 N Mill St (Mon–Fri 8.30am–5pm; ☎970 925 1940, ⓦaspenchamber.org); Wheeler Opera House Visitor Center, 320 E Hyman Ave (Daily: summer 9am–5pm, rest of year 11am–6pm; ☎970 920 7148, ⓦwheeleroperahouse.com).

ACCOMMODATION   SEE MAP PAGE 65

Stay Aspen Snowmass Central Reservations (☎970 925 9000, ⓦstayaspensnowmass.com) runs a helpful service and also arranges package deals combining accommodation with lift tickets. Rates vary considerably even in winter, and are lowest in the "value seasons" (last week in Nov, first two weeks of Dec and first two weeks of

April). Prices also reduce dramatically during the summer, when **camping** is also a good cheap option; there are nine USFS campgrounds around Aspen, of which only a handful can be reserved (☎518 885 3639, ⓦrecreation.gov). Aspen is also well represented on ⓦairbnb.com.

Mountain Chalet 333 E Durant Ave,

1

@mountainchaletaspen.com. Friendly mountain lodge with large, comfortable rooms, pool, hot tub, gym and fine buffet breakfast. Some dorm-style beds are available in winter, along with more straightforward rooms. Dorms $$, doubles winter $$$$, doubles summer $$$

St Moritz Lodge 334 W Hyman Ave, @stmoritzlodge.com. A short walk from central downtown, with well-priced dorms and private rooms that tend to be booked way in advance. Facilities include a small heated pool and a comfortable common room. Continental breakfast included in winter. Dorms $$, doubles $$$

★ **W Aspen** 550 S Spring St, @marriott.com. Opened in 2019 with 88 chic rooms, the W offers luxurious amenities, a ski shop, rooftop bar and pool and fire pits. Also features *39°*, an underground cocktail bar and grotto. Rates soar in the peak ski season. $$$$

EATING
SEE MAP PAGE 65

Big Wrap 520 E Durant Ave, ☎970 544 1700. Cheap eats in central Aspen? No wonder this place is so popular, with tasty, wholesome wraps, and nutrient-rich smoothies. Cash only. $

Pyramid Bistro (Explore Booksellers) 221 E Main St, @pyramidbistro.com. Fantastic bookstore with a shady roof terrace and an upstairs café serving creative vegetarian and "nutritarian" dishes; mango spring rolls, sunflower seed crusted Cajun salmon, veggie curry bowls and salads. $$

Red Onion 420 E Cooper Ave, @redonionaspen.com. Aspen's oldest pub, dating from 1892, delivers decent beers and burgers and serves bar snacks and big plates (pan-seared mountain trout). $$

DRINKING AND NIGHTLIFE
SEE MAP PAGE 65

Nightlife in Aspen is at its peak in the après-ski winter season, but there's always something going on year-round. In summer, downtown hosts several top-notch festivals, including the summer-long Aspen Music Festival (@aspenmusicfestival.com), when orchestras and operas feature well-known international performers, as well as promising students.

Aspen Tap 121 S Galena St, @aspenbrewingcompany.com. Check out the tap room of Aspen's very own microbrewery, serving beers such as the hoppy Independence Pass Ale, and the malty Brown Bearale.

Woody Creek Tavern 2858 Upper River Rd, Woody Creek, @woodycreektavern.com. Rustic tavern in tiny Woody Creek, 7 miles northwest of Aspen along Hwy-82, where ranch hands, tourists and the occasional celebrity local (Hunter S. Thompson was a frequent patron) shoot pool, guzzle fresh lime-juice margaritas and eat good Tex-Mex.

Vail

Compared to most other Colorado ski towns, **VAIL**, 97 miles west of Denver on I-70, is a new creation: just a handful of farmers lived here before the resort opened in 1962. Today the town sprawls eight miles or so along the narrow Gore Creek valley floor, comprising a series of village districts beginning with **Vail Village** – the area's main social centre – and running west to Lionshead, Cascade Village and West Vail. Vail Resorts (@vail.com), which operates the ski area at Vail, owns an even more exclusive gated resort, **Beaver Creek**, eleven miles further west on I-70 (the small towns of Avon, Eagle-Vail and Edwards extend the resort area still further along the valley). Each area is pedestrianized and linked by **free shuttle buses** between them and the ski lifts. The villages themselves are mostly uninspiring collections of Tyrolean-style chalets and concrete-block condos, pockmarked by pricey fashion boutiques and often painfully pretentious restaurants; the real highlights are the stunning mountain scenery and activities on offer. Indeed, given the exceptional quality of the snow, and the sheer size and variety of terrain available, Vail is a formidable winter sport destination. In summer, you can use the lifts to go **mountain biking**, best at Vail, and **hiking**, best at the quieter Beaver Creek. Note, however, that unlike Aspen, Vail is essentially just a big resort, and often deserted out of season.

ARRIVAL AND INFORMATION
VAIL

By plane From Denver Airport, several companies offer shuttles to Vail and Beaver Creek, including Epic Mountain Express (☎970 926 9800, @epicmountainexpress.com). More convenient (hence more expensive) flights are available to Eagle County Regional Airport (@flyvail.com), just 35 miles west of Vail.

Vail Welcome Center 241 South Frontage Rd, top deck of the parking garage (daily 8.30am–5pm; summer Mon–Thurs & Sun 9am–7pm, Fri & Sat 9am–8pm; @visitvailvalley.com).

1

ACCOMMODATION

Sonnenalp Hotel 20 Vail Rd, ⓦsonnenalp.com. For the full Vail experience splash out on this luxury hotel bang in the centre of Vail, with an excellent spa, Alpine theme and spacious suites with Bavarian furniture, fireplaces and large bathrooms with heated floors. $\overline{\$}\overline{\$}\overline{\$}\overline{\$}$

Tivoli Lodge 386 Hanson Ranch Rd, ⓦtivolilodge.com. Family-owned hotel with comfy rooms, pool, whirlpool and sauna; rates include a continental breakfast, and you can find bargains online (off season). $\overline{\$}\overline{\$}\overline{\$}\overline{\$}$

EATING

Alpenrose Vail 100 E Meadow Drive, ⓦalpenrose-vail. com. Lauded German and Austrian restaurant since the 1970s, with a menu of hearty goulash, dumplings, kässpätzle, tomato fondue and a range of traditional desserts such as marillenknödel, dampfnudeln and apple strudel. $\overline{\$}\overline{\$}\overline{\$}$

★ **Little Diner** 616 W Lionshead Circle, ⓦthelittlediner. com. Legendary 1950s style diner, best experienced over a lazy breakfast, though you may have to wait: it only seats twenty around a U-shaped counter. There's a selection of grilled and cold sandwiches for lunch. $\overline{\$}$

Slope Room 352 E Meadow Drive, ⓦsloperoom.com. Good for a splurge, this is a little gem among many posh restaurants in Vail; organic, farm-to-table dishes include truffle asparagus and Scottish salmon. $\overline{\$}\overline{\$}\overline{\$}$

Westside Café 2211 N Frontage Rd W, ⓦwestsidecafe. net. Dressed up like a Colorado mining shack with outdoor seating, this is a top breakfast spot, best known for its twists on eggs Benedict. $\overline{\$}\overline{\$}$

Glenwood Springs

Bustling, touristy **GLENWOOD SPRINGS** sits at the western end of impressive Glenwood Canyon, 157 miles west of Denver on I-70 and within striking distance of both Vail and Aspen; as such, it offers those with their own vehicle a budget base for either destination. Just north of the confluence of the Roaring Fork and Colorado rivers, the town was long used by the Ute people as a place of relaxation thanks to its **hot springs**, which became the target for unscrupulous speculators who broke treaties and established resort facilities in the 1880s. North from downtown and across the Eagle River is the town's main attraction, the huge **Glenwood Hot Springs Pool**, 410 N River St (daily: summer 7.30am–10pm; rest of year 9am–10pm; charge; ⓦhotspringspool. com), offering spa services in addition to two large pools and several waterslides. More intimate are the natural, subterranean steam baths of the nearby **Yampah Spa Vapor Caves**, 709 E 6th St (daily 9am–9pm; charge; ⓦyampahspa.com), where you can relax on cool marble benches set deep in ancient caves and enjoy a variety of classy spa treatments. Also on the north side of town is the **Glenwood Caverns Adventure Park**, 508 Pine St (summer daily 9am–9pm, rest of year hours vary; charge; ⓦglenwoodcaverns.com), with thrill rides, horseback rides and caverns that extend for two miles, with chambers reaching 50ft.

ARRIVAL AND INFORMATION
GLENWOOD SPRINGS

By bus Greyhound buses stop 2 miles west of downtown at Alta Convenience, 51171 US-6, just off I-70. RFTA buses (BRT) run every 12–30min to Aspen (1hr; ⓦrfta.com). Destinations Denver (2 daily; 3hr 35min); Grand Junction (2 daily; 1hr 35min); Vail (2 daily; 1hr 10min). By train Amtrak services arrive at 413 7th St in the heart of downtown.

Destinations Denver (1 daily; 6hr 28min); Grand Junction (1 daily; 2hr 4min); Salt Lake City (1 daily; 9hr 12min). Visitor centre 802 Grand Ave (Mon–Fri 8am–5pm, Sat 10am–4pm; also Sun 10am–4pm summer only; ☏ 970 945 6589, ⓦvisitglenwood.com).

ACCOMMODATION AND EATING

Glenwood Canyon Brewpub Hotel Denver, 402 7th St, ⓦglenwoodcanyon.com. Cooks up reliable pub grub, great burgers and produces excellent hand-crafted microbrews. $\overline{\$}\overline{\$}$

Glenwood Springs Inn 141 W 6th St, ⓦglenwoodspringsinn.com. This good-value, family-owned motel has clean, comfortable rooms a couple of blocks away from the hot springs. Offers complimentary shuttle to and from the train station. $\overline{\$}\overline{\$}$

Hotel Colorado 526 Pine St, ⓦhotelcolorado.com. Grand historic hotel opened back in 1893, steps from the hot springs themselves. The elegant rooms are dressed with Victorian décor and there's an excellent restaurant on-site . $\overline{\$}\overline{\$}\overline{\$}$

Hotel Denver 402 7th St, ⓦthehoteldenver.com. Dating back to 1915, the grandfather of Glenwood resort hotels features an elegant, 1920s theme, though rooms come with modern amenities. On-site coffee house with a river fron patio features. $\overline{\underline{\$\$\$}}$

Rosi's Little Bavarian Restaurant 141 W 6th St, ☎970 928-9186. Great breakfast joint, with Vienna crêpes, wholewheat pancakes and bratwurst plates in addition to the usual items. Don't miss the home-made Bavarian pastries. $\overline{\underline{\$\$}}$

Grand Junction and around

The immediate environs of **GRAND JUNCTION**, 87 miles west of Glenwood Springs on I-70, are awash in outdoor opportunities, and within a fifty-mile stretch you can trace the transition from fertile alpine valley to full-blown desert. Although initial impressions are unfavourable – a sprawl of factory units and sales yards lines the I-70 Business Loop – the tiny **downtown** is much nicer, with leafy boulevards hemming in a small, tree-lined historic district dotted with sculptures and stores. Nevertheless, the main attractions lie in the surrounding rugged and spectacular high desert country.

Museum of the West

462 Ute Ave • May–Sept Mon–Sat 9am–5pm; Oct–April Tues–Sat 10am–4pm • Charge • ⓦ museumofwesternco.com

The absorbing **Museum of the West** offers a hands-on trip through regional history, from virtual "rides" in a stagecoach and displays of Ute and Fremont native rock art, to guns used by Buffalo Bill and Kit Carson and rare Spanish Colonial artefacts from the wreck of the *El Matancero*, a Spanish merchant ship that sank off Mexico in 1741 (recovered by local scuba diver Hans Schmoldt).

Dinosaur Journey Museum

550 Jurassic Court, Fruita • May–Sept daily 9am–5pm; Oct–April Mon–Sat 10am–4pm, Sun noon–4pm • Charge • ⓦ museumofwesternco.com

Although the Colorado section of Dinosaur National Monument (ⓦnps.gov/dino) is ninety miles north of Grand Junction, the town of **Fruita**, just twelve miles west of town, contains the intriguing **Dinosaur Journey Museum**. The interactive museum features robotic displays of several kinds of dinosaurs, as well as a collection of giant, locally excavated bones – all helping to create a vivid picture of these prehistoric beasts.

Colorado National Monument

1750 Rim Rock Drive, Fruita • Daily 24hr • Charge • **Visitor centre** Daily: June–Aug 8am–6pm; Sept–May 9am–4.30pm • ⓦ nps.gov/colm

Grand Junction's main attraction is the mesmerizing scenery of **Colorado National Monument**, where more than two hundred million years of wind and water erosion have gouged out rock spires, domes, arches, pedestals and balanced rocks along a line of cliffs a few miles south of the city; the colourful result makes for an enthralling painted desert of warm reds, stunning purples, burnt oranges and rich browns. The park has two entrances at either end of twisting, 23-mile **Rim Rock Drive**, which links a string of spectacular overlooks with the **visitor centre** at the north end of the park (exit 19, I-70). Short hikes along the way afford views of several monoliths, while longer treks get right down to the canyon floor.

MOUNTAIN BIKING GRAND JUNCTION

The Grand Junction area is prime mountain biking territory, with a network of local trails just outside the city; visit Ruby Canyon Cycles at 301 Main St (ⓦrubycanyoncycles.com) for trail information and rentals. You can also try the smooth, rolling single-track trails in nearby Fruita; Over the Edge Sports, 202 E Aspen Ave (ⓦotesports.com), in the centre of town, has trail information and rental bikes.

1

By bus Greyhound buses stop at 230 S 5th St on the edge of downtown, three blocks east of the train station.
Destinations Denver (2 daily; 5hr 15min–6hr); Glenwood Springs (2 daily; 1hr 35min); Las Vegas (2 daily; 9hr 35min); Vail (3 daily; 2hr 50min–3hr 10min).
By train The Amtrak station is at 339 South 1st St on the edge of downtown.

Destinations Denver (1 daily; 8hr 15min); Glenwood Springs (1 daily; 1hr 47min); Salt Lake City (1 daily; 6hr 55min).
Visitor centre 740 Horizon Drive (summer Mon–Fri 8.30am–6pm, Sat & Sun 9am–6pm, rest of year Mon–Fri 8.30am–5pm, Sat & Sun 10am–4pm; ☎ 970 256 4060, ⓦ visitgrandjunction.com).

ACCOMMODATION AND EATING

Castle Creek Manor 638 Horizon Drive, ⓦ castlecreekmanor.com. Cosy B&B north of downtown, offering a huge breakfast buffet and plush, spotless rooms – owners Ron and LeeAnn Unfred are especially friendly. $$
Kannah Creek Brewing Co 1960 N 12th St, ⓦ kannahcreekbrewingco.com. This popular brewpub, with outdoor seating, serves decent pizza, pastas, salads, wine and cider on tap and tasty microbrewed beers. $

Main St Café 504 Main St, ☎ 970 242-7225. Tasty breakfasts and lunches are available at this retro 1950s diner; try the Elvis burger (green chilli burger with cheddar) or the fish (beer-battered cod) sandwich. $
Palomino Inn 2400 North Ave, ⓦ elpalominomotel. com. Older-style 1950s motel but great value, with clean, quiet rooms, decent continental breakfast, flatscreen TVs and pool. $$

Black Canyon of the Gunnison National Park

Hwy-347 (off US-50, 15 miles east of Montrose) • Daily 24hr • **South Rim Rd** April to mid-Nov • Charge • **South Rim Visitor Center** Daily: late May to early Sept 8am–6pm; late April to late May & early Sept to Oct 8am–5pm; Nov to late April 9am–4pm • ⓦ nps.gov/blca

Containing a narrow, precipitous gorge a mind-boggling one-mile deep, **BLACK CANYON OF THE GUNNISON NATIONAL PARK** lies seventy miles southeast of Grand Junction. The view down into the fearsome, black rock canyon to the foaming Gunnison River below is as foreboding as mountain scenery gets. Over two million years, the river has eroded a deep, narrow gorge, leaving exposed cliffs and jagged spires of crystalline rock more than 1.7 billion years old. The one-way aspen-lined **South Rim Road** leading through the park to the top of the canyon winds uphill until the trees abruptly come to an end, the road levels out and the scenery takes a dramatic turn – stark black cliffs, with the odd pine clinging to a tiny ledge in desperation. The road is lined with **viewpoints: Gunnison Point** behind the visitor centre, the **Pulpit Rock** overlook and **Painted View Wall**, where the vast scale and height of the streaky cliffs really hits home, are the best. South Rim Road ends at **High Point** (8289ft), and the Warner Point Trail (1.5 miles return).

Crested Butte

The beautiful Victorian mining town of **CRESTED BUTTE** (pronounced like "beaut"), 153 miles east of Grand Junction and ninety miles from the Black Canyon, sits 8885ft up on a flat, alpine plain surrounded by snowy peaks. The town boomed after it was

---

BIKING CRESTED BUTTE

In summer, **mountain bikes** all but outnumber cars around Crested Butte, especially during **Fat Tire Week** in late June (now officially dubbed **Crested Butte Bike Week**), one of the oldest festivals in the sport; the original evolved from a race over the rocky 21-mile Pearl Pass to Aspen in 1976, now commemorated at the **Pearl Pass Mountain Bike Tour** (Sept).

You can still ride the route to Aspen – 190 miles shorter than the road – but some of the most exciting trails are much nearer the town and include the gorgeous 401 trail with its wide-open vistas; the thickly wooded Dyke Trail; and the long, varied and occasionally challenging Deadmans. The Alpineer, 419 6th St (ⓦ alpineer.com), rents mountain bikes.

1

founded in the 1870s but almost died off in 1952 after its coal deposits were exhausted and the **Big Mine** closed. However, the development of 11,875ft **Mount Crested Butte**, four miles north of the town, into a world-class **ski resort** in the 1960s, and its further transformation into **mountain bikers'** paradise two decades later means that today it can claim to be the top year-round resort in Colorado (there's also fishing, hiking and kayaking in the summer). The old town is resplendent with gaily painted clapboard homes and businesses, with all the action taking place among the low-rise, historic buildings, bars and restaurants on **Elk Avenue**.

Crested Butte Mountain Resort

12 Snowmass Rd • ⓦ skicb.com

In skiing and snowboarding circles, **Crested Butte Mountain Resort** is best known for its extreme terrain, with lifts serving out-of-the-way bowls and faces that would only be accessible by helicopter at other resorts; unsurprisingly, the resort hosts both the US extreme skiing and snowboarding championships. That said, plenty of long beginner runs are mixed in over the mountain's one thousand skiable acres, with sixteen chairlifts linking 121 usually uncrowded runs. In summer the action switches to zip-line tours, rafting, horseback riding and the trails of **Crested Butte Mountain Bike Park.**

ARRIVAL, GETTING AROUND AND INFORMATION   CRESTED BUTTE

By plane A 5hr drive southwest from Denver along mostly minor highways, Crested Butte is not easy to reach, though the roads are almost always open. Many skiers fly from Denver to Gunnison Airport (ⓦ flygunnisonairport.com), 28 miles south, a 40min trip to Crested Butte via the Alpine Express (☎ 970 641 5074, ⓦ letsride.co/locations/crested-butte).

By bus Dolly's Mountain Shuttle (☎ 970 349 2620,

ⓦ crestedbutteshuttle.com) provides transport to Aspen and Denver (six-person minimum or equivalent price in summer). Mountain Express (free; ⓦ mtnexp.org) buses ply the 3 miles between the town and resort (every 15–20min, 7.35am–midnight).

Visitor centre 601 Elk Ave (daily 9am–5pm; ☎ 970 349 6438, ⓦ gunnisoncrestedbutte.com).

ACCOMMODATION

The choice of accommodation is between the ski area or downtown; in season, you're likely to flit between the two areas every day, so it's only worth staying at the generally more expensive mountainside lodgings if you're obsessed with getting first tracks. Crested Butte Mountain Resort (see page 71) can book rooms and advise on package deals – reserve well in advance during winter. Airbnb lists over 300 properties in the Crested Butte area, from $70 a night.

Elk Mountain Lodge 129 Gothic Ave, ⓦ elkmountainlodge.com. Compact but comfy rooms,

breakfast and a shared hot tub (indoors) in this old mining boarding house built in 1919. $$$

Old Town Inn 708 6th St, ⓦ oldtowninn.net. Standard motel rooms with great home-made breakfasts, free bikes and cookies and coffee in the afternoon. $$

★ **Purple Mountain Lodge** 714 Gothic Ave, ⓦ purplemountainlodge.com. Extremely comfortable B&B (more blueish than purple), with bright, cheery rooms, its own day spa, a hot tub and free bikes in summer. No kids under 16. $$$

EATING AND DRINKING

Brick Oven Pizzeria & Pub 223 Elk Ave, ⓦ brickovencb.com. Wildly popular for its outdoor patio (with bar), thirty beers on tap and decent pizza such as the "Hurricane Hanna" (sliced meatballs, bacon and mushrooms, drizzled with pesto). $$

The Eldo 215 Elk Ave, ⓦ eldobrewery.wordpress.com. The coolest place to be on a sunny afternoon, the second-floor deck of this brewpub is always packed; the Wild West timber exterior is faux but handsome, and the third-of-a-pound burgers and veggie burgers are excellent. $

Kochevar's 127 Elk Ave, ☎ 970 349 6745. Timber-frame beauty from 1891, the original saloon established by Jacob

Kochevar, with cheap drinks and bar snacks. Pool tables inside. $

Montanya Distillers 212 Elk Ave, ⓦ montanyarum.com. Housed in the old electric plant of 1901, this award-winning rum maker offers all sorts of cocktails, free tastings and tours along with classy shared plates of snacks and Mountain Oven breads. $

Wooden Nickel 222 Elk Ave, ⓦ woodennickelcb.com. One of the oldest saloons in town (the old wooden bar dates from the 1890s); the atmospheric restaurant is the focus these days, with perfect steaks, elk stew and Rocky Mountain trout. $$$

1

Durango

Thanks to a splendid setting amid the San Juan Mountains, **DURANGO**, founded in 1880 as a refining town and rail junction to serve Silverton, 45 miles north, is southwest Colorado's largest town. A friendly, ebullient place, it's home these days to a mixed population of teleworkers and outdoor enthusiasts, who enjoy its year-round activities, excellent restaurants and flourishing arts scene.

INFORMATION AND ACTIVITIES
DURANGO

Visitor centres Downtown at 802 Main Ave (daily 9am–7pm; ☎ 970 247 3500, ⓦ durango.org), and near the train station at 111 S Camino del Rio (June–Sept Mon–Fri 8am–6pm, Sat 9am–5pm, Sun 11am–4pm; Oct–May Mon–Fri 8am–5pm).

River-rafting Several operators run river-rafting excursions on the Animas River. Full-day expeditions are offered with Mild to Wild Rafting (ⓦ mild2wildrafting.com). Brief float trips are operated by Flexible Flyers (ⓦ flexibleflyersrafting.com).

ACCOMMODATION

Lightner Creek Campground 1567 Lightner Creek Rd, ⓦ camplightnercreek.com. Peaceful riverside campground, 5 miles west of town, with well-shaded tent sites, basic wooden cabins, a summer-only pool and small store. Closed mid-Oct to April; two-night minimum stay for cabins. Tents $. Cabins $$. RVs $

★ **Rochester Hotel** 721 E 2nd Ave, ⓦ rochesterhotel.com. Charming, intimate nineteenth century B&B, where the differing Wild West themes of the fifteen very comfortable rooms, some of which have kitchenettes, are inspired by classic, locally filmed Westerns. Includes a relaxing secret garden. $$$

★ **Strater Hotel** 699 Main Ave, ⓦ strater.com. Major downtown landmark that's bursting with frontier elegance. Mostly small, antique-furnished rooms, plus a lively Western saloon, restaurant, and even a melodrama theatre. $$$

EATING AND DRINKING

Chimayo Stone Fired Kitchen 862 Main Ave, ⓦ chimayodurango.com. Stylish modern restaurant where stone hearth ovens deliver perfect pizzas, and substantial main dishes such as delicious stuffed poblano chillis. $$

James Ranch Grill James Ranch, 33846 US-550, ⓦ jamesranch.net. Organic farm, 11 miles north of Durango, where you order at the counter then enjoy the superb burgers, sandwiches and salads at picnic tables near the river. $$

Jean-Pierre Bakery & Cafe 601 Main Ave, ☎ 970 247 7700. French bakery/restaurant offering exquisite breads and pastries, plus sandwiches, salads and quiches, and full meals such as mussels or beef with crab. Live music on Fri & Sat. $$

Steamworks Brewing Co 801 E 2nd Ave, ⓦ steamworksbrewing.com. Large brewpub, perched a block above Main Ave; enjoy wood-fired pizzas on its sunny open-air patio, or home-brewed beer in the bustling, cavernous interior. $

Silverton

The turnaround point for the narrow-gauge railroad from Durango comes at **SILVERTON**: "silver by the ton", allegedly. Spread across a small flat valley and hemmed in entirely by the tall peaks of the San Juan Mountains, it's one of Colorado's most evocative (and secluded) mountain towns, where wide, dirt-paved streets lead off toward the surrounding heights. Silverton's zinc- and copper-mining days only came to an end in 1991, and the population has dropped since then, with those who remain generally relying on the seasonal tourist train – winters here are harsh and largely quiet. Although the false-fronted stores along "Notorious Blair Street" may remind one of the days when Wyatt Earp dealt cards here, the town is defined by the restaurants and gift shops that fill up around noon, when train passengers are in town.

ACCOMMODATION AND EATING
SILVERTON

Avalanche Brewing Company 1067 Blair St, ⓦ avalanchebrewing.com. A welcome contrast to Silverton's run-of-the-mill steakhouses, this friendly hangout is both coffee bar and microbrewery, serving home-brewed ales as well as espressos, sandwiches and pizzas. $

The Avon 144 E 10th St, ⓦ avonsilverton.com. This hotel and hostel offers great value, with simple but stylish rooms in a grand 1904 building with its own saloon. Popular with skiers in winter, book ahead. The cheapest rooms feature bunk beds and shared bathrooms. Bar and basement music venue feature. $\overline{\$\$}$

Triangle Motel 848 Greene St, ⓦtrianglemotel.com. Behind its rather ugly facade, this motel at the south end of town is very well maintained, offering good facilities, with two-room suites available. $\overline{\$\$}$

Ouray

The attractive mining community of **OURAY** lies 23 miles north of Silverton, on the far side of 11,018ft **Red Mountain Pass**, where the bare rock beneath the snow really is stained red by mineral deposits. The **Million Dollar Highway** twists and turns to get here, passing abandoned mine workings and rusting machinery in unlikely and inaccessible spots; trails and backroads into the San Juans offer rich pickings for hikers or 4WD drivers.

Ouray itself is squeezed into a verdant sliver of a valley, with the commercially run **Ouray Hot Springs** beside the Uncompahgre River at the north end of town. A mile or so south, a one-way-loop dirt road leads to Box Canyon Falls Park (daily 8am–dusk; charge), where a straightforward 500ft trail, partly along a swaying wooden parapet, leads into narrow Box Canyon and the namesake falls that thunder through a tiny cleft in the mountain at the far end.

ACCOMMODATION AND EATING
OURAY

Box Canyon Lodge 45 3rd Ave, ⓦboxcanyonouray. com. Old-style timber motel below the park, where guests can bathe in natural hot tubs. The guest rooms are cosy and snug, with good furnishings. $\overline{\$\$}$

★ **Hot Springs Inn** 1400 Main St, ⓦhotspringsinn. com. All the very pleasant rooms at this comfortable upscale modern inn, at the north end of town, have deck

balconies facing the river, and the staff are hugely helpful. Closed mid-Oct to mid-May. $\overline{\$\$}$

Maggie's Kitchen 705 Main St, ☎970 325 0259. Hugely popular central diner, where every square inch is covered in all-but-indecipherable graffiti. The blackboard lists grilled cheese, hot dogs and assorted sandwiches, but it's the fabulous burgers that draw in the crowds. No credit cards. $\overline{\$}$

Telluride

Set in a picturesque valley, at the flat base of a bowl of vast steep-sided mountains, **TELLURIDE** is a 74-mile drive from Silverton, even though as the crow flies, across the mountains, they're barely ten miles apart. This former mining village was briefly home to the young Butch Cassidy, who robbed his first bank here in 1889. These days, it's better known as a top-class **ski resort** that rivals Aspen for celebrity allure. Happily, preserved low-slung buildings along its wide main street. Healthy young bohemians with few visible means of support but top-notch ski equipment seem to form the bulk of the twelve hundred inhabitants, while most visitors tend to stay two miles up from town in **Mountain Village**, served by a free, year-round gondola service. Summer **hiking** opportunities are excellent; one three-mile round-trip walk leads from the head of the valley, where the highway ends at Pioneer Mill, up to the 431ft **Bridal Veil Falls**, the tallest in Colorado.

ACCOMMODATION AND EATING
TELLURIDE

Baked in Telluride 127 S Fir St, ⓦbakedintel.com. Takeout deli-bakery, just off the main drag, that's great for

1

morning espressos and pastries, and has a nice little terrace where you can enjoy soup, sandwiches or pizza. $

The Butcher & The Baker 217 E Colorado Ave, ⓦbutcherandbakercafe.com. Bright, friendly contemporary café/bistro, feeding health-conscious locals with fresh organic produce. Serves delicious "small plate" salads, larger mains such as burgers, brisket or chicken schnitzel. $

Manitou Lodge 333 S Fir St, ⓦtelluridehotels.com. While it calls itself a B&B, Manitou Lodge looks more like an old-fashioned national-park lodge. The cosy comforts of its 11 renovated rooms can't be faulted, though, and neither can its riverside setting. $$$

New Sheridan Hotel 231 W Colorado Ave, ⓦnewsheridan.com. Restored 1895 hotel in the heart of town, where the large, very luxurious rooms have stylish antique furnishings but modern bathrooms and fittings. The cheapest face inwards, though. Great roof-top bar with stunning 360-views of Telluride. Closed late Oct to late Nov. $$$$

Smuggler Union Restaurant & Brewery 225 S Pine St, ⓦsmugglerunion.com. Lively, convivial hangout, with a wide-ranging pub-grub menu – the "ancient grain" salad is excellent – and exceptional house brews. $

Mesa Verde National Park

Fifteen miles up from US-160, 10 miles east of Cortez and 35 miles west of Durango • Entry late May to early Sept • Charge; tickets valid for a week

The only US national park devoted exclusively to archeological remains, **MESA VERDE NATIONAL PARK** is set high on a densely wooded plateau, so remote that its extensive **Ancestral Puebloan** ruins remained unseen by outsiders until late in the nineteenth century.

During the thousand or so years up to 1300 AD, Ancestral Puebloan peoples expanded to cover much of the area now known as the "**Four Corners**". While their earliest dwellings were simple pits in the ground, they ultimately developed the architectural sophistication needed to build the spectacular multistorey apartments that characterize Mesa Verde, nestled in rocky alcoves high above the sheer canyons that bisect the southern edge of the Mesa Verde plateau. The region's inhabitants eventually migrated into what's now New Mexico to establish the pueblos where their descendants still live.

All the park's ruins are located twenty or more tortuous miles up from the roadside visitor centre. The access road forks to reach the two main constellations of remains: **Chapin Mesa** to the south, and **Wetherill Mesa** to the west.

Chapin Mesa

Ruins Road, the driving route around **Chapin Mesa** (April to late Oct, daily 8am–sunset) consists of two one-way, six-mile loops, which provide access to assorted sites including the park's two best-known attractions.

Tucked 100ft below an overhanging ledge of pale rock, and the largest Ancestral Puebloan cliff dwelling to survive anywhere, **Cliff Palace** holds 217 rooms and 23 *kivas*, each thought to have belonged to a separate family or clan. Probably a ceremonial or storage centre rather than a communal habitation, it may have been home to 120 people. Guided tours (see page 75) offer the chance to walk through the empty plazas and peer down into the mysterious *kivas*. If you don't have a ticket you can still get a great view from the overlook where the tour groups gather.

Built around 1240, **Balcony House** was remodelled during the 1270s to make it even more impregnable; access is very difficult, and it's not visible from above. Guided tours involve scrambling up three hair-raising ladders and crawling through a narrow tunnel. It's a spectacular site, with two circular *kivas* standing side by side, but those who don't share the fearless Ancestral Puebloan attitude to heights should give it a miss.

Wetherill Mesa

The tortuous twelve-mile drive onto **Wetherill Mesa** beyond the main park road is open in summer only (late May to Oct, daily 8am to sunset), and even then for ordinary sized vehicles only.

From the parking lot at the far end, a free **miniature train** loops around the tip of the mesa. Its main stop is at **Long House**, the park's second largest ruin, where hour-long tours descend sixty or so steps to reach its central plaza, then scramble around its 150 rooms and 21 *kivas*.

INFORMATION AND TOURS	MESA VERDE NATIONAL PARK

Visitor centre Beside US-160 at the entrance to the park, around 40min drive below the mesa-top sites (daily: mid-April to late May & early Sept to Oct 8am–5pm, late May to early Sept 7.30am–7pm, Nov to mid-April 8.30am–4.30pm; ☎ 970 529 4465, ⓦ nps.gov/meve).

Ruins tours The three main ruins in the park – Balcony House and Cliff Palace on Chapin Mesa, and Long House on Wetherill Mesa – can only be visited on timed, guided tours. Buy tickets at the visitor centre as soon as you arrive.

ACCOMMODATION AND EATING

Far View Lodge 15 miles up from US-160, ⓦ visitmesaverde.com. Peaceful lodge offering the only rooms at Mesa Verde. Standard rooms have private balconies, while "Kiva" rooms are more luxurious; all have wi-fi but not phones or TVs. The Metate Room is a pretty good restaurant that's open daily for dinner only; mains such as elk tenderloin cost up to $32. Open mid-April to late Oct. Standard ⑤⑤, kiva ⑤⑤

Morefield Campground 4 miles up from US-160, ⓦ visitmesaverde.com. The park's official campground – so large it's almost never full – is a long way down from the ruins. Reservations available, but seldom necessary. Open mid-April to late Oct. One or two vehicles ⑤. Hookups ⑤

Spruce Tree Terrace Near Chapin Mesa museum, ⓦ visitmesaverde.com. The one place in the park to offer food year-round, this straightforward cafeteria serves sandwiches, salads and Navajo tacos at very affordable prices, and has a pleasant shaded terrace. ⑤

Wyoming

Pronghorn antelope all but outnumber people in wide-open **WYOMING**, the ninth largest but least populous state in the union, with just over 577,000 residents. This is classic **cowboy country** – the inspiration behind *Shane, The Virginian* and countless other Western novels – replete with dude ranches, rodeos and country-music dance halls. The state emblem, seen everywhere, is a hat-waving cowboy astride a bucking bronco, and a favourite bumper sticker reads, "Wyoming *is* what America *used* to be".

Unlikely as it may seem, this conservative state was the first to grant **women the right to vote** in 1869 – a full half-century before the federal government, on the grounds that the enfranchisement of women would attract settlers and increase the population, thereby hastening statehood (which came in 1890). The "Equality State" also elected the **first female US governor**, Nellie Tayloe Ross, in 1924. Today the home state of former vice president Dick Cheney is solidly Republican.

Politics aside, Wyoming is home to two of America's most famous natural attractions, the simmering geothermal landscape of **Yellowstone National Park**, and the spectacular mountain vistas of adjacent **Grand Teton National Park**. With millions of visitors pouring in to both parks every year, all roads tend to lead to this northwestern corner of the state, but there is plenty to see en route. Wyoming is effectively a giant plateau broken by a series of precipitous mountain ranges, with its eastern third high-elevation prairie – a sea of rolling grassland and scrub. Much of the state's history is associated with the great wagon trails that led across this vast, generally empty landscape, littered with old army forts, dinosaur fossils and likeable Old West towns such as **Cody** and **Buffalo**.

Cheyenne

Dwarfing the outlying neighbourhoods, the sky above **CHEYENNE** appears gargantuan, with the snow-crested Rockies looming in the distance and sun-bleached grasslands encircling the city. Established in 1867 as little more than a hardscrabble camp for workers on the Union Pacific railroad, the capital of Wyoming has grown to around

1

AMERICA'S DINOSAUR GRAVEYARD

Wyoming has become a **dinosaur** hotspot since the first major fossils were excavated in the 1870s – it even has a "state dinosaur", the triceratops. Since its sedimentary layer was geologically active throughout the Paleozoic, Mesozoic and Cenozoic eras, Wyoming is studded with over 500 million years' worth of fossils. Though numerous specimens have been shipped out of the state, there are still several sites to excite budding paleontologists.

The best place to start is the **Wyoming Dinosaur Center** in Thermopolis (daily; mid-May to mid-Sept 8am–6pm; mid-Sept to mid-May 10am–5pm; charge; ⑩ wyomingdinosaurcenter. org), which displays twenty full-size dino skeletons and is crammed with interpretive exhibits. You can play paleontologist for a day by helping dig for bones at nearby excavation sites (extra charge).

Peruse the Green River Formation at **Fossil Butte National Monument** (visitor centre daily: late May to Aug 8am–6pm, Sept 8am–5pm, Oct to late May 8am–4.30pm; free; ⑩ nps. gov/fobu), a massive collection of fossilized fish as well as fossils of a 13ft crocodile and the world's oldest-known bat, or visit the **University of Wyoming Geological Museum** in Laramie (Mon–Sat 10am–4pm; free; ⑩ uwyo.edu/geomuseum), which displays a rare 75ft Apatosaurus skeleton.

65,000, though its sleepy centre rarely feels busy. Much activity revolves around its **F.E. Warren Air Force Base**, one of the nation's largest intercontinental missile bases. Cowboy culture is big here, too, as the ranchwear stores and honky-tonks attest.

Downtown

Today only freight trains trundle through the handsome 1886 **Union Pacific depot**, now the **Cheyenne Depot Museum**, 121 W 15th St (May–Aug Mon–Fri 9am–6.30pm, Sat 9am–5pm, Sun 11am–3pm; Sept–April Mon–Fri 9am–3pm, Sat 9am–3pm, Sun 11am–3pm; charge; ⑩ cheyennedepotmuseum.org), though it still anchors Cheyenne's compact **downtown**. A few blocks north, the elegant but restrained Renaissance Revival-style **Wyoming State Capitol**, with its distinctive gold-leaf smothered dome, was completed in 1890 (open for self-guided tours Mon–Fri 8am–5pm; free; ⑩ wyomingcapitolsquare.com). Nearby **Wyoming State Museum**, 2301 Central Ave (Mon–Sat 9am–4.30pm; free; ⑩ wyomuseum.state.wy.us), chronicles the history of the state with hands-on displays, with special emphasis on its mineral resources and its Native American cultures (don't miss the Great Turtle Petroglyph). Two blocks away at 300 E 21st St, the stately Georgian-style **Historic Governors' Mansion** (June–Sept Mon–Sat 9am–5pm, Sun 1–5pm; Dec & Jan–May Wed–Sat 9am–5pm; free; ☎ 307 777 7878) was completed in 1904, its period rooms reflecting the modest tastes of its tenants (the governors moved out in 1976).

ARRIVAL AND INFORMATION CHEYENNE

By bus Greyhound buses stop at the Big D Gas Station at 5404 Walker Rd, on the outskirts of town.
Destinations Billings (1 daily; 10hr); Denver (2 daily; 1hr 35min–2hr 30min); Laramie (1 daily; 55min); Salt Lake City

(1 daily; 8hr 35min).
Visitor centre In the Union Pacific depot (same hours as museum – see page 76; ☎ 307 778 3133, ⑩ cheyenne. org).

ACCOMMODATION AND EATING

Freedom's Edge Brewing Co 1509 Pioneer Ave, ⑩ freedomsedgebrewing.com. Popular microbrewery in the heart of downtown; sup a pint of 1890 IPA, Wyoming Wit or Horchachacha (a stout based on the traditional cinnamon-spiked horchata). No food, but there's usually a wood-fired pizza truck outside that delivers to your table. $

Historic Plains Hotel 1600 Central Ave, ⑩ theplainshotel.com. Opened in 1911 but refurbished in 2002, this was one of the first luxury hotels to open in Wyoming. Whilst there is plenty of historical ambience, the standard ("Queen") rooms remain fairly small and bare-bones (the mattresses tend to be spongy). $$

Luxury Diner 1401 W Lincolnway, ⓦluxurydiner. com. Classic old diner in a converted railroad dining car from 1926, serving all the home-made classics made from scratch; huge breakfasts, excellent corned beef, BLTs with amazing sweet potato fries and the hefty "Luxury Burger". Great cheesecake, too. ⑤

Nagle Warren Mansion 222 E 17th St, ⓦnaglewarrenmansion.com. This historic B&B is the pick of Cheyenne's non-motel accommodation (book ahead); built in 1888, the house contains twelve luxurious rooms decked out in elegant Victorian West style and period antiques. ⑤⑤

To Yellowstone: the southern routes

Heading west from Cheyenne to Yellowstone National Park, I-80 and then US-287 cut across the vast high plains of southern and central Wyoming, via **Laramie** and **Rawlins**. At the Wind River Range the main route continues northwest via **Dubois**, while an alternative is to take US-191 to **Pinedale** and Jackson, gateway to Grand Teton National Park.

Laramie

Founded in 1868 as another "Hell on Wheels" camp for the Union Pacific, **LARAMIE** is far more genteel today thanks to the **University of Wyoming** (UW), whose campus spreads east from the town centre. The town lies fifty miles west of Cheyenne via either I-80 or the spectacular Hwy-210 (Happy Jack Rd), the latter slicing through the **Medicine Bow National Forest** and studded with bizarrely shaped boulders and outcrops. At first Laramie seems typical of rural Wyoming, but behind downtown's Victorian facades lurk vegetarian cafés, day spas and secondhand bookstores.

Wyoming Territorial Prison Historic Site

975 Snowy Range Rd • May–Sept, daily 8am–7pm; Oct–April Wed–Sat 10am–3pm • Charge • ⓦ wyoparks.wyo.gov

The centrepiece of the ambitious **Wyoming Territorial Prison Historic Site**, just west of town, is the old **prison** itself, in business from 1872 to 1903. Its minuscule cells and rooms contain informative displays on the history of the site along with some of its colourful ex-convicts – there's a whole room dedicated to **Butch Cassidy**, incarcerated here for eighteen months in 1896 for the common crime of cattle-rustling. Other buildings include the broom factory where prisoners were set to work, historic log structures and the 1910 horse barn.

ACCOMMODATION, EATING AND DRINKING   LARAMIE

Buckhorn Bar 114 E Ivinson St, ⓦbuckhornbarlaramie. com. The town's oldest tavern, open since 1900 and sprinkled with historic relics. Live music Fridays and club nights with live DJs on Saturdays. Daily 9am–2am.

★ **Cavalryman Steakhouse** 4425 S 3rd St (US-287), ⓦwyomingsteakhouse.com. This classic steakhouse is housed in an old, wood-panelled clubhouse on the former site of Fort Sanders. Steaks are tasty and well-priced. ⑤⑤

THE DADDY OF 'EM ALL

Founded back in 1897 as a way to boost the local economy, **Cheyenne Frontier Days** (ⓦcfdrodeo.com) in late July is now one of the nation's premier Western festivals (hence its slogan, "the daddy of 'em all"), attracting thousands to its huge outdoor rodeo, big-name C&W concerts, parades, chuckwagon races, air shows and cook-outs. The action takes place at the specially built grounds in Frontier Park on Carey Avenue, a couple of miles north of downtown. At other times you can visit **Cheyenne Frontier Days Old West Museum**, in Frontier Park at 4610 Carey Ave (daily 9am–5pm; charge; ☎307 778 7290), which chronicles the history of the festival and displays a wonderful collection of vintage stagecoaches and horse-drawn carriages from the 1860s on. Look out also for a rare elk hide painting by Shoshone leader Chief Washakie.

1

TRACING THE OREGON-CALIFORNIA TRAILS

North of Cheyenne, Wyoming's largely untouched high prairies have preserved numerous sites associated with the great wagon trails that cut across the nation to California and Oregon in the mid-nineteenth century. Get an overview at the **National Historic Trails Interpretive Center**, 1501 N Poplar St in Casper (summer Tues–Sun 8am–5pm; rest of year Tues–Sat 9am–4.30pm; free; ⓦnhtcf.org), before moving on to **Fort Laramie National Historic Site** (visitor centre daily: summer 9am–7pm, rest of year 8am–4.30pm; free; ⓦnps.gov/fola), established as a private fur-trading fort in 1834, and later the largest military post on the Northern Plains. Nearby in Guernsey, the names of pioneers are etched into **Register Cliff** (open sunrise–sunset; free), overlooking the North Platte River. Some 58 miles southwest of Casper, imposing **Independence Rock** (open 24hr; free) was a major landmark on the trails and is also inscribed with pioneer graffiti. A few miles southwest, **Devil's Gate**, a gorge on the Sweetwater River, was another dramatic trail landmark, now accessible from the **Mormon Handcart Historic Site**, 47600 Hwy-220, Alcova (daily: summer 9am–9pm, rest of year 9am–4pm; free; ☎307 328 2953). This major Mormon pilgrimage site commemorates the Mormon handcart pioneers (who actually pulled their own carts all the way to Salt Lake City, horses being too expensive) and especially the tragic circumstances of companies stranded near here at Martin's Cove in 1856 – students re-enact portions of the trek each year. Finally, **Historic South Pass** (elevation 7412ft), 180 miles west of Casper, was the easiest Rockies crossing point used by trail emigrants, today traversed by Hwy-28, with wagon ruts still visible in several places.

Gas Lite Motel 960 N 3rd St, ☎307 742 6616. Rare independent motel among the chains, with a kitchsy Old West theme, ageing but adequate rooms near the centre of town and friendly owners – great value. $$

Lovejoy's Bar & Grill 101 E Grand Ave, ⓦelmerlovejoys.com. Busy diner/bar in the old 1900 *Johnson Hotel* downtown, with inventive starters and substantial mains like the "Crunch Burger", potato bowl or fried shrimp basket. $

Night Heron Books & Coffeehouse 107 E Ivinson St, ⓦnightheronbooks.com. Decent coffee, cakes, quiche and sandwiches among antique books downstairs and newer books upstairs. $

Vee Bar Guest Ranch 2091 Hwy-130, ⓦveebar.com. If you're looking for a rural place to lay your head, travel about 20 miles west out of Laramie to this ranch where you can relax in a cosy creekside cabin and enjoy a hearty cooked breakfast (they offer week-long riding and ranching holidays in summer). Minimum stay three nights. $$$

Wyoming Frontier Prison

500 W Walnut St, Rawlins • Mon–Thurs 9am–noon & 1–4pm (tours 10.30am &1.30pm) • Charge • ⓦwyomingfrontierprison.org

There would be little reason to stop at the tiny prairie town of **RAWLINS**, one hundred miles west of Laramie on I-80, but for the unmissable **Wyoming Frontier Prison**. In service from 1901 till 1981, this huge jail with dingy cells, peeling walls and echoing corridors can make for a creepy experience – not least due to the fascinating anecdotes told by the exceptional guides. The darkest moment comes as the gas chamber (in use from 1937 until 1965) is revealed. From Laramie, the **Snowy Range Scenic Byway** is a more alluring route to Rawlins, snaking over the Medicine Bow Mountains via the tiny Wild West village of **Centennial** and Snowy Range Pass (10,847ft).

The Wind River Indian Reservation

Heading northwest to Grand Teton and Yellowstone from Rawlins and I-80, roads skirt the **WIND RIVER RANGE**, the state's longest and highest mountains. No roads cross the mountains; you can either see them from the east by driving through the **Wind River Reservation** on US-287, or from the less accessible west, by taking US-191. The reservation is centred on the small town of **Fort Washakie**, where the **Shoshone Tribal Cultural Center** at 90 Ethete Rd (Mon–Fri 9am–4pm when school is open; free; ☎307 332 9106) usually displays exhibits related to the Shoshone tribe. Ask here, or at the **Wind River Trading Co** (Mon–Sat 9am–6pm, Sun 9am–5pm; ☎307 332 3267) on the main road, for directions to the **Sacajawea Cemetery** (resting place of the Shoshone heroine), and the memorial to **Chief Washakie**.

Dubois

The former logging town of **DUBOIS** ("dew-BOYS"), squeezed into the tip of the Wind River valley north of the reservation, is an oasis among the badlands. The town turned to tourism after its final sawmill closed in 1987; it doesn't hurt that it's located sixty miles southeast of Grand Teton National Park via dramatic **Togwotee Pass** (9544ft). Home to the biggest herd of bighorn sheep in the lower 48 states, Dubois celebrates that fact with the impressive **National Bighorn Sheep Interpretive Center**, a half-mile northwest of town on US-287 (10 Bighorn Lane; June–Aug daily 9am–5pm; Sept–Dec & April–May Mon–Sat 10am–4pm, Jan–March Tues–Sat 10am–4pm; charge; ⓦbighorn.org). Along with running 3–4 hour 4WD sheep-spotting tours (Nov–March only; charge, reservations required), the centre provides self-guided tours and has exhibits on the majestic mascot of the Rockies.

ACCOMMODATION AND EATING   DUBOIS

Cowboy Café 115 E Ramshorn St, ⓦcowboycafewyo.com. Tasty country breakfasts, fresh, juicy buffalo burgers and crispy home-made fries – the coconut cream pie is pretty good, too. $̶$̶

Trail's End Motel 511 W Ramshorn St, ⓦtrailsendmotel. com. Immaculate, peaceful log-and-pinewood motel with units on the Wind River and a riverside deck. $̶$̶

Twin Pines Lodge & Cabins 218 W Ramshorn St, ⓦtwinpineslodgeandcabins.com. Comfy rooms in the main log building or spacious rustic cabins dating from 1934 (with wi-fi and microwaves). $̶$̶

Pinedale

On the west side of the Wind River Range, a scenic 77-mile drive from Jackson on US-189/191, tiny **PINEDALE** offers excellent access to outdoor pursuits, while the **Museum of the Mountain Man**, 700 E Hennick Rd (May–Oct daily 9am–5pm; charge; ⓦmuseumofthemountainman.com), commemorates its role as a rendezvous for fur trappers in the 1830s.

A sixteen-mile road winds east from Pinedale past Fremont Lake to **Elkhart Park Trailhead**, from where horse-worn paths lead past beautiful **Seneca Lake** and up rugged Indian Pass to glaciers and 13,000ft peaks.

ACCOMMODATION AND EATING   PINEDALE

★ **Log Cabin Motel** 49 E Magnolia St, ⓦthelogcabinmotel.com. Rustic lodge dating from 1929 dripping in atmosphere, with old Western-style log cabins, many with kitchens and all with modern amenities (satellite TV etc). Cabins $̶$̶, doubles $̶$̶

Wind River Brewery 402 Pine St, ⓦwindriverbrewingco.com. Serves interesting beers such as the Sweetwater (a sour ale made from a red prickly pear) and Coffee Beer. Expect good, fresh Western burgers and the occasional live local music. $̶$̶

To Yellowstone: the northern route

Heading west from South Dakota and the Black Hills to Yellowstone National Park, I-90 and then US-14 slices across the vast open spaces and mountain ranges of **northern Wyoming** for some 430 miles, beginning with **Devils Tower**, 25 miles northwest of I-90.

THE PEOPLE OF WIND RIVER

The **Wind River Reservation** is shared by the Eastern Shoshone (population 3500) and Northern Arapaho (population 9400) – many of the latter are descendants of the Sand Creek Massacre of 1864. Sadly, poverty is endemic here, and the average life expectancy is 49 (as grimly depicted in the 2017 movie *Wind River*). Other than the usual spread of casinos, the reservation is best known for the monument to **Sacagawea**, the Shoshone guide of Lewis and Clark's expedition, erected here in 1963. The best and safest way to experience the local Native American culture is to attend a **powwow** – gatherings of both spiritual and social significance – held mainly in summer, and generally open to the public. Contact the **Shoshone Tribal Cultural Center** or check ⓦwindriver.org for details.

1

Devils Tower National Monument

Monument Daily 24hr · **Visitor centre** Early April to late Nov daily 9am–4pm · Charge · Camping (May–Oct) · ⓦ nps.gov/deto

Though Congress designated **DEVILS TOWER**, in far northeastern Wyoming, as the country's first national monument in 1906, it took Steven Spielberg's inspired use of it as the alien landing spot in *Close Encounters of the Third Kind* to make this eerie 1267ft volcanic outcrop a true national icon. Plonked on top of a thickly forested hill above the peaceful Belle Fourche River, it resembles a giant wizened tree stump; however, it can be hauntingly beautiful when painted ever-changing hues by the sun and moon. Plains tribes such as the Arapaho and Crow consider it sacred and call it "Bear Lodge" – June is an especially sacred month during which there is a voluntary climbing ban. Four short **trails** loop the tower (where deer and wild turkey are often spotted), beginning from the **visitor centre** at its base, three miles from the main gate.

Buffalo

Snuggled among the southeastern foothills of the Bighorn Mountains, easy-going **BUFFALO** remains largely unaffected by the bustle of the nearby I-90/I-25 junction; winters here are mild compared to other areas of Wyoming, thus prompting locals to refer to the town as the state's "banana belt". Although Main Street, now lined with frontier-style stores, used to be an old buffalo trail, the place was actually named after Buffalo, New York. The **Jim Gatchell Memorial Museum**, 100 Fort St (summer Mon–Sat 9am–5pm, Sun noon–5pm; rest of year Mon–Fri 9am–4pm; charge; ⓦ jimgatchell.com), houses a fine collection of Old West curiosities pertaining to soldiers, ranchers and Native Americans.

ACCOMMODATION AND EATING
BUFFALO

Bozeman Trail Steakhouse 675 E Hart St, ⓦ thebozemantrailsteakhouse.com. Casual, Western-themed, family-friendly steakhouse with a menu that features quality Angus beef, elk and bison, plus a range of craft beers on tap. $$

★ **Occidental Hotel** 10 N Main St, ⓦ occidentalwyoming. com. Wonderfully restored historic hotel dating back to 1880, where you can stay in the Owen Wister Suite, where the writer wrote a chunk of *The Virginian*. The sumptuous lobby is a sight in itself, and many rooms feature vintage radios tuned to old-time music on the hotel's own micro-frequency. There's also bluegrass music in the bar on some nights. $$$

The Bighorn Mountains

Of the three scenic highways that wind through the **Bighorn Mountains**, US Alt-14 from **Burgess Junction**, fifty miles west of **Sheridan**, is the most spectacular. The road (typically closed Nov–May due to snow), edges its way up **Medicine Mountain**, on whose windswept western peak the mysterious **Medicine Wheel** (1.5 miles on gravel road, then a 3-mile return hike; 24hr; free, rangers summer only 8.30am–6pm) – the largest such monument still intact – stands protected behind a wire fence. Local Native American legends offer no clues as to the original purpose of these flat stones, arranged in a circular "wheel" shape with 28 spokes and a circumference of 245ft – though the pattern suggests sun worship or early astronomy.

Cody

The "rodeo capital of the world", located along US-14 and the North Fork of the Shoshone River, **CODY** was the brainchild of investors who, in 1896, persuaded **"Buffalo Bill" Cody** to become involved in their development company, knowing his approval would attract homesteaders and visitors alike. Despite Bill spending much of his later life in the town, his wife had the hero buried in Golden, Colorado in 1917 (see page 53); Wyoming has argued for the body's "return" ever since. In stark contrast, the town's other famous son, painter **Jackson Pollock**, who was born here in 1912, is rarely mentioned.

In summer, tourism is huge business here, but underneath all the Buffalo Bill-connected attractions and paraphernalia, Cody manages to retain the feel of a rural Western settlement. The wide main thoroughfare, **Sheridan Avenue**, holds souvenir and ranchwear shops and hosts parades during early July's annual **Cody Stampede Rodeo** (ⓦcodystampederodeo.com). In summer the **Cody Nite Rodeo** takes place nightly at the open-air arena at 519 W Yellowstone Ave on the western edge of town (June–Aug daily 8pm; charge; same contact info).

Just east of the rodeo grounds off US-14 (at 1831 Demaris Drive), the 1890s buildings gathered at **Old Trail Town** (mid-May to Sept daily 8am–6pm; charge; ⓦoldtrailtown.org), include cabins and saloons frequented by Butch Cassidy and the Sundance Kid.

Buffalo Bill Center of the West

720 Sheridan Ave • May to mid-Sept daily 8am–6pm; mid-Sept to Oct daily 8am–5pm; March, April & Nov daily 10am–5pm; Dec–Feb Thurs–Sun 10am–5pm • Charge • ⓦ centerofthewest.org

By far the biggest year-round attraction in Cody is the massive **Buffalo Bill Center of the West**, a complex of five interconnected museums. The most intriguing is the **Buffalo Bill Museum**, charting the extraordinary life of William Cody himself, from frontier legend to one of the first global celebrities thanks to his Wild West show. The **Plains Indian Museum** tackles aspects of Native American culture by theme not tribe (with just one tiny section on the wars of the nineteenth century). Its huge collection of rare artefacts ranges from headdresses and shields to clubs and painted buffalo hides. The **Whitney Western Art Museum** contains a high-quality collection of Western-themed paintings from Albert Bierstadt and Charles Russell, a whole room dedicated to Frederic Remington, John James Audubon engravings, George Catlin lithographs and the iconic *Medicine Robe* by Maynard Dixon. The **Draper Natural History Museum** focuses on the fauna and flora of the Yellowstone region, while the **Cody Firearms Museum** is one of the largest collections of guns in the world.

ACCOMMODATION AND EATING   CODY

Buffalo Bill's Antlers Inn 1213 17th St, ⓦantlersinncody.com. Clean and comfortable motel, which stands out as good value, especially in the summer; breakfast (donuts and hot coffee) and cable TV included. $$
Irma Hotel 1192 Sheridan Ave, ⓦirmahotel.com. This historic gem was built by Buffalo Bill in 1902 (named for his daughter), and retains a superb original cherrywood bar (a gift to Bill from Queen Victoria) in its namesake downstairs restaurant. $$$
Proud Cut Saloon 1227 Sheridan Ave, ⓦproudcutsaloon.com. Cowboy-style bar (with game trophies on the walls) and steakhouse serving decent bacon burgers, barbecue and steaks, as well as deep-fried cheese curds and fried green tomatoes. $$

Yellowstone National Park

Daily 24hr • Charge (tickets good for a week) • Two of the five main entrances to Yellowstone are in Wyoming, via Cody to the east and Grand Teton National Park to the south. The others are in Montana: West Yellowstone (west), Gardiner (north) and Cooke City (northeast). Due to winter snow, most roads are open from early May to Oct only

America's oldest and easily its most famous national park, **YELLOWSTONE NATIONAL PARK** attracts over four million visitors every year (97 percent of them in summer), for good reason; the sheer diversity of what's on offer is mind-bending. Not only does Yellowstone deliver jaw-dropping mountain scenery, from the scintillating colours of the **Grand Canyon of the Yellowstone** to the deep-azure **Yellowstone Lake** and wild-flower-filled meadows, but it's jam-packed with so much **wildlife** you might think you've arrived at a safari park. Shambling grizzly bears, vast herds of heavy-bearded bison (buffalo) and horned elk mingle with marmots, prairie dogs, eagles, coyotes and more than a dozen elusive wolf packs on the prowl. What really sets Yellowstone apart, however, is that this is one of the world's largest **volcanoes**, with thermal activity providing half the world's **geysers**, thousands of **fumaroles** jetting plumes of steam, **mud pots** gurgling with acid-dissolved muds and clays, and of course, **hot springs**. The park might not look like a volcano, but that's because the caldera is so big – 34 by 45 miles – and because, thankfully, it hasn't exploded for 640,000 years.

1

The following account runs clockwise around the Loop Road, beginning at Mammoth Hot Springs five miles south of the North Entrance. Of course, no trip to Yellowstone is complete without at least one **hike**, be it to a waterfall or geyser; each visitor centre has free day-hiking handouts for its area.

Mammoth Hot Springs

The small village-like centre of **Mammoth Hot Springs**, at the northern tip of the Loop Road (with lodgings, general stores and petrol station), was once **Fort Yellowstone**, with most of the stolid buildings constructed here between 1891 and 1913 now used for park administration. Elk are often seen grazing on the grass in winter. Today, the old bachelor officers' quarters of 1909 houses the **Albright Visitor Center & Museum**, with movies and exhibits on the human history of the park and a small art gallery of Yellowstone-related paintings (some by Thomas Moran). The main attraction here, though – the **hot springs** – are clearly visible south of the centre; terraces of barnacle-

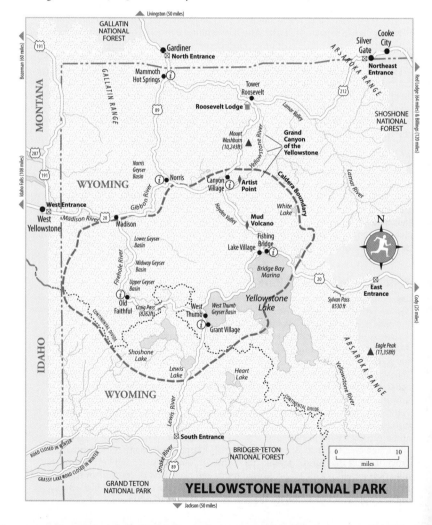

WINTER IN YELLOWSTONE

Blanketed in several feet of snow between November and April, Yellowstone takes on a new appearance in **winter**: a silent and bizarre world where waterfalls freeze in mid-plunge, geysers blast towering plumes of steam and water into the crisp air and bison – beards matted with ice – stand in huddles. It's undeniably cold, and transport can require some hefty pre-planning, but crowds are nonexistent and wildlife-spotting opportunities are superb. Only the fifty-mile road from Gardiner to Cooke City via Mammoth Hot Springs is kept open (although beyond that, the Beartooth Highway is closed). The park's sole winter lodging is available at *Mammoth Hot Springs Hotel & Cabins* or *Old Faithful Snow Lodge & Cabins* (both accessible only by snowcoach and snowmobile, and closed for Nov and much of Dec).

Xanterra operates **snowcoach** trips and tours of the park over the closed roads from West Yellowstone, Flagg Ranch to the south, Old Faithful and Mammoth Hot Springs. **Snowmobile** rental is generally cheapest in West Yellowstone; only a limited number of snowmobiles are allowed in the park at any one time, so reserve ahead (see ⓦyellowstoneadventures.com). Much less expensive is **cross-country skiing** and **snowshoeing**, with groomed or blazed trails throughout the park.

like deposits cascade down a vapour-shrouded mountainside. Tinted a marvellous array of greys, greens, yellows, browns and oranges by algae, they are composed of travertine, a form of limestone which, having been dissolved and carried to the surface by boiling water, is deposited as tier upon tier of steaming stone.

Tower-Roosevelt and the Lamar Valley

The main landmark of Yellowstone's **Tower** and **Roosevelt** area, twenty miles east of Mammoth Hot Springs, is the high peak of **Mount Washburn**; its lookout tower can be reached by an enjoyable hike (5 or 6 miles return, depending on which trailhead you use) or a gruelling cycle ride. For an easier hike, take the trail that leads down to the spray-drenched base of 132ft **Tower Fall**, 2.5 miles south of Tower Junction.

From Tower Junction, the Northeast Entrance highway wanders through the meadows of serene **Lamar Valley** – often called "North America's Serengeti" for its **abundant wildlife**, where life-and-death struggles between predators (grizzlies, wolves, mountain lions) and prey (elk, pronghorn, mule deer and especially bison) play out daily. This is the most spectacular route to Montana, via the Beartooth Highway.

The Grand Canyon of the Yellowstone

The Yellowstone River roars and tumbles for twenty miles between the sheer red, pink and golden-hued cliffs of the **Grand Canyon of the Yellowstone** (some 800–1200ft high), its course punctuated by two powerful **waterfalls**: 109ft **Upper Falls** and its downstream counterpart, thunderous 308ft **Lower Falls**. On the south rim, **Artist Point** looks down hundreds of feet to the river canyon, where frothing water swirls between mineral-stained walls. Nearby, **Uncle Tom's Trail** descends steeply to a spray-covered platform in the canyon, gently vibrating in the face of the pounding Lower Falls. A few miles south, the river widens to meander through tranquil **Hayden Valley**, one of the finest spots in Yellowstone to view wildlife from the road.

To get oriented, visit the modern **Canyon Visitor Education Center** (daily: late April to mid-June & Sept–Oct 9am–5pm; mid-June to Sept 8am–6pm; closed Nov to late April; ☏307 344 2550) in **Canyon Village**, the most visitor-friendly centre in the park; all the services, shops and restaurants are close together on a horseshoe-shaped cul-de-sac. The centre highlights the natural wonders of the park and its "supervolcano" status through multimedia exhibits and films – it's the best overall introduction to Yellowstone.

1

Norris Geyser Basin

Some twelve miles west of Canyon Village is the less crowded **Norris Geyser Basin**, where two separate trails explore a pallid landscape of whistling vents and fumaroles. **Steamboat** is the world's tallest geyser, capable of forcing near-boiling water over 300ft into the air; full eruptions are entirely unpredictable. The **Echinus Geyser** is the largest acid-water geyser known; every 35 to 75 minutes it spews crowd-pleasing, vinegary eruptions of 40 to 60ft. Get oriented at the **Norris Geyser Basin Museum** (late May to mid-Oct daily 9am–5pm; ☎307 344 2812), which chronicles the history of Yellowstone's geothermal activity. Nearby, the modest **Museum of the National Park Ranger** (late May to late Sept daily 9am–4pm; ☎307 344 7353) charts the development of the park ranger since 1916 with exhibits and films in an old army log cabin.

Yellowstone Lake

North America's largest alpine lake, deep and deceptively calm **Yellowstone Lake** fills a sizeable chunk of the eastern half of the Yellowstone caldera. At 7733ft above sea level, it's high enough to be frozen half the year, and its waters remain perilously cold through summer. You'll see the lake sixteen miles south of Canyon Village (passing the **Mud Volcano** and **Sulphur Caldron**), where the small **Fishing Bridge Museum & Visitor Center** (see page 85) has displays on lake biology and stuffed waterbirds found around here, including Trumpeter swans.

Nearby **Lake Village** has hotels and places to eat, while rowboats, along with larger motorboats and powerboats, can be rented from the **Bridge Bay Marina** (May–Sept; ☎307 242 3876), also the place to catch scenic cruises (mid-June to early Sept).

At **West Thumb Geyser Basin**, 21 miles south from Lake Village, where hot pools empty into the lake's tranquil waters and fizz away into nothing, it's easy to see why early tourists would have made use of the so-called **Fishing Cone** by cooking freshly caught fish in its boiling waters. A couple of miles south, the **Grant Visitor Center** (daily: late May to Aug daily 8am–7pm, Sept to mid-Oct 9am–5pm; ☎307 344 2650) has a small exhibit examining the role of forest fires in Yellowstone, using the major fires of 1988 as examples.

Old Faithful and around

For well over a century, the dependable **Old Faithful** (17 miles west from West Thumb) has erupted more frequently than any of its higher or larger rivals, making it the most popular geyser in the park – for many, this is what Yellowstone is all about. As a result, a half-moon of concentric benches, backed by a host of visitor facilities, now surround it at a respectful distance on the side away from the Firehole River. On average, it "performs" for expectant crowds every 65 to 92 minutes; approximate schedules are displayed nearby. The first sign of activity is a soft hissing as water splashes repeatedly over the rim; after several minutes, a column of water shoots to a height of 100 to 180ft as the geyser spurts out a total of eleven thousand gallons. As soon as it stops,

---

PLANNING A YELLOWSTONE VISIT

The key to appreciating the park is to take your time, plan carefully and – particularly in summer – exercise patience with the inevitable crowds and traffic. While you can explore a representative proportion in a day-trip, allow for a stay of at least three days to see the park fully. The majority of Yellowstone's top sights are signposted within a few hundred yards of the 142-mile **Loop Road**, a figure-of-eight circuit fed by roads from the park's five entrances, though the traditional **North Entrance** is the one marked by the 1903 **Roosevelt Arch**. Although the speed limit is a radar-enforced 45mph, journey times are very difficult to predict. Wildlife traffic jams, usually caused by stubborn herds of bison parking themselves on the pavement, are not unusual and should be expected; also for this reason, it's advisable to avoid night driving in Yellowstone.

everyone leaves, and you'll suddenly have the place to yourself. The **Old Faithful Visitor Education Center** (see below) features interactive exhibits explaining Yellowstone's thermal features and plenty of activities for kids. Check out also the **Old Faithful Inn** while you're here (see below), a Yellowstone landmark built in 1904, featuring the oldest log-and-wood-frame structures in the world and a seven-storey lobby.

Two miles of boardwalks lead from Old Faithful to dozens of other geysers in the Upper Basin. If possible, try to arrive when **Grand Geyser** is due to explode. This colossus blows its top on average just twice daily, for twelve to twenty minutes, in a series of four powerful bursts that can reach 200ft. Other highlights along the banks of the Firehole River, usually lined with browsing bison, include the fluorescent intensity of the **Grand Prismatic Spring** at **Midway Geyser Basin**, particularly breathtaking in early evening when human figures and bison herds are silhouetted against plumes of mineral spray.

INFORMATION   YELLOWSTONE NATIONAL PARK

Albright Visitor Center Near the north entrance at Mammoth (daily: mid-June to Aug 8am–6pm; Sept to mid-June 9am–5pm; ☎ 307 344 2263, ⓦ nps.gov/yell); the park's sole year-round information centre.

Fishing Bridge Museum & Visitor Center At Yellowstone Lake, one mile off Grand Loop Road on East Entrance Road (daily: late May to Aug 8am–7pm; Sept to mid-Oct 9am–5pm ☎ 307 344 2450).

Old Faithful Visitor Education Center Daily: late April to late May, Oct & mid-Dec to mid-March 9am–5pm; late May to Sept 8am–8pm; closed mid-March to mid-April & Nov to mid-Dec (☎ 307 344 2751).

Gas You'll find gas stations throughout the park (summer only).

ACCOMMODATION

IN THE PARK

All indoor lodging within Yellowstone is run by Xanterra (☎ 307 344 7311, ⓦ yellowstonenationalparklodges.com). Unless otherwise indicated, all the properties listed below are open late May to early Oct. Reservations, always strongly recommended, are essential over holiday weekends. Every major "village" has a dining room (most close by 9.30pm), and sometimes a laundry, grocery store, petrol station, post office and gift shop.

Canyon Lodge & Cabins Canyon Village 41 Clover Lane. Plush en suite hotel rooms and the recently restored Western Cabins, dating back to the park's first major revamp in 1957 and located half a mile from Grand Canyon of the Yellowstone. *Cascade Lodge* and *Dunraven Lodge* were added in the 1990s. Doubles $̄$̄$̄, cabins $̄$̄$̄$̄

Lake Lodge Cabins 459 Lake Village Rd. Fabulous rustic log building (built 1920–26), acting as the focus for nearly 186 en suite budget cabins close to the lake – visit the lobby even if you're not staying. The cheapest cabins have one double bed and are a very basic "pioneer" style; others have two doubles and can accommodate four people. $̄$̄$̄

Lake Yellowstone Hotel & Cabins 235 Yellowstone Lake Rd. Alarmingly yellow, this huge 1891 Colonial Revival-style hotel on the lake features comfy rooms and lake cottages. Its *Sun Room*, overlooking the lake, is a terrific spot for an evening drink. Doubles $̄$̄$̄$̄, cottages $̄$̄$̄$̄

Mammoth Hot Springs Hotel & Cabins 2 Mammoth Hotel Ave. Venerable 1936 behemoth (though the oldest wing dates from 1911), offering a range of cabins and hotel rooms. The Map Room is worth a look regardless of whether you stay, featuring a giant wall map made of more than 2500 pieces of wood. Open May to early Oct & mid-Dec to Feb. Doubles $̄$̄$̄$̄, cabins $̄$̄$̄, shared-bath cabins $̄$̄

★ **Old Faithful Inn** 3200 Old Faithful Inn Rd. One of the most beautiful lodges around, this magnificent 1904 inn has a wide range of rooms (the nearby Old Faithful Lodge Cabins offers cheaper digs). You can watch Old Faithful erupt from the terrace bar. Doubles $̄$̄$̄$̄, shared-bath doubles $̄$̄$̄

Old Faithful Snow Lodge & Cabins 2051 Snow Lodge Ave. This comparatively new lodge (1999) holds modern rooms, alongside attractive slightly older cabins. Open mid-May to mid-Oct & mid-Dec to Feb. Doubles $̄$̄$̄$̄, cabins $̄$̄

Roosevelt Lodge Cabins 100 Roosevelt Lodge Rd. More than eighty cabins, from sparsely furnished to motel-like, grace this attractive property, built in 1920 with log buildings designed to give a dude ranch effect – the most serene and atmospheric of all the lodges in the park. $̄$̄$̄, shared-bath cabins $̄$̄

CAMPING

Official campgrounds Of Yellowstone's twelve campgrounds, Xanterra operates five (rates are per night for up to six people) – *Bridge Bay* ($̄), *Canyon* ($̄), *Grant Village* ($̄), *Madison* ($̄) and *Fishing Bridge* (RVs only; $̄), all of which can be reserved in advance while the park service runs the other seven on a first-come, first-served basis; arrive early in the day to get a site during summer months, as most are full by 11am. The campgrounds open any time from late April until early June and start closing in mid-Sept. All have toilet facilities, but few have showers.

1

Backcountry camping To camp in the backcountry, you'll need a permit (late May to mid-Sept charge, free otherwise) from visitor centres, information stations and ranger stations; these can be collected no earlier than 48hr in advance of your camping trip. The park is so busy it's now possible to reserve backcountry campsites, at ⓦ recreation. gov or in person (and by calling ☎ 307 344 2860 or by email, April to mid-May only) – they cannot be made over the phone or by email in peak season (mid-May to early Nov).

GATEWAY TOWNS

In addition to Jackson (see page 90) and Cody (see page 80) in Wyoming, the towns just outside the park's western and two northern gates offer cheaper lodging. West Yellowstone, the largest town, is somewhat disfigured by gift stores and fast-food joints and can be overwhelmed with crowds in the summer. Friendly Western-themed Gardiner lies just 5 miles from Mammoth Hot Springs. Less developed, the one-street town of Cooke City is 3 miles from the isolated northeast entrance on US-212, which closes just east of town in winter.

Elk Horn Lodge 103 Main St, Cooke City, ⓦ elkhornlodgemt.com. Two cabins (3-night minimum in

summer) and six motel rooms, all with full bath, TV, mini-fridges, microwaves and coffeemakers. Doubles $\overline{\underline{SS}}$, cabins $\overline{\underline{SSS}}$

Madison Hotel 139 Yellowstone Ave, West Yellowstone, ⓦ madisonhotelmotel.com. This historic 1912 hotel includes an adjacent motel (with cabin-themed rooms), and one of the few hostels in the region; the attractive, log-hewn main building includes single-sex dorm rooms that sleep up to four. Open late May to early Oct. Dorms $\overline{\underline{S}}$, hotel doubles $\overline{\underline{SS}}$, motel doubles $\overline{\underline{SSS}}$

Three Bear Lodge 217 Yellowstone Ave, West Yellowstone, ⓦ threebearlodge.com. Large motel housing 75 sizeable rooms and two-bedroom family units that sleep six. On-site amenities include a friendly diner, pool and hot tub. Snowmobile packages are usually available. $\overline{\underline{SSSS}}$

Yellowstone Village Inn 1102 Scott St, Gardiner, ⓦ yellowstonevinn.com. On the edge of town, this high-end motel has 43 tidy rooms, most themed around wildlife or Western Americana, including a John Wayne room. Substantially lower rates off-season. $\overline{\underline{SSSS}}$

EATING

IN THE PARK

Each of Yellowstone's lodges and villages boasts official dining rooms, typically open May–Sept 7–10am, 11.30am–2.30pm and 5–10pm, offering similar menus of pricey but usually high-quality food: breakfast buffets that include fresh fruit, cereals, pastries and standard cooked items; lunches such as smoked trout; and more elaborate dinners such as mesquite smoked chicken. Each location also usually features a workaday cafeteria open similar hours with cheaper options such as bison burgers and sandwiches, as well as soda fountains and general stores, where burgers and fries along with ice cream and shakes are served.

Lake House Restaurant 1095 Grant Marina Rd, Grant Village, ☎ 307 344 7311. Casual dining and a decent pub-style menu (bison burgers and the like) take second place to the view: this restaurant is literally right on Lake Yellowstone. $\overline{\underline{SS}}$

Roosevelt Lodge Dining Room 100 Roosevelt Lodge Rd, ☎ 307 344 7311. The best of the resort restaurants features applewood-smoked BBQ ribs, wild game chili and breakfast mains. It also does an addictive Yellowstone "caldera" (warm chocolate torte with molten middle). $\overline{\underline{SS}}$

GATEWAY TOWNS

Beartooth Café 207 E Main St, Cooke City, ☎ 406 838 2475. Cooke City's best restaurant throughout the day (but no breakfast), serving buffalo burgers, smoked trout and sandwiches. $\overline{\underline{S}}$

The Corral 711 Scott St, Gardiner, ☎ 406 848 7627. The place for burgers since 1960; huge, half-pound burgers made with bison, elk or organic beef. $\overline{\underline{S}}$

★ **Log Cabin Cafe** 106 Hwy-212, Silver Gate, ⓦ thelogcabincafe.com. Highly atmospheric diner and B&B since 1937, just down the road from Cooke City (near the park entrance), serving a menu rich in organic and local produce – the local trout is highly recommended, as are the steaks. The dessert menu is worth a perusal too, with freshly made pies and cakes. The pumpkin bread is the star of the show, topped off with Montana ice cream and local clover honey. $\overline{\underline{SS}}$

Running Bear Pancake House 538 Madison Ave, West Yellowstone, ⓦ runningbearph.com. Serves an enjoyable breakfast and lunch, highlights include home-made cinnamon rolls, pies, fresh soups and of course, lavish stacks of pancakes. For coffee lovers there's an extensive specials menu including a Pumpkin Brickle Latte. $\overline{\underline{S}}$

Grand Teton National Park

Open daily 24hr • Charge (tickets good for 1 week)

The jagged tooth-like peaks of **GRAND TETON NATIONAL PARK**, stretching for fifty miles south from Yellowstone to Jackson, are more dramatic than the mountains of its superstar neighbour park to the north. These sheer-faced cliffs make a magnificent spectacle, rising abruptly to tower 7000ft above the valley floor. A string of gem-like lakes is set tight at the foot of the mountains; the park also encompasses the broad, sagebrush-covered **Jackson Hole** river basin (a "hole" was a pioneer term for a flat, mountain-ringed valley), broken by the gently winding Snake River, rich in elk, bison and moose – it's a lot more common to see the latter here than in Yellowstone.

Colter Bay Village and around

While no road crosses the Tetons, those that run along their eastern flank were designed with an eye to the mountains, affording stunning views at every bend. Coming from Yellowstone, Hwy-89 swoops down to Jackson Lake and **Colter Bay Village** for your first taster of the jaw-dropping views to come. The "village" contains shops, a petrol station, cabins (see page 89) and a marina (summer daily 7am–7pm) where boats can be rented. The **Colter Bay Visitor Center** (see page 89) displays 35 artefacts from the David T. Vernon Indian Arts Collection, an ensemble of rare Native American artwork donated to the park by billionaire Laurance Rockefeller in 1976.

Jackson Lake Lodge and around

Five miles south of Colter Bay, **Jackson Lake Lodge** is a gorgeous park hotel, built in 1955, with fabulous views of the mountains from its bar and back terrace – stop in even if you're not staying here. Nearby **Oxbow Bend Turnout** on the Snake River is a good place to spot wildlife in the early morning, while further south on Teton Park Road the narrow side road up **Signal Mountain** (7727ft) offers a breathtaking panorama of the Tetons and especially the wide valley of Jackson Hole.

Jenny Lake

From Jackson Lake Lodge, Teton Park Road continues fourteen miles south to crystal-clear **Jenny Lake**, a hub for boating, kayaking and wonderfully scenic hiking trails that is subsequently heavily overcrowded in peak season. Down at the boat dock, **ferries** shuttle across the lake (daily 8am–6pm, every 15min; charge; ⓦjennylakeboating.com) for a face-to-face encounter with towering, partly hunchbacked 13,770ft **Grand Teton** (Wyoming's second highest mountain) at **Inspiration Point** (a one-mile uphill hike from the dock) via cascading **Hidden Falls** (also reachable by a two-mile hike along the south shore of the lake). Note that at peak periods in July you might have to wait over an hour to take the shuttle. You can also take one-hour scenic cruises of the lake here (mid-May to Sept 11am, 2pm & 5pm; charge; reservations recommended ☏307 734 9227).

GRAND TETON ADVENTURES

Cycling the flat roads of Jackson Hole is a joy; bikes can be rented at Adventure Sports within the *Dornan's* complex in Moose (May–Sept; ⓦdornans.com), where an eight-mile, paved trail runs to Jenny Lake (or twelve miles south to Jackson). To admire the Tetons from water, rent a **canoe** or **kayak** from the same outfit or take a ten-mile **Barker-Ewing Scenic Float Trip** (ⓦbarkerewing.com) along the Snake River.

The Tetons also offer excellent **rock-climbing** opportunities; Exum Mountain Guides (ⓦexumguides.com) runs classes and guided trips from a summer office, steps from Jenny Lake.

Official park activities run by Grand Teton Lodge Co (ⓦgtlc.com) include scenic Snake River float trips, park bus tours, horseback riding (from Colter Bay) and 1hr 30min **Jackson Lake cruises** from Colter Bay. Boat rentals on Jackson Lake includes canoes and kayaks, and motorboats (also from Colter Bay). Advance reservations are highly recommended. Swimming is free and allowed in all lakes.

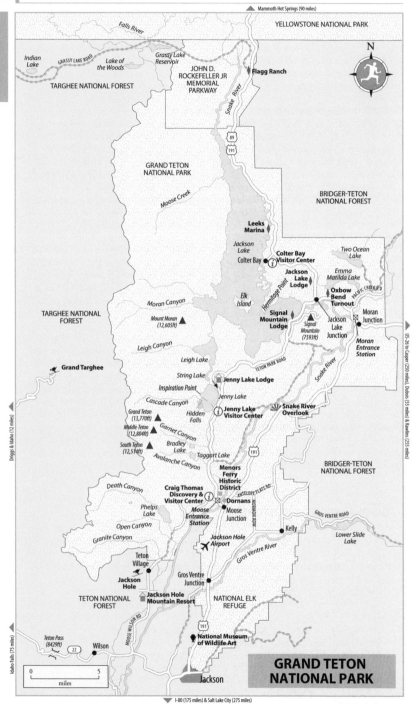

Mammoth Hot Springs (90 miles)

YELLOWSTONE NATIONAL PARK

Falls River

Indian Lake

GRASSY LAKE ROAD

Lake of the Woods

Grassy Lake Reservoir

JOHN D. ROCKEFELLER JR MEMORIAL PARKWAY

Flagg Ranch

TARGHEE NATIONAL FOREST

Snake River

89 191

GRAND TETON NATIONAL PARK

Moose Creek

BRIDGER-TETON NATIONAL FOREST

Leeks Marina

Jackson Lake

Colter Bay Visitor Center

Colter Bay

Two Ocean Lake

Jackson Lake Lodge

Emma Matilda Lake

Hermitage Point

PACIFIC CREEK RD

TARGHEE NATIONAL FOREST

Moran Canyon

Mount Moran (12,605ft)

Elk Island

Signal Mountain Lodge

Oxbow Bend Turnout

Moran Junction

Leigh Canyon

Signal Mountain (7593ft)

Jackson Lake Junction

Moran Entrance Station

Leigh Lake

US-26 to Casper (250 miles), Dubois (55 miles) & Rawlins (255 miles)

String Lake

Jenny Lake Lodge

TETON PARK ROAD

Grand Targhee

Inspiration Point

Cascade Canyon

Jenny Lake

Grand Teton (13,770ft)

Hidden Falls

Jenny Lake Visitor Center

Snake River Overlook

Snake River

Driggs & Idaho (12 miles)

Middle Teton (12,804ft)

Garnet Canyon

South Teton (12,514ft)

Bradley Lake

Taggart Lake

191

BRIDGER-TETON NATIONAL FOREST

Avalanche Canyon

Death Canyon

Menors Ferry Historic District

ANTELOPE FLATS RD

Craig Thomas Discovery & Visitor Center

Dornans

Phelps Lake

Moose Entrance Station

Moose Junction

MORMON ROW

Kelly

GROS VENTRE ROAD

Open Canyon

Granite Canyon

Jackson Hole Airport

Gros Ventre River

Lower Slide Lake

Idaho Falls (75 miles)

Teton Village

Jackson Hole

Gros Ventre Junction

NATIONAL ELK REFUGE

TETON NATIONAL FOREST

Jackson Hole Mountain Resort

MOOSE WILSON RD

Teton Pass (8429ft)

22

Wilson

191

National Museum of Wildlife Art

0   5
miles

GRAND TETON NATIONAL PARK

Jackson

1

GRAND TETON TOP HIKES

Hiking trails in Grand Teton National Park waste no time in getting to the highlights. To climb one of the craggy Tetons themselves you need to be an experienced mountaineer: guides can usually take fit newbies up Grand Teton in two days after two days of training – contact Exum Mountain Guides (see page 87).

Leigh Lake Easy and popular walk following the sandy beaches of Leigh Lake, where the imposing 12,605ft Mount Moran, named after American landscape artist Thomas Moran, bursts out dramatically from the shore.
Bradley & Taggart Lakes Moderate hike of just over 5 miles around these lakes at the base of the Tetons; lots of wildlife and wild flowers en route.

Phelps Lake Overlook Pleasant stroll of just under 2 miles from the Death Canyon Trailhead, with views of the lake, the canyon and Jackson Hole.
Death Canyon A more adventurous, but suitably rewarding amble heads up the macabrely named Death Canyon itself, reaching a verdant plateau after 4 miles on a well-graded trail adjacent to crashing creek waters.

Moose and around

Just before Teton Park Road crosses the Snake River and rejoins Hwy-89 it passes through **Moose**, eight miles south of Jenny Lake, the small park headquarters. It's also home to the beautifully designed **Craig Thomas Discovery & Visitor Center** (see page 89), where the park's geology, ecology and human history (including some artefacts from the Vernon Indian Art Collection) are explained through illuminating exhibits, artwork and movies (it also has free wi-fi). Nearby, **Menors Ferry Historic District** on the Snake River preserves Bill Menor's 1894 homestead cabin and store, and the 1916 **Maud Noble Cabin**, with exhibits on the portentous meeting that took place here in 1923 to discuss the formation of the park. Before exiting the park south, detour to **Mormon Row**, a short drive off Hwy-89 via Antelope Flats Road. This is where Mormon homesteaders settled in the early 1900s, and several timber barns and homes remain standing; look for the Moulton Barn, positioned photogenically with the snow-capped Tetons in the background.

INFORMATION

GRAND TETON NATIONAL PARK

Craig Thomas Discovery & Visitor Center 100 Discovery Way, Moose. Daily: April 10am–4pm; May & Oct 8am–5pm; June–Sept 8am–7pm (☎307 739 3399).
Colter Bay Visitor Center 640 Cottonwood Way. Daily: May & Sept 8am–5pm; June–Aug 8am–7pm (☎307

739 3594). Check the park website for the latest weather conditions (ⓦ nps.gov/grte).
Jenny Lake Visitor Center 403 South Jenny Lake Drive. Daily mid-May to late Sept 8am–7pm (☎307 739 3392).

ACCOMMODATION

Most rooms and activities within the park are managed by Grand Teton Lodge Company (☎307 543 3100, ⓦ gtlc.com); reservations are absolutely essential in summer.
Colter Bay Village Cabins ⓦ gtlc.com/lodges/colter-bay-village. Utilitarian and somewhat ageing cabins just off Jackson Lake (some date back to the 1920s and 1930s), with no a/c or TVs, and wi-fi only in select locations around the site. In high summer, "tent cabins" – canvas cabins with bunk beds (bed linen available to rent), wood-burning stove and outdoor barbecue grill – are also available. Open late May to late Sept. Tent cabins $̄$̄, cabins $̄$̄$̄
★**Jackson Lake Lodge** ⓦ gtlc.com/lodges/jackson-lake-lodge. Choose from rooms in the beautiful main lodge or spacious, modern cabins (phones and free wi-fi throughout, but no TVs). Outdoor pool and shops on-site. Open mid-May to early Oct. Cottages & non-view rooms

$̄$̄$̄$̄, mountain-view rooms $̄$̄$̄$̄
★**Jenny Lake Lodge** ⓦ gtlc.com/lodges/jenny-lake-lodge. Luxurious timber lodge getaway, smaller and much quieter than the other options, but much pricier – rates do include breakfast and dinner. Open June to early Oct. Cabins $̄$̄$̄$̄
Signal Mountain Lodge ⓦ signalmountainlodge.com. Independently run lodge in a great location beside Jackson Lake, with a wide range of options, from somewhat bland motel-style units to much nicer rustic one- or two-room log cabins. Includes on-site shop, restaurants and bar. Guided fishing tours also available. Open mid-May to mid-Oct. Doubles $̄$̄$̄$̄, cabins $̄$̄$̄$̄

CAMPING

Campgrounds All five park campgrounds are only open in

1

summer (dates vary between mid-May and mid-Oct) and operate on a first-come, first-served basis ($/site, for RVs and for hikers). Individual campgrounds tend to fill June to August in roughly the following order: *Jenny Lake* (49 tents; no RVs; full before 10am), *Signal Mountain* (81 pitches; fills between 8am and 10am), *Lizard Creek* (fills between noon and 3pm; 60 pitches), *Colter Bay* (335 pitches; fills in the afternoon) and *Gros Ventre* (355 pitches).

Backcountry camping Backcountry permits are available from park visitor centres or at ⓦ recreation.gov. Backpackers are required to carry approved bear-resistant canisters except where food storage boxes are provided.

EATING AND DRINKING

★ **Blue Heron Lounge** Jackson Lake Lodge, ⓦ gtlc. com. Be sure to earmark time for an evening drink at this hotel bar, where you can recline in comfortable chairs and ogle through huge picture windows the warm blues, greys, purples and pinks of a Teton sunset.

Dornan's Moose, ⓦ dornans.com. Right on the Snake River with Teton views from the rooftop bar or lawn, this log-frame food complex dates back to 1920. Today it boasts

two main eating options: the summer-only *Chuckwagon* and *Dornan's Pizza Pasta Co*, open year-round (except Nov). $$

Pioneer Grill Jackson Lake Lodge, ⓦ gtlc.com. *Jackson Lake Lodge* does offer fine dining in the *Mural Room* but this is the cheaper, excellent alternative, laid out like a 1950s diner with great breakfast plates, sandwiches, soups and salads. $

Jackson

Crammed with touristy boutiques, art galleries, Old West bars and excellent restaurants, **JACKSON** makes for an enjoyable base, five miles from Grand Teton National Park's southern boundary. Centred around shady **Town Square**, marked by an arch of tangled elk antlers at each corner, the Old West-style boardwalks of **downtown** burst with visitors in summer; the free **Town Square Shoot Out** recreates a Western gunfight (Mon–Sat 6pm) and the family-friendly **Jackson Hole Rodeo** (June–Aug Wed & Sat 8pm; charge; ⓦ jhrodeo.com) adds to the Western kitsch. In winter, time is best spent visiting the 25,000-acre **National Elk Refuge** on the north edge of town, where you can take a horse-drawn sleigh ride among a 11,000-strong herd of elk (mid-Dec to early April daily 10am–4pm; charge; ⓦ fws.gov/refuge/national_elk_refuge); buy tickets at Jackson Hole's visitor centre, and you'll be taken by shuttle bus to the departure point. Within town, **Snow King Resort** (ⓦ snowkingmountain.com) is an affordable, family-friendly ski resort that's also lit for night skiing; in summer you can take the chairlift (charge) up to the summit of Snow King Mountain (7808ft) for fine views of Jackson.

North of town on Hwy-89, in a building that looks like a castle, the **National Museum of Wildlife Art** (May–Oct daily 9am–5pm, Nov–April Tues–Sat 9am–5pm, Sun 11am–5pm; charge; ⓦ wildlifeart.org) houses an impressive collection from all over the world.

Jackson Hole Mountain Resort and Teton Village

While busiest in summer with road-tripping national park visitors, Jackson remains a year-round draw thanks to **Jackson Hole Mountain Resort** (winter season late Nov to early April; ⓦ jacksonhole.com), where the slopes are among the finest in the US for confident intermediates and advanced skiers and boarders. Twenty minutes' drive from downtown Jackson lies **Teton Village** at the base of the resort: in the summer you can ride the **Aerial Tram** (late May to early Oct 9am–6pm; 10min; charge; includes gondola) some 4139ft straight up to Rendezvous Mountain (10,450ft) for hiking and mind-bending views, or the **Bridger Gondola** (late June to mid-Sept daily 9am–9pm) to Gondola Summit (9095ft) for fine dining (you can also hike between the two points). There's also a popular **downhill bike park** on the slopes, while back in Teton Village kids will enjoy the pop jet fountains, climbing wall and bungee trampolines.

ARRIVAL AND GETTING AROUND   JACKSON

By plane Jackson Hole Airport (ⓦ jacksonholeairport. com), 8 miles north in Grand Teton National Park, is linked to town by taxis. The main flights here are from Denver (United) and Salt Lake City (Delta). Rental cars are available at the airport.

By bus Salt Lake Express (ⓦsaltlakeexpress.com) runs the only regular public transport to Jackson, from Idaho Falls (2 daily; 2hr), with connections to Salt Lake City, Boise and Butte. START buses (daily 6.30am–10pm, every 30min; ⓦjacksonwy.gov/363/START-Bus), provide free transport within Jackson Hole (up to the Wildlife Art Museum), and charges for trips to Teton Village.

INFORMATION AND ACTIVITIES

Visitor centre 532 N Cache St (daily: late June to late Sept 8am–7pm; late Sept to late June 9am–5pm; ☎307 733 3316, ⓦjacksonholechamber.com).

Bike tours Guided bike tours with Teton Mountain Bike Tours, 545 North Cache St (☎307 733 0712, ⓦtetonmtbike.com).

Rafting Dozens of rafting companies, including Sands

Whitewater & Scenic River Trips (☎307 733 4410, ⓦsandswhitewater.com), offer whitewater trips on the Snake River south of town; expect to pay about $80 for a half-day trip, including transport and outerwear.

Dogsled tours Dogsled tours (late Nov to early April) with Continental Divide Dogsled Adventures (☎307 455 30522, ⓦdogsledadventures.com).

ACCOMMODATION

Accommodation in Jackson is fairly expensive in summer; rates drop by around 25 percent in winter and are good value for a ski vacation. In Teton Village, on the other hand, the ski-in ski-out accommodation is at a premium come winter. Explore possibilities quickly using Jackson Hole Central Reservations (☎307 733 4005, ⓦjacksonholewy.com) or ⓦairbnb.com.

★ **The Alpine House** 285 N Glenwood St, ⓦalpinehouse.com. You won't receive better service at five-star resorts than you'll get at this cosy, 22-room B&B on a quiet street a few blocks from the town square. Breakfasts are equally extraordinary. $̄$̄$̄$̄

★ **Anvil Hotel** 215 N Cache St, ⓦanvilhotel.com. This former 1950s motel has been redesigned as a rustic chic boutique hotel with an American West/Shaker theme. Rooms feature custom beds and furnishings, rainforest showers and Co. Bigelow products. Coffee is supplied by

Jackson's Snake River Roasters, with breakfast pastries by local bakery Persephone. $̄$̄$̄$̄

The Hostel 3315 Village Drive, Teton Village, ⓦthehostel.us. Excellent slopeside hostel featuring a lounge with fireplace, TV and games room, laundry and ping-pong and pool tables. Dorm beds and private rooms, either with king bed or four twin beds. Dorms $̄$, doubles

The Inn at Jackson Hole 3345 W Village Drive, Teton Village, ⓦinnatjacksonhole.com. Boasts 83 mid-size rooms, along with a few lofts. Amenities include heated outdoor pool and hot tub, plus laundry. There's also a chic on-site bar and grill restaurant. $̄$̄$̄$̄

The Wort Hotel 50 N Glenwood St, ⓦworthotel.com. Built in 1941, the *Wort* is the most venerable high-end property in town, combining old-world style with modern facilities that include hot tubs. $̄$̄$̄$̄

EATING AND NIGHTLIFE

JACKSON

Million Dollar Cowboy Bar 25 N Cache St (Town Square), ⓦmilliondollarcowboybar.com. Built in the early 1930s, this watering hole is a touristy but essential pit stop, with saddles for bar stools and live C&W; downstairs the *Million Dollar Cowboy Steakhouse* has pinewood booths and knocks out a mean elk chop. $̄$̄$̄

Silver Dollar Bar & Grill 50 N Glenwood St, ⓦworthotel.com. More than 300 Morgan silver dollar coins from 1921 are inlaid into the bar here; admire it over the potent Bartender's Margarita. The restaurant has outdoor seating and a menu featuring house smoked trout, delicious corn chowder and marinated lamb T-bone. $̄$̄$̄

Snake River Brewing Co 265 S Millward St, ⓦsnakeriverbrewing.com. Great locals' brewpub a few blocks southwest of Town Square. Reasonably priced bison burgers and wood-fired pizzas are well worth trying, but it's the award-winning beers that pack 'em in (order the

sampler tray). $̄$̄

★ **Snake River Grill** 84 E Broadway (Town Square), ⓦsnakerivergrill.com. This local favourite does Old West with elegance, offering a fresh, seasonal menu, famed beer-battered onion rings (served on a branding iron), potato pancake with smoked salmon, steak tartare pizza and its lauded Eskimo Bars dessert (chocolate-covered bars of cake and warm caramel dipping sauce). $̄$̄$̄

TETON VILLAGE

Mangy Moose 3295 Village Drive, ⓦmangymoose.com. Legendary ski-bum hangout, famed for its après-ski sessions that segue into evenings of live rock or reggae. The bustling upstairs dining room (daily 5–10pm) serves decent burgers, chicken and pasta, alongside an extensive selection of cocktails and local beers. Cover charge for live music. $̄$̄

★ **Piste Mountain Bistro & The Deck** Jackson Hole Mountain Resort, ⓦjacksonhole.com. Take the Bridger

Gondola (free at night) to dine at 9095ft up the mountain; *Piste* specializes in local farm-to-table American cooking – try the lamb tagliatelle or Colorado striped bass. *The Deck* serves up drinks and bar snacks with stellar views (happy hour 5–6pm). $$$

Montana

Believe the hype: **MONTANA** really is Big Sky country, a region of snow-capped summits, turbulent rivers, spectacular glacial valleys, heavily wooded forests and sparkling blue lakes beneath a vast, deep blue sky that seems to stretch for a million miles. The Blackfeet and Shoshone once hunted bison here and today the state remains a bastion of Western culture, a land of cowboys, ranches, small cities and nineteenth-century ghost towns (when the gold ran out so did the people). In Montana, so the jokes go, locals keep snow tyres on till June, the speed limit is 80mph but you'll still be passed on the highway, and half the licence plates are Canadian. Cheap Charlie Russell prints line every wall, and all the railway stations are now bars, offices or restaurants. Grizzly bears, elk and bighorn sheep are found in greater numbers in Montana than just about anywhere else on the continent.

The scenery is at its most dramatic and heavily trafficked in the **western** side of the state, especially the phenomenal **Glacier National Park** and the surrounding mountain chains, landscapes that featured heavily in 1990s movies *A River Runs Through it* and *The Horse Whisperer* (both filmed in part on Dennis Quaid's Montana ranch). In contrast, the **eastern** two-thirds is dusty high prairie – sun-parched in summer and wracked by blizzards in winter – that attracts far fewer visitors.

Each of Montana's small cities has its own proud identity, and most of them are conveniently located off the east–west I-90 corridor. Enjoyable **Missoula** is a laidback college town, a glimmer of liberalism in this otherwise libertarian state; the historic copper-mining hub of **Butte** was once a union stronghold; the elegant state capital **Helena** harkens back to its prosperous gold-mining years; and **Bozeman**, just to the south, is one of the hippest mountain towns in the USA, buzzing with out-of-towners in the peak months.

Little Bighorn Battlefield National Monument

756 Battlefield Tour Rd, Crow Agency (1 mile east of I-90 exit 510, on US-212) • Daily; late May to Aug site 8am–8pm, visitor centre daily 8am–7.30pm; April to late May & Sept site & visitor centre 8am–6pm; Oct–March site & visitor centre 8am–4.30pm • Charge; bus tours summer daily 10am, 11am, noon, 2pm & 3pm (extra charge) • ⓦ nps.gov/libi

With the exception of Gettysburg, no other US battle has gripped the American imagination like the **Battle of the Little Bighorn** in June 1876, the biggest defeat of US forces by Native Americans in the West and the scene of the much-mythologized "Custer's Last Stand". Once seen as a tragic hero, Custer is better known today for a series of blunders leading up to the battle, and the decisive Native American victory – of combined Arapaho, Lakota Sioux and Cheyenne warriors – helped shape the legends of leaders Sitting Bull and Crazy Horse (see box page 93).

The battlefield is located on the current Crow Indian Reservation in the Little Bighorn Valley, and you can trace the course of the battle on a **self-guided driving tour** through the grasslands, between the visitor centre and Last Stand Hill itself, and the Reno-Benteen Battlefield five miles away – there are also several **hiking trails**. What makes Little Bighorn so unique is that the landscape has remained virtually unchanged since 1876; equally unusual, white headstone markers show where each cavalryman was killed (Custer himself was reburied in 1877 at the West Point Military Academy in New York State), while red granite markers do the same for Native American warriors, making for an extremely evocative experience. The **visitor centre** only contains a small exhibit on the battle, so to get the most out of the site listen to a **ranger talk** or take

CUSTER'S LAST STAND

During an erratic career, **George Armstrong Custer** was one of the major American military icons of the mid- to late nineteenth century. Though he graduated last in his class at West Point in 1861, he became the army's youngest-ever brigadier general, seeing action at Gettysburg and national fame through his presence at the ultimate Union victory at Appomattox, with his own troops blocking the Confederate retreat. However, he was also suspended for ordering the execution of deserters from a forced march he led through Kansas, and found notoriety for allowing the murder in 1868 of almost one hundred Cheyenne women and children at the Battle of Washita River. His most (in)famous moment, though, came on June 25, 1876, at the **Battle of the Little Bighorn**, known to native tribes as the **Battle of the Greasy Grass**.

Custer's was the first unit to arrive in the **Little Bighorn Valley**. Disdaining to await reinforcements, he set out to raze a village along the Little Bighorn River – which turned out to be the largest-ever gathering of Plains Indians. As a party of his men pursued fleeing women and children, they were encircled by two thousand Lakota and Cheyenne warriors emerging from either side of a ravine. The soldiers dismounted to attempt to shoot their way out, but were soon overwhelmed; simultaneously, Custer's command post on a nearby hill was wiped out.

Although American myth up to the 1960s established Custer as an unquestioned hero, archeologists and historians have since discounted the idea of **Custer's Last Stand** as a heroic act of defiance in which Custer was the last cavalryman left standing; the battle lasted less than an hour, with the white soldiers being systematically and effortlessly picked off. This most decisive Native American victory in the West – led by Sitting Bull and warriors like Crazy Horse – was also their final great show of resistance. With a total 268 US combatants killed, an incensed President Grant piled maximum resources into a military campaign that brought about the effective defeat of all Plains Indians by the end of the decade.

a **free ranger tour**; there are also fascinating hour-long **bus tours** with Crow-operated Apsaalooke Tours, and you can also use your phone to access audio tour commentary.

Billings and around

With a population of around 110,000, **BILLINGS** is Montana's big city, with a booming economy and even a couple of skyscrapers (though the state's tallest building, First Interstate Tower, is a modest 272ft). Founded in 1882, Billings was originally a railroad town; today the nearby Bakken and Heath shale oil fields continue to fuel the city's explosive growth. **Downtown**, bounded on its north side by the 400ft crumpled sandstone cliffs of the **Rimrock** (or just "the Rims"), centres on the tent-like **Skypoint** structure covering the intersection of Second Avenue and Broadway. While there are plenty of shops and restaurants here, this isn't likely to be the version of Montana you've come to experience – make time instead for the city's cultural attractions and the intriguing historic sites nearby.

Moss Mansion

914 Division St • June–Aug Tues–Sat 10am–4pm, Sun noon–3pm (1hr guided tours Tues–Sat 10am & 1pm); Sept–May Tues–Sun noon–3pm (1hr guided tours Fri & Sat 1pm) • Charge • ⦿ mossmansion.com

The most prominent historical property downtown is the **Moss Mansion**, a sturdy 1903 red-sandstone manse built for **P.B. Moss** (1863–1947), an entrepreneur who made a fortune running most of the businesses and utilities in Billings from the 1890s. His daughter lived in this house virtually unaltered until it became a museum in 1984, so the contents are in mint condition, lavishly furnished and decorated in various styles, from a Moorish-themed entrance hall and sombre English oak dining room to a pretty pink French parlour.

1

Yellowstone Art Museum

401 N 27th St • Tues, Wed & Fri–Sun10am–5pm, Thurs 10am–8pm • Charge (free parking on site) • ⓦ artmuseum.org

The modest **Yellowstone Art Museum**, partly housed in the town's 1910 jail, is mostly filled with travelling art exhibits, but the excellent permanent collection galleries on the ground floor specialize in Montana art from the mid-twentieth century on; work rotates here, but highlights include the Western books, paintings and posters by cowboy illustrator **Will James** (1892–1942), who lived here in later life, and contemporary works from **Theodore Waddell**, who was born in Billings in 1941 (ironically, both spent time in the jail's drunk tank). Make time also for the **Visible Vault** at 505 N 26th St, behind the museum (included), where all seven thousand-plus items in the permanent collection are stored and you can view resident artists at work.

Pompeys Pillar National Monument

3039 Hwy-312 (exit 23, I-94) • May–Sept daily 9am–6pm, Oct 9am–4pm • Charge per vehicle • ⓦ pompeyspillar.org

Just 28 miles northeast of Billings, overlooking the Yellowstone River, **Pompeys Pillar National Monument** would just be a 150ft-tall sandstone outcrop with modest appeal if not for its fascinating historical connections: the rock was named by explorer **William Clark** for Sacagawea's son when he passed here in 1806, but he also **carved his signature** into its stone flanks. It's now protected by glass (surrounded by graffiti going back to the 1880s and reached via a boardwalk), but history buffs will get chills being up close to the only physical evidence of the Corps of Discovery's 1804–06 expedition. The excellent **visitor centre** provides details of the expedition.

ARRIVAL AND INFORMATION
BILLINGS AND AROUND

By plane Billings Logan International Airport (ⓦ flybillings. com) is just 2 miles northwest of downtown. Taxis meet most flights and local MET Transit bus #1 (ⓦ ci.billings. mt.us/259/MET-Transit) runs downtown every 30min or so.
By bus The Greyhound/Jefferson Lines bus station is downtown at 1830 4th Ave N.

Destinations Bismarck (1 daily; 6hr 55min); Bozeman (2 daily; 2hr 20min); Butte (2 daily; 3hr 35min–4hr); Missoula (2 daily; 5hr 45min–6hr).
Visitor centre 815 S 27th St, downtown (Mon–Fri 8.30am–5pm; ☎ 406 252 4016, ⓦ visitbillings.com).

ACCOMMODATION AND EATING

C'mon Inn 2020 Overland Ave S, ⓦ cmoninn.com. Fun place to stay, with lush garden court-yard with waterfalls and spacious rooms with fireplaces, jacuzzis, flatscreen TVs and fridges, plus continental breakfast. $$
★ Stella's Kitchen and Bakery 2525 1st Ave N (ClockTower Inn), ⓦ stellaskitchenandbakery.com. Local favourite for its hearty breakfasts and pastries, especially

the hefty pancakes, cinnamon buns and apple pie. $
Überbrew 2305 Montana Ave, ⓦ uberbrew.beer. With ten breweries in the metro area, Billings has more craft beer makers than any other community in Montana. Get acquainted at this superb brewpub, with excellent *hefeweizen* (wheat beer) and bar food such as bison burgers and elk sausage. $

Red Lodge and Beartooth Scenic Highway

The small but popular resort town of **RED LODGE** lies along Bear Creek, sixty miles south of Billings at the foot of the awe-inspiring **Beartooth Mountains** – whose jagged peaks and outcrops contain some of the oldest rocks on earth – and in winter acts as a base for skiers using the popular **Red Lodge Mountain**, six miles west on US-212 (ⓦ redlodgemountain.com).

Originally founded to mine coal for the trans-continental railroads, Red Lodge's future was secured by the construction of the 65-mile **Beartooth Scenic Highway** (usually open late May to early Oct) connecting to Cooke City at the northeastern entrance to Yellowstone National Park (see page 81), a jaw-dropping ride of tight switchbacks, steep grades and vertiginous overlooks (allow 2–3hr to the park entrance). Even in summer the springy tundra turf of the 10,940ft **Beartooth Pass** is covered with

1

snow that (due to algae) turns pink when crushed. All around are gem-like corries, deeply gouged granite walls and huge blocks of roadside ice.

ACCOMMODATION	**RED LODGE AND BEARTOOTH SCENIC HWY**

★ **Pollard Hotel** 2 N Broadway, ⓦ thepollardhotel. com. Handsome 1893 brick hotel with some of the cheery, Victorian-themed rooms offering jacuzzis and balconies, plus pool, sauna and a comfortable old library. $\overline{5}\overline{5}\overline{5}$

Yodeler Motel 601 S Broadway, ⓦ yodelermotel.com. Offers a quirky Bavarian-German theme to go with its clean and basic motel rooms; most of the water is heated by solar power. $\overline{5}\overline{5}$

EATING AND DRINKING

Café Regis 501 S Word Ave, at 16th St W, ⓦ regiscafe.com. Best place in town for breakfast, with local ingredients and home-baked goods; wholesome salads, generous sandwiches and wraps, wild salmon and tasty corn cakes feature. $\overline{5}$

Más Taco 304 N Broadway, ⓦ eatmastaco.com. Popular, family joint on the northern edge of town, serving authentic tacos; pork "al Pastor", *carne asada*, slow-roasted chicken and shrimp (also empanadas and burritos). Be sure to check out the daily specials featuring Baja-style fish tacos and vegetarian empanada. $\overline{5}$

Red Box Car 1300 S Broadway, ☎ 406 446-2152. A

must-try experience on the southern edge of town, this 100-year old boxcar has been a diner since 1972, knocking out tasty, cheap burgers and exquisite "box car burgers" (all-steak patties) – great shakes, onion rings and Indian tacos. Sit outside overlooking the river. $\overline{5}$

Red Lodge Ales (Sam's Tap Room) 1445 N Broadway, ⓦ redlodgeales.com. The local micro-brewery knocks out some excellent ales, from its highly drinkable IPA to some intriguing seasonal beers, as well as appewood smoked specials, deli sandwiches and light bites. $\overline{5}$

Bozeman

Founded in 1864, **BOZEMAN** lies at the north end of the lush Gallatin Valley some 145 miles west of Billings, a small, affluent college town of around forty thousand with a pleasant, lively **Main Street** and a couple of worthwhile museums. The city is also a gateway to Yellowstone (just ninety miles south), and home to **Montana State University** (MSU), whose **Bobcats** sports teams enjoy enthusiastic support among locals. The biggest game of the year is the (American) football match with bitter rivals Missoula-based University of Montana (the **Grizzlies**), dubbed the "**Brawl of the Wild**" (usually in Nov; see ⓦ msubobcats.com).

Museum of the Rockies

600 W Kagy Blvd (off S 7th Ave) • Summer daily 8am–6pm; rest of year daily 9am–5pm (Living History Farm: summer daily 10am–4pm) • Charge • ⓦ museumoftherockies.org

South of downtown Bozeman, the huge **Museum of the Rockies** is best known for its exceptional **dinosaur** collection, almost all of it obtained from digs in Montana. Among the many highlights is the world's largest-known skull of a *T-rex*, a large ensemble of giant *Triceratops* skulls and skeletons and landmark *Deinonychus* finds (the nasty little ancestor of the *Velociraptor*) that revolutionized the way scientists thought about dinosaurs (that modern-day birds are direct descendants of dinosaurs is a big theme of the museum). The section on Native American culture of the northern Rockies is comprehensive but a bit drier, and there is also a section of pioneer history, a decent planetarium showing movies throughout the day (included) and, in summer, the **Living History Farm**, an 1889 farmhouse and blossom-filled garden manned by costumed guides.

Gallatin History Museum

317 W Main St • Tues–Sat: summer 11am–5pm; rest of year 11am–4pm • Charge • ⓦ gallatinhistorymuseum.org

The small **Gallatin History Museum** is crammed with all sorts of historical bits and pieces relating to the history of Bozeman and Gallatin County, from exhibits on MSU and Gary Cooper (who went to high school here), to city founder, gambler and womanizer John Bozeman and **Fort Ellis**, the army camp that operated near Bozeman 1867 to 1886. The museum occupies the old jail of 1911 (in operation till 1982), with several of the old cells still intact; you can also see the gallows where the jail's one execution took place in 1924.

1

ARRIVAL AND DEPARTURE
BOZEMAN

By plane Bozeman Yellowstone International Airport (⍵ bozemanairport.com) is 7 miles northwest of downtown, with taxis meeting flights.

By bus Greyhound/Jefferson Lines stop at the Walmart at 1500 N 7th Ave (just off I-90, junction 306), 1.5 miles from

the centre of Bozeman.

Destinations Billings (2 daily; 2hr 20min); Butte (2 daily; 1hr 20min–1hr 40min); Missoula (2 daily; 3hr 30min–3hr 40min).

ACCOMMODATION

Howlers Inn 3185 Jackson Creek Rd, ⍵ howlersinn. com. True to its name, this delightful hotel sits next to a

small wolf sanctuary and features a jacuzzi, sauna and modern rooms with DVD-players and microwaves. $\overline{5}\overline{5}\overline{5}$

EATING AND DRINKING

Cateye Café 23 N Tracy St, one block north of Main St, ⍵ cateyecafe.com. Cool, quirky, feline-themed place, knocking out classic American comfort food such as chicken pot pie with corn bread and burgers. $\overline{5}$

★ **Co-op Downtown** 44 E Main St, at Black Ave, ⍵ bozo. coop. Spacious, clean self-serve café (buffet priced by the pound) with terrific vegetarian dishes, deli sandwiches, salads, curries and mouthwatering desserts. $\overline{5}\overline{5}$

Copper Whiskey Bar & Grill 101 E Main St, at Black Ave, ⍵ coppermontana.com. Hoppin' bar and restaurant serving interesting dishes such as bison burgers and brisket

tacos along with 125 types of whiskey. $\overline{5}\overline{5}$

★ **Granny's Gourmet Donuts** 3 Tai Lane, at W Lincoln St, ⍵ facebook.com/grannysgourmetdonuts. This tiny hole-in-the-wall near the MSU campus has garnered something of a cult following for its freshly made donuts, from the addictive orange-cream flavour to the zingy strawberry. Cash only. $\overline{5}$

Montana Ale Works 611 E Main St, ⍵ montanaaleworks.com. Offers dozens of quality local microbrews along with solid steaks and bison burgers, sandwiches and even bison dumplings. $\overline{5}\overline{5}$

Butte and around

Eighty miles west of Bozeman, the former copper-mining colossus of **BUTTE** (rhymes with "mute") burst into life after gold was discovered here in 1862. Set on the slopes of a steep hill, today it sports massive black steel headframes – "gallus frames" (gallows frames) to miners – grand architecture, Cornish pasties and Irish and Serbian churches, all a legacy of its turbulent mining heyday. Though mining still takes place here, Butte's population has been reducing for years, with around 34,500 current inhabitants and large areas of the centre boarded up or simply empty lots. The historical section is known as **Uptown**, while below Front Street lies **The Flats**, where most people live today. At dusk it's all oddly attractive, when the golden light casts a glow on the mine-pocked hillsides, and the old neon signs illuminate historic brick buildings.

Berkeley Pit Viewing Stand

300 Continental Drive • March–Nov daily 9am–5pm • Charge • ⍵ pitwatch.org

In 1954 Anaconda Mining decided to open up the **Berkeley Pit**, an incredibly productive move that led to some 320 million tons of copper being extracted before the mine closed in 1982 (thanks to the collapse in copper prices). Unfortunately, the company had to demolish half of Butte to create this giant hole, 1800ft deep, one mile wide and 1.25 miles long; and when the whole thing flooded after closing, it became some of the most toxic water in the US. At the viewing stand you can take in the vast size of it all, and learn about the long-term efforts to clean it up.

World Museum of Mining

155 Museum Way (at the end of West Park St) • April–Oct Mon–Sat 9am–6pm, Sun 10am–6pm (2–3 underground mine tours daily, reservations required) • Charge • ⍵ miningmuseum.org

The excellent **World Museum of Mining**, on the far side of the Montana Tech on the University of Montana campus, is packed with fascinating memorabilia, and outside,

DURANGO AND SILVERTON NARROW GAUGE RAILROAD, CO

1

beyond the scattered collection of rusting machinery – from jackhammers to mine carts – the museum's fifty-building **Hell Roarin' Gulch** re-creates a cobbled-street mining camp of the 1890s, complete with saloon, bordello, church, schoolhouse and Chinese laundry. Above it all looms the 100ft headframe of the 3200ft-deep **Orphan Girl** mineshaft, which closed in 1955; below it all you can take in an **underground tour** (65ft Level Tour is 45–60min; the 100ft Level Tour is 1hr 30min) of some of the rickety old facilities, walking through tunnels below ground (the mine is completely flooded below 100ft).

Copper King Mansion
219 W Granite St • Tours (1hr) May–Sept daily 10am–4pm • Charge • Ⓦ copperkingmansion.com

Few mining baron estates are grander than the 34-room **Copper King Mansion**, completed for copper magnate **William A. Clark** in 1888. Clark was already a successful businessman when he came to Butte in 1872, but his investments in copper made him a multimillionaire. Along with frescoed ceilings, handcrafted mahogany and bird's-eye maple chandeliers and fireplaces, the "modern Elizabethan"-style mansion has been restocked with an incredible collection of period antiques, dolls, toys, clocks, paintings and carpets; it also has the draw of being a B&B (see page 98).

Charles W. Clark Chateau
321 W Broadway • May–Oct Thurs–Sun noon–4pm, Sept–April Sat & Sun noon–4pm • Charge • Ⓦ clarkchateau.org

Charles W. Clark, the eldest son of William Clark (see page 94), built the 26-room **Charles W. Clark Chateau** in 1898, a mock-French castle with a splendid spiral staircase, exotic-wood-inlaid rooms and wrought-iron decor. It now contains Victorian furniture and antiques, as well as a rotating selection of contemporary regional art.

Mai Wah Museum
17 W Mercury St • Early June to late Sept Tues–Sat 10am–4pm • Charge • Ⓦ maiwah.org

Hard to imagine today, but Butte once had a thriving Chinese community, at its peak in the 1910s and commemorated at the **Mai Wah Museum**. The museum occupies two historic buildings; the **Wah Chong Tai**, erected in 1899 and a general store operated by the Chinn family until 1941; and the **Mai Wah Noodle Parlour**, built in 1909. The Wah Chong Tai section is crammed with all its original contents frozen in time (a collector had bought the shop's whole stock in 1941 hoping to open his own museum). There's also an excellent exhibit on the 2007 excavations across the street, and a detailed section on Butte's Chinatown, which emerged around here in the 1870s. Despite considerable anti-Chinese prejudice from the 1890s on, the community thrived until the mining declined – by the 1940s most Chinese had gone and many nearby buildings were demolished.

ARRIVAL, INFORMATION AND TOURS
BUTTE AND AROUND

By bus Greyhound/Jefferson Lines buses drop off downtown at 1324 Harrison Ave.

Destinations Billings (2 daily; 3hr 35min–3hr 40min); Bozeman (2 daily; 1hr 20min); Missoula (2 daily; 1hr 50min).

Chamber of Commerce Just off I-90, exit 126, at 1000 George St (summer Mon–Sat 8am–6pm, Sun 9am–4pm; rest of year Mon–Fri 9am–5pm; ☎ 406 723 3177,

Ⓦ butteelevated.com).

Walking tours For more on the town's colourful history, take a 90min walking tour with Old Butte Historical Adventures, 117 N Main St (April–Oct Mon–Sat 10am–2pm; ☎ 406 498 3424, Ⓦ buttetour.info), which covers the area's architecture, mines, railway lines, a speakeasy and even journeys to the region's ghost towns (prices vary; by appointment only).

ACCOMMODATION

★ **Copper King Mansion** 219 W Granite St, Ⓦ thecopperkingmansion.com. Staying at this historic B&B really is like staying in a museum (see page 98); checkout is 9am to allow tours of the rooms to begin, and

much of the interior – bedrooms and bathrooms – contain exhibits. Sleeping here is a spellbinding experience; the place drips with history and the breakfasts are excellent. No TVs or wi-fi in rooms, and one shared shower (most rooms

have old-style baths). $\overline{\underline{5}}\overline{\underline{5}}$
Toad Hall Manor 1 Green Lane, ⓦtoadhallmanor.com. Stylish B&B in a stately neo-Georgian house, whose

four units variously come with jacuzzis, fridges, microwaves and courtyards. In-room massages and free off-site gym facilities available. $\overline{\underline{5}}\overline{\underline{5}}$

EATING

★ **Oro Fino Coffee** 68 W Park St, ⓦorofinocoffee.com. Best coffee in town, with beans sourced from Revel Coffee Roasters in Billings (including the exceptional Ethiopian Wush Wush), served with delicious pastries from nearby North 46. $\overline{\underline{5}}$

Pekin Noodle Parlor 117 S Main St, ☎406 782 2217. The last of Butte's historical Chinese noodle parlours, this gem has been going strong since 1911; inside is a line of pink wooden booths, with curtains for privacy – the food is cheap and solid American Chinese, Cantonese and Sichuan fare. $\overline{\underline{5}}$

Pork Chop John's 8 W Mercury St, ⓦporkchopjohns.com. For more rib-stuffing, lunch-bucket fare, head to

another old-time favourite (since 1932) for its fried breaded pork sandwiches (served like burgers), hamburgers and grilled-chicken sandwiches. $\overline{\underline{5}}$

Sparky's Garage 222 E Park St, ⓦsparkysrestaurant.com. Fun restaurant loaded with auto memorabilia and old cars; you can eat in a pickup truck. Great comfort food including slow-cooked baby back ribs and Southern-fried catfish. $\overline{\underline{5}}\overline{\underline{5}}$

★ **Uptown Cafe** 47 E Broadway, ⓦuptowncafe.com. The best place in Butte for a splurge, with an eclectic menu that might include Yugoslavian chicken stew, the beef eater sandwich, chicken farfalle and a range of delicious desserts. $\overline{\underline{5}}\overline{\underline{5}}$

Helena

Some seventy miles north of Butte on I-15 and framed by the Rocky Mountains, **HELENA** is Montana's relaxed, tiny state capital, founded in 1864 when a party of gold prospectors hit the jackpot at Last Chance Gulch. During the boom years, more than $20 million in gold was extracted from the gulch, and fifty successful prospectors remained here as millionaires. **Last Chance Gulch** is now the town's attractive main street (the water still runs underground), whose stately Victorian buildings are home to gift shops, diners and bars. Contrast this with the far more modest digs southwest of town in **Reeder's Alley** (ⓦreedersalley.com), a collection of miners' bunkhouses, wooden storehouses and other humble stone and brick structures built between 1875 and 1884, now refurbished into smart shops and restaurants. Helena has an unexpected Hollywood connection, too: **Gary Cooper** was born here in 1901 and almost became a real cowboy before heading to Hollywood in the 1920s to play one on screen, while actress **Myrna Loy** lived here as a child.

Montana State Capitol

1301 E 6th Ave • Mon–Fri 8am–5pm, Sat & Sun 9am–3pm (self-guided tours only) • Free • ⓦmhs.mt.gov/education/Capitol

The Montana legislative branch has worked since 1902 out of the elegant **Montana State Capitol**, topped with a copper-clad dome and featuring an ornate, French Renaissance interior adorned with stained-glass skylights and numerous murals. The most famous artwork lies in the House Chamber, where a huge mural completed by Montana artist **Charles M. Russell** in 1911 depicts a dramatic encounter between native tribes and Lewis and Clark.

Montana's Museum

225 N Roberts St • Mon–Sat 9am–5pm • Charge • ⓦmhs.mt.gov

The illuminating **Montana's Museum**, opposite the Capitol, chronicles the history of the state in great detail with clear explanations and rare artefacts from each period. It's especially good on prehistory and the region's Native American cultures, as well as having a modern, family-friendly hall depicting Montana at the time of Lewis & Clark's 1805 expedition. Don't miss the small gallery dedicated to Western artist Charles M. Russell, and upstairs "Big Medicine", the rare (and revered) white buffalo that died and was preserved here in 1959. The Montana Historical Society runs the museum and also tours of the **Original Governor's Mansion** (mid-May to mid-Sept Tues–Sat noon, 1pm, 2pm & 3pm; mid-Sept to mid-May Sat noon, 1pm, 2pm & 3pm).

1

By plane Helena Regional Airport (ⓦhelenaairport.com) is 2 miles northeast of downtown; you'll need to call a taxi (ⓣ406 449 5525) or arrange a hotel shuttle.

By bus Salt Lake Express (ⓣ208 656 8824, ⓦsaltlakeexpress.com) operates shuttle buses from Helena's transit centre at 1415 N Montana Ave, northeast of downtown. There's one daily service south to Butte (11.15am; 1hr 15min) and north to Great Falls (2.55pm; 1hr 35min).

Visitor centre 105 Reeder's Alley (June–Aug Mon–Fri 8am–6pm, Sat 10am–2pm; rest of year Mon–Fri 8am–5pm; ⓣ406 449 2107, ⓦhelenamt.com).

ACCOMMODATION, EATING AND DRINKING

Barrister Bed & Breakfast 416 N Ewing St, ⓦthebarristermt.com. Gorgeous 1874 Victorian mansion near the cathedral and originally used as priests' quarters, now offering five graceful rooms. $$

★ **Big Dipper Ice Cream** 58 N Last Chance Gulch, ⓦbigdippericecream.com. Local gem – the original is in Missoula (see page 101) – with unusual and delicious concoctions such as strawberry pink peppercorn sorbet. $

Lewis & Clark Tap Room 1517 Dodge Ave, ⓦlctaproom.com. Stop at the local microbrewery tap room for bar snacks, live music and 12 craft beers on tap, including the highly rated Pompey's Pilsner or Prickly Pear Pale Ale. $

The Sanders 328 N Ewing St, ⓦsandersbb.com. Justly popular B&B in a home from 1875, whose seven old-fashioned rooms come with Western decor and antiques, some with clawfoot tubs and fireplaces. $$$

Windbag Saloon 19 S Last Chance Gulch, ⓣ406 443 9669. Big old barn of a place – and former brothel – that reopened in 2016 after a major remodel, serving rib-stuffing seafood, burgers and steaks. $$

Gates of the Mountains

Some 25 miles north of Helena off Hwy-287 • late May to late Sept hours vary, generally hourly Mon–Fri 11am–2pm or 3pm, Sat & Sun 10am–4pm • Charge • ⓦgatesofthemountains.com

One of the region's more worthwhile excursions is the two-hour guided **boat tour** through the stunning **Gates of the Mountains**. This dramatic stretch of the Missouri River, also known as Great White Rock Canyon, is a six-mile gorge between sheer 1200ft-tall limestone cliffs named by explorer Meriwether Lewis. While not as grand as Glacier National Park, the gentle cruise does offer plenty of raw, scenic splendour not to mention an eye-opening array of wildlife, including resident pelicans and bald eagles, bighorn sheep and occasionally mountain lions and black bears (August is the best time for the latter).

Missoula and around

Framed by the striking Bitterroot and Sapphire mountains, vibrant and friendly **MISSOULA** is full of contrasts – bookstores, continental cafés and gun shops – a place where students from the local University of Montana (UM) provide much of the town's energy. Founded in 1866, it's now the second biggest city in Montana and the fastest growing city in the state.

Missoula Art Museum

335 N Pattee St • Tues–Sat 10am–5pm • Free • ⓦmissoulaartmuseum.org

One sign of Missoula's dynamism is its **Missoula Art Museum**, which displays challenging contemporary work in digital photography, painting and sculpture, and a range of eye-opening pieces by contemporary Native American artists.

Montana Museum of Art & Culture

Meloy and Paxson galleries, inside PARTV Center (off of E 6th St, University of Montana) • Tues–Sat noon–6pm (closed university holidays) • Charge • ⓦumt.edu/montanamuseum

On the UM campus, the **Montana Museum of Art & Culture** boasts an incredibly rich collection of art highlighted by interesting Renaissance-era Flemish tapestries, paintings and prints by Rembrandt, Delacroix, Joan Miró, Picasso and Toulouse-Lautrec, and American art from Frederic Remington, Warhol, Rockwell and many others.

1

HIKING, BIKING AND CAMPING AROUND MISSOULA

Missoula is a particularly good base for outdoor activities. Worthwhile hikes traverse the sixty thousand acres of the **Rattlesnake National Recreation Area**, which, despite the name, claims to be serpent-free; find more information at the local **ranger station**, at Fort Missoula, Building 24 (Mon–Fri 8am–4.30pm; ⊛ fs.usda.gov/lolo). Missoula is excellent for cycling, too, and another good source of information and **trail maps** is the Adventure Cycling Association, 150 E Pine St (⊛ adventurecycling.org); the Bicycle Hangar, 1801 Brooks St (⊛ bicycle-hangar. com), rents out good-quality mountain bikes.

The most developed of the city's small ski areas is **Montana Snowbowl**, twelve miles northwest, which has a range of slopes for all abilities and boasts a summer **chairlift** (July to early Sept daily noon–5pm; charge; extra for bikes; ⊛ montanasnowbowl.com). For state-park **camping** you'll need to backtrack east, either 25 miles on I-90 to small **Beavertail Hill** (May–Oct; day-use fee and camping charge; ⊛ fwp.mt.gov/stateparks/beavertail-hill), which also has two replica tipis to stay in, or forty miles on Hwy-200 and a brief jog on Hwy-83 north to **Salmon Lake** (⊛ fwp.mt.gov/salmon-lake), which is great for its fishing and swimming in the Clearwater River.

Elk Country Visitor Center

5705 Grant Creek Rd • May–Nov Mon–Fri 8am–5pm, Sat & Sun 9am–5pm; Dec–April Mon–Fri 8am–5pm, Sat 10am–5pm • Free • ⊛ rmef.org

Operated by the pro-conservation/pro-hunting Rocky Mountain Elk Foundation just outside town, the **Elk Country Visitor Center** provides exhibits about the prodigious, especially horned, creatures in the region, with a short walking trail providing on-site examples of a few of the creatures you can expect to see on more rugged hikes.

Smokejumper Center

5765 W Broadway St • **Visitor centre** Summer daily 8.30am–5pm • Free • ⊛ smokejumpers.com

Fires are common in this part of the country during the dry season, and the associated dangers are highlighted at the Forest Service **Smokejumper Center**, ten miles out of town on US-93. A small **visitor centre** explains methods used to train smokejumpers here – highly skilled firefighters who parachute into forested areas to stop the spread of wildfires. Free guided tours (6 daily; 45min) are also given of the parachute loft and training facilities.

ARRIVAL AND INFORMATION

MISSOULA AND AROUND

By plane Missoula International Airport (⊛ flymissoula. com) is just 4 miles northwest of downtown on W Broadway; taxis and Mountain Line public buses (Mon–Fri 11 daily; free; ⊛ mountainline.com) serve the airport.

By bus Greyhound/Jefferson Lines pulls in at 1660 W Broadway, on the edge of downtown.

Destinations Billings (2 daily; 5hr 45min); Bozeman (2 daily; 3hr 25min–3hr 40min); Butte (2 daily; 2hr); Coeur D'Alene (2 daily; 3hr); Spokane (2 daily; 4hr).

Visitor centre 101 E Main St (summer Mon–Fri 9am–5pm, Sat & Sun 10am–4pm; rest of year closed Sat & Sun; ☎ 406 532 3250, ⊛ destinationmissoula.org).

ACCOMMODATION

Doubletree Missoula-Edgewater 100 Madison St, ⊛ doubletree3.hilton.com. Best of the chain hotels, near the university right on the Clark Fork River – on which you can conveniently fly-fish – with nice rooms and suites and gym, pool and hot tub. Just a fifteen-minute walk from downtown Missoula. 5̶5̶5̶5̶

Goldsmith's Airbnb 803 E Front St, ⊛ missoulabedandbreakfast.com. This quaint 1911 Victorian three-story, brick home with nice riverside views transitioned from a B&B into a series of rental apartments after the Covid-19 pandemic, with seven rooms and suites variously offer balconies and fireplaces. 5̶5̶

EATING AND DRINKING

★ **Big Dipper Ice Cream** 631 S Higgins, ⊛ bigdippericecream.com. Local icon, serving innovative ice cream flavours such as huckleberry and El Salvador coffee. 5̶

Kettlehouse Brewing Co 602 Myrtle St, ⊛ classic.

kettlehouse.com. Lovingly known as the "K-hole", this tap room doesn't serve food, just quality handcrafted beers such as Hemp Pale Ale.

Second Set Bistro 111 N Higgins St, ⊛ secondsetbistro.

com. Opening in the historic Florence Building in 2019, this fine dining option features seasonal, locally-sourced menus of pasta, steaks, and shared plates such as smoked trout tacos and crispy Brussels sprouts. $\overline{\underline{5}}\overline{\underline{5}}$

The Shack 222 W Main St, ⓦ theshackcafe.com. Solid breakfast option, with tasty omelettes and moderately priced Mexican food, pasta and sandwiches for lunch. $\overline{\underline{5}}$

Wally & Buck 319 E Front St, ⓦ wallyandbuck.com. Slick, modern restaurant serving superb burgers, "salt-n-pepa fries" and some excellent veggie burger alternatives. $\overline{\underline{5}}$

Garnet Ghost Town

Garnet Range Rd (11 miles south of Hwy-200) • Daily 9.30am–4.30pm • Charge • ⓦ garnetghosttown.org • Road open May–Dec 15 only

To get an in-depth look at the rugged days of the Old West, travel east from Missoula some forty miles on I-90, then another ten bumpy miles by single-lane Bear Gulch Road, to **Garnet Ghost Town**. In the late 1890s this site was home to thousands of hard-rock gold miners doing a tough, perilous job – by 1905 many of the mines were abandoned and the town's population had shrunk to about 150. By the 1940s Garnet was a ghost town, and since the buildings have been kept in their semi-decayed state, the atmosphere is quite arresting: the quiet and lonely spectre of vacant, wood-framed saloons, cabins, stores and a jail, set amid acres of rolling hills that invite a leisurely stroll.

National Bison Range

58355 Bison Range Rd (Hwy-212), Moiese • **Visitor centre** Mid-May to Sept daily 8am–5pm • **Red Sleep Mountain Drive** Mid-May to early Oct daily 6.30am–8.30pm • Charge • ⓦ bisonrange.org

Conveniently located just off the route between Missoula and Glacier National Park, the 18,500-acre **National Bison Range** lies near the town of Moiese, twenty miles west of St Ignatius on Hwy-212. Beyond the small **visitor centre** the nineteen-mile **Red Sleep Mountain Drive** loop road rises into the hills for stellar views of the surrounding mountains, before dropping down to plains that harbour small herds of 350–500 bison – you might also see black bears, and plenty of pronghorn and deer. Note that it's strictly forbidden to leave your car, except on two marked hiking trails. The preserve was carved out of the Flathead Indian Reservation in 1908; after a long legal battle, the Confederated Salish and Kootenai Tribes became the steward of the bison herd and range in 2020.

Flathead Lake and around

The alpine charms of 28-mile-long **Flathead Lake** provide a welcome diversion on the long route north toward Glacier National Park, reached by following US-93 north from I-90. Between **Polson** in the south and **Somers** in the north, US-93 follows the lake's curving western shore, while the narrower Hwy-36 runs up the east below the **Mission Mountains**, and is the summer home to countless roadside cherry and berry vendors. Surrounded by low-lying mountains, both routes offer handsome views of the deep blue waters, and the lake is a great place for hiking, boating or just lazing on the shore for a few hours, though there are plenty of amusements in the nearby towns: the small resort of **Bigfork** in the northeast is the most pleasant place to stay.

Wild Horse Island State Park

US-93 is closest to **Wild Horse Island** (daily dawn–dusk; charge; ⓦ fwp.mt.gov/wild-horse-island), the lake's largest island, which you can reach by boat. Hiking on its terrific range of moderate-to-steep trails, which lead past knolls and buttes up to fine lookouts over the lake, you're apt to see mule deer and the odd group of bighorn sheep – though the eponymous untamed animals are few and rarely visible (there are just five). To visit the island rent a motorboat or kayak, or contact **Pointer Scenic Cruises** at 452 Grand Drive in Bigfork (May–Nov Mon–Sat only; ⓦ wildhorseislandboattrips.

com) or **Big Arm Boat Rentals and Rides** (ⓦboatrentalsandrides.com) which operate a shuttle (round-trip; charge) to the island from the village of Big Arm.

ACCOMMODATION AND EATING   FLATHEAD LAKE AND AROUND

Bridge Street Cottages 309 Bridge St, Bigfork, ⓦbridgestreetcottages.com. Ten cosy, luxurious self-catering one-bedroom cottages and smaller cottage suites close to town and the Swan River, with fully equipped kitchens (washer and dryer) and fireplaces. Rates halve in winter. Suites $̄$̄$̄, cabins $̄$̄$̄$̄

Echo Lake Cafe 1195 Hwy-83, ⓦecholakecafe.com. Best place for breakfast or lunch, serving up solid omelettes and burgers, with some veggie options, too. $̄

★ **Eva Gates** 456 Electric Ave, Bigfork, ⓦevagates.com. For souvenirs and picnic items don't miss the fudges, jams and sweets made with huckleberries at this local institution, established in 1949.

The Inn on Bigfork Bay 416 Electric Ave, Bigfork, ⓦbigforkbayinn.com. This beautiful inn sits right on the lake, with four comfy rooms (all en suite, with mini fridge and microwave). It also has boats and kayaks for use on the lake. $̄$̄$̄

Whitefish

The old logging town of **WHITEFISH**, just 25 miles west of Glacier National Park, is now one of the most popular resorts in Montana, perched on the south shore of beautiful **Whitefish Lake** in the shade of the **Whitefish Mountain Ski Resort** (ⓦskiwhitefish.com). As one of the area's big-name wintersports draws, the resort is also excellent for **hiking** in summer, when you can trudge four hard miles up to a restaurant on top of the mountain or take a chairlift ride or **cycle** the roads around the lake and foothills – bikes can be rented from Glacier Cyclery, 326 E 2nd St (ⓦglaciercyclery.com).

ACCOMMODATION   WHITEFISH

Grouse Mountain Lodge 2 Fairway Drive, ⓦglacierparkcollection.com. Large, luxurious modern hotel with a lodge theme, open all year-round, with a golf course on site and useful shuttle service (free) to take you into town or up the mountain. $̄$̄$̄$̄

Hidden Moose Lodge 1735 E Lakeshore Drive, ⓦhiddenmooselodge.com. Charming timber-chic B&B,

excellent for its outdoor hot tub, hearty breakfasts and rooms with jacuzzis or private decks. $̄$̄$̄$̄

North Forty Resort 3765 Hwy-40 W, ⓦnorthfortyresort.com. Stay at one of these 22 homely log cabins (minimum five people), which come equipped with fireplaces, kitchens, DVD players, free wi-fi and outdoor barbecues. $̄$̄$̄$̄

EATING AND DRINKING

Great Northern Bar & Grill 2 Central Ave, ⓦgreatnorthernbar.com. Fun sports bar and restaurant, with hefty sandwiches, burgers, fish tacos and lasagne, plus pool and ping-pong tables. Live music every Thurs– Sat (plus Tues and Wed in the summer). $̄

LouLa's Café 300 2nd St E, ⓦwhitefishrestaurant.com. Great local café, best known locally for its sumptuous pies, such as the freshly made coconut cream and the huckleberry peach combo. $̄

Montana Coffee Traders 110 Central Ave, ⓦcoffeetraders.com. Cool boho café with the best

espresso in the state (made with Costa Rican beans). Coffee but also oven-toasted wraps, sandwiches, and excellent quiche. $̄

★ **Sweet Peaks Ice Cream** 419½ 3rd St, ⓦsweetpeaksicecream.com. Irresistible in summer, when you might end up visiting daily for the luscious huckleberry, salty caramel and maple bacon flavours. $̄

★ **Tupelo Grille** 17 Central Ave, ⓦtupelogrille.com. The most esteemed dining experience in town, giving your stomach a (pricey) Southern treat with crawfish cakes, Creole chicken and good ol' shrimp and grits. $̄$̄$̄

Glacier National Park

Open year-round 24hr • Charge, good for seven days

Two thousand lakes, a thousand miles of rivers, thick forests, breezy meadows and awe-inspiring peaks make up one of America's finest attractions, **GLACIER NATIONAL PARK** – a haven for bighorn sheep, mountain goats, black and grizzly bears, wolves and mountain lions. Although the park does hold 25 small (and rapidly retreating) glaciers, it really takes its name from the huge flows of ice that carved these immense valleys

1

twenty thousand years ago. In the summer months this is prime **hiking** and **whitewater rafting** territory, while **huckleberries** litter the slopes in autumn. Outside of summer, the crisp air, icy-cold waterfalls and copious snowfall give the impression of being close to the Arctic Circle; in fact, the latitude here is lower than that of London.

Note that Glacier is one of the few national parks you can happily explore without a car; Amtrak runs up to the park entrance, where shuttle buses ply up and down the mind-bending **Going-to-the-Sun Road**.

Going-to-the-Sun Road

The fifty-mile **Going-to-the-Sun Road** across the heart of Glacier National Park is one of the most mesmerizing drives in the country, and driving it from west to east can take several hours, creating the illusion that you'll be climbing forever – with each successive hairpin bringing a new colossus into view. Beginning at **West Glacier**, the road runs east along ten-mile **Lake McDonald** before starting to climb, as snowmelt from waterfalls gushes across the road, and the winding route nudges over the **Continental Divide** at **Logan Pass** (6680ft) – a good spot to step out and enjoy the views.

The most popular **trail** in the park begins at Logan Pass, following a boardwalk for a mile and a half across wildflower-strewn alpine meadows framed by towering craggy peaks, en route to serene **Hidden Lake**. Four miles on, there's an overlook at **Jackson Glacier**, one of the few glaciers visible from the roadside. From here the road descends to **St Mary Lake** and the east gate at St Mary, right on the edge of the Great Plains.

Many Glacier

If you have time, explore some of the more remote sections of the park by car, bike or on foot, beginning with **Many Glacier**, twenty miles northwest of St Mary. At Swiftcurrent Lake an easy two-mile loop trail runs along the lakeshore, and an exciting five-mile, one-way trail heads to Iceberg Lake, so called for the blocks of ice that float on its surface even in midsummer. Another popular option is to take the trip to the foot of the **Grinnell Glacier** via two boat trips and two hikes (charge; ⓦglacierparkboats.com).

Southern loop

US-2 runs around the **southern border** of the park, for 85 miles between West Glacier and St Mary. It's not as dramatic as Going-to-the-Sun Road, but still very scenic; you'll pass **Goat Lick Overlook**, a good place to spot mountain goats, the remote village of **East Glacier Park** and the entrance to the **Two Medicine** section of the park, a less crowded centre for hiking and boating.

ARRIVAL AND INFORMATION   GLACIER NATIONAL PARK

By car The park's main, western entrance is at West Glacier, 25 miles east of Whitefish and just 35 miles south of the Canadian border. The east gate is at St Mary. Going-to-the-Sun Rd is the one through-road between the two entrances, usually passable between June and mid-Oct, though in recent years road closures for constructions have made travel more intermittent. The southern border of Glacier is skirted by US-2, which remains open all year and is an attractive alternative drive.

By train Amtrak trains between Chicago and Seattle/Portland follow the route of US-2, stopping at West Glacier, a short walk from the west gate; East Glacier Park, 30 miles south of St Mary (1hr 40min by train from West Glacier);

and Essex (summer only), in between (40min from West Glacier).

Visitor centres There are several visitor centres (all ☎ 406 888 7800, ⓦnps.gov/glac). One is at the park's main, western entrance at Apgar (mid-May to mid-June daily 9am–4.30pm; mid-June to Aug daily 8am–6pm; Sept to mid-Oct daily 8am–5pm; mid-Oct to mid-May Sat & Sun 9am–4.30pm), and another at the east gate at St Mary (daily: late May to mid-June 8am–4.30pm; mid-June to Aug 8am–6pm; Sept to early Oct 8am–5pm). The Logan Pass (daily: late June to Aug 9am–7pm, Sept 9.30am–4pm) visitor centre stands at the top of Going-to-the-Sun Rd.

GETTING AROUND, TOURS AND ACTIVITIES

By "jammer bus" Travellers arriving by public transport   can travel around the park via the bright-red 1936 "jammer" buses (so called because of the need to jam the gears into place) that provide narrated sightseeing tours from the main lodges (east side early June to late Sept; west side late May to late Oct; ☎ 406 892 2525, ⓦ glaciernationalparklodges. com/red-bus-tours).

By Glacier Shuttles Free Glacier Shuttles operate on two routes along Going-to-the-Sun Road: one between Apgar Transit Center, several miles from the park gate, and Logan Pass (9am–5pm every 40–60min; 1hr 30min–2hr trip), and one between Logan Pass and St Mary Visitor Center (9am–5pm, every 1hr; 1hr); both run July 1 to Sept only.

Guided tours Sun Tours (June–Sept; ☎ 406 226 9220, ⓦ glaciersuntours.com) offers daily half-day and full-day guided tours led by members of the Blackfeet tribe (from St Mary Visitor Center and Apgar Visitor Center).

Boat tours and rentals Tour boats explore all of the large lakes, and the major ones have kayak rentals. Contact Glacier Park Boat Co (☎ 406 257 2426, ⓦ glacierparkboats. com).

Rafting Several companies offer excellent whitewater rafting trips in and around Glacier National Park, mostly based at West Glacier. The Glacier Raft Company is a reputable operator offering half-day and full-day excursions (☎ 406 888 5454, ⓦ glacierraftco.com).

ACCOMMODATION

WITHIN THE PARK

Most accommodation within the park is run by the Xanterra Travel Collection (☎ 855 733 4522, ⓦ glaciernationalparklodges.com); most of the lodges are open from June into Sept. Limited wi-fi is now available in most hotel lobbies (note there is limited mobile [cell] phone service in the park).

Lake McDonald Lodge 10 miles from western entrance. This grand hotel opened in 1914 with an ideal shoreline location and a picturesque Swiss chalet design, offering spacious lodge rooms or small rustic cabins outside the complex. Lodge rooms ₷₷₷₷, cabins ₷₷₷

Many Glacier Hotel 12 miles west of Babb and US-2. Stately, alpine-style lodge built by the Great Northern Railway in 1915, right on Swiftcurrent Lake, with pricey lakeside suites and value rooms for half that price. Doubles ₷₷₷₷, suites ₷₷₷₷

Rising Sun Motor Inn 5.5 miles west of St Mary. Near the shores of St Mary Lake, 7 miles in from the east gate at St Mary, this 1941 inn is more rustic than the big lodges, but closer to the trails and Logan Pass. ₷₷₷

Swiftcurrent Motor Inn Many Glacier, 13 miles west of Babb and US-2. The park's cheapest accommodation, featuring cabins dating from the 1930s with or without bathrooms, and good for its access to trails on the northeast side. Cabins ₷₷, en suite ₷₷

Village Inn at Apgar Apgar Village. Fronting Lake McDonald overlooking the mountains and the water, a 1950s hotel with just 36 rooms; the views are the main draw. ₷₷₷

CAMPING

The park's thirteen campgrounds (₷) often fill up by late morning during July and Aug; ask at any visitor centre for locations and availability or call ☎ 406 888 7800. Most are open from June to mid-Sept, though St Mary and the Apgar Picnic area open year-round (no charge Dec–March). All sites are first-come, first-served, with the exception of Fish Creek and St Mary, which you can reserve six months

in advance (₷; ☎ 518 885 3639, ⓦ recreation.gov). There are showers available at the Rising Sun and Swiftcurrent campstores (St Mary and Fish Creek campgrounds have free showers for guests only).

Backcountry camping Backcountry sites can be reserved in advance (online only) starting March 15 for groups of 1-8 campers (with application fee); otherwise permits are available the day before your stay, from visitor centres (half of all sites are set aside for walk-in campers). A camping fee is payable per night May–Oct (free Nov–April).

OUTSIDE THE PARK

Belton Chalet 12575 US-2, West Glacier (2 miles outside the western entrance), ⓦ glacierparkcollection. com. This quaint 1910 lodge offers simple yet elegant digs, the three-bedroom cottages have fireplaces and balconies; no phone or TV. Open late June to late Sept (cottages also available Oct–May). ₷₷₷

★ **Glacier Park Lodge** East Glacier Park (close to the Amtrak station), ⓦ glacierparkcollection.com. Wide range of cosy lodge rooms, but best known for the massive Douglas-fir and cedar columns (bark still attached) in its huge, phenomenal lobby, brought over from the Pacific Northwest in 1913 by Great Northern Railway (non-guests are welcome to look). ₷₷₷₷

Great Northern Resort 12127 US-2, West Glacier, ⓦ greatnorthernresort.com. Just outside the main western gate to the park, this hotel was modelled on the much more expensive Glacier Park Lodge, with attractive alpine-style log cabins, all with kitchens and fireplaces. ₷₷₷

Izaak Walton Inn 290 Izaak Walton Inn Rd, Essex, ⓦ izaakwaltoninn.com. Halfway between the east and west park gates is Essex, where this atmospheric 1939 inn is the site of the Amtrak stop. As well as cosy wood-panelled rooms, it provides four fun, remodelled train cabins, and has a serviceable restaurant for fish and burgers. Doubles ₷₷₷, cabins ₷₷₷₷

North Fork Hostel 80 Beaver Drive, Polebridge, ⓦ nfhostel.com. Up in Polebridge, 28 miles north of the

1

park's west entrance, largely via gravel road, this laidback, extremely cosy hostel offers camping pitches, dorm beds, small private chalets and log cabins. Free wi-fi. Open late May to early Sept. Camping $\overline{5}$, dorms $\overline{5}$, chalets $\overline{55}$, cabins $\overline{55}$

EATING

Serrano's 29 Dawson Ave, East Glacier Park, Ⓦ serranosmexican.com. The decent Mexican food served in this historic 1909 cabin makes a pleasant change (tacos, *chiles rellenos*), and it also serves local microbrews. $\overline{55}$

Two Sisters Café 3600 Hwy-89, Babb, Ⓦ twosistersofmontana.com. This multicoloured roadhouse, famous for its outlandish decor, is great for home-made huckleberry pie, rainbow trout, bison burgers, chilli and desserts. $\overline{5}$

Whistle Stop 1024 Hwy-49, East Glacier Park, ☎ 406 226 9292. Best of a cluster of places here, worth a stop for its famous huckleberry pie (all berries, with a thin crust), with adequate meaty dinners, burgers and even better breakfasts. Often long waits for tables. $\overline{5}$

Idaho

Declared a state in 1890 after much political wrangling, **IDAHO** was the last of the Western regions to be penetrated by white settlers – in 1805, **Lewis and Clark** described central Idaho's bewildering labyrinth of razor-edged peaks and wild waterways as the most difficult leg of their epic trek. Often assumed to be all potato country, Idaho has most of the world fooled; much of its mind-blowing scenery deserves national park status, but it has always lacked the major showstoppers (and therefore the crowds) of its neighbouring states, a situation its famously conservative citizens have long been happy to maintain.

The state capital, **Boise**, is surprisingly urbane and friendly, but above all, this is a destination for the outdoors enthusiast. The state is laced with incredibly **scenic highways**, especially through the jaw-dropping **Sawtooth Mountains**, with Red Fish Lake offering some of the most mesmerizing scenery in the Rockies. Other natural wonders include **Hells Canyon**, America's deepest river gorge, and the black, barren **Craters of the Moon**. Hikers and backpackers have the choice of some eighty mountain ranges, interspersed with virgin forest and lava plateaus, while the mighty **Snake** and **Salmon rivers** offer endless **fishing** and especially **whitewater rafting**. And you'll eat well here: the **fresh trout** is superb, and the state is also known for hops (and therefore microbrews), lamb and of course, fine potatoes.

Craters of the Moon National Monument

US-20, 18 miles west of Arco • Daily 24hr; visitor centre daily: summer 8am–6pm; rest of year 8am–4.30pm • Charge (good for 7 days); Lava Flow campground extra charge (May–Nov) • Ⓦ nps.gov/crmo

The eerie, 83-square-mile **Craters of the Moon National Monument**, ninety miles west of Idaho Falls, comprises a surreal cornucopia of lava cones, tubes, buttes, craters, caves

---

HEMINGWAY IN SUN VALLEY

Ernest Hemingway completed *For Whom the Bell Tolls* as a guest of the *Sun Valley Lodge* in 1939, and lived in Ketchum for the last two years of his life before his shotgun suicide in 1961. His simple, flat gravestone can be found in Ketchum Cemetery, 1026 N Main St (Hwy-75; Ⓦ ketchumcemetery.org), next to those of his wife and son. The Hemingway Memorial (a bronze bust of the writer erected in 1966) is just off Trail Creek Road, one mile east from *Sun Valley Lodge*; it's inscribed with Hemingway's own words, ending "…*Now he will be a part of them forever*".

The Nature Conservancy (Ⓦ nature.org) actually owns Hemingway's last home in the valley, on a private drive off East Canyon Run Blvd (Mary Hemingway lived here until 1986), but it remains closed to the public.

1

and splatter cones, with trees battered by the fierce winds into bonsai-like contortions. These arose from successive waves of lava pouring from wounds in the earth's crust throughout the millennia; the most recent event occurred two thousand years ago.

The park **visitor centre** is on US-20. A seven-mile **loop road**, open late April to mid-November, takes you around myriad lava fields, where trails of varying difficulty lead past assorted cones and monoliths – don't stray from the paths, as the rocks are razor-sharp and can reach oven-like temperatures. Highlights include the one-mile trail past hollow **tree moulds** where the ancient wood ignited, leaving craggy holes; the steep half-mile trek to the top of the **Inferno Cone**, with commanding views of the region; and the eight-mile **Wilderness Trail** (free backcountry permit required, from the visitor centre), which leads deep into the backcountry past cinder cones, ropy lava flows and the blown-out expanse of **Echo Crater**.

Sun Valley

Some 160 miles east of Boise, in wonderfully scenic country, **Sun Valley** is the common label for the entire Wood River Valley area – though technically it is just the name of a **ski resort** (ⓦsunvalley.com). Here in the gentle foothills of the Sawtooths near the old sheep-ranching village of **KETCHUM**, the world's first chairlift was built in 1936, and the resort attracted the likes of Clark Gable, Gary Cooper and **Ernest Hemingway**, who came to hunt and fish. Today it becomes the centre of the media world every July during the enormously influential **Allen & Company Sun Valley Conference**, held at the Sun Valley Lodge.

Sun Valley Resort is based around **Bald Mountain**, the 9100ft peak on which most of the serious skiing occurs, and nearby **Dollar Mountain**, the 6600ft peak with easier runs for beginner skiers. The **season** runs from late November to April; as well as downhill skiing, you can also set off cross country. Ketchum itself is a lively little town with plenty of accommodation (it's undergoing something of a building boom), and even a bit of nightlife. Among **summer** outdoor activities are **cycling** along thirty miles of excellent trails, as well as **mountain biking** on the superb lift-accessed trails on Bald Mountain and **rafting** on the rivers to the north.

ARRIVAL, GETTING AROUND AND INFORMATION   SUN VALLEY

By shuttle Sun Valley Express (ⓣ 208 576 7381, ⓦctcbus. com) runs once-daily shuttles from Boise airport to Sun Valley and back (around 3hr).

By bus Mountain Rides buses link Sun Valley resort with Ketchum and other locations in the valley (rides free; ⓣ 208 788 7433, ⓦmountainrides.org)

Visitor centre In *Starbucks* at 491 Sun Valley Rd E (Mon–Sat 9am–5pm, Sun 10am–4pm; ⓣ 208 726 3423, ⓦvisitsunvalley.com).

ACCOMMODATION

Inn at Ellsworth Estate 702 3rd Ave S, Hailey (13 miles south of Sun Valley), ⓦellsworthestate.com. Nine clean and tasteful B&B rooms with smart modern furnishings, some with fireplaces and DVD players. $$$

Sun Valley Inn 1 Sun Valley Rd, ⓦsunvalley.com. Resort lodgings opened in 1937, offering a mock-Swiss Alps design but relatively new, remodelled rooms. Amenities include restaurant, bar and outdoor pool. $$$$

★ **Sun Valley Lodge** 1 Sun Valley Rd, ⓦsunvalley. com. This luxurious 600-room resort, built in 1936, is as expensive as you'd expect, with flatscreen TVs, high-speed internet and DVD players, and suites with parlours and fireplaces. Also famed for the swans that glide around the pond at the main entrance. $$$$

EATING, DRINKING AND NIGHTLIFE

The Kneadery 260 N Leadville Ave, Ketchum, ⓦkneadery.com. This has been a breakfast staple in the valley since the 1970s, serving plates of organic breads, huge omelettes, seasonal fruit and top-quality meats. It also does lunch, with a range of excellent sandwiches, salads and soups. $

Pioneer Saloon 320 N Main St, Ketchum, ⓦpioneersaloon.com. Most popular joint in town, crammed with all sorts of bizarre Old West memorabilia (stuffed bison heads) and serving up fabulous aged steaks, grilled trout and an Idaho baked potato. $$

Sawtooth Club 231 N Main St, Ketchum,

1

IDAHO'S BIG RIVER ADVENTURE

Taking a five-day rafting trip down the Middle Fork of the **Salmon River** is perhaps the most exhilarating and unforgettable experience in Idaho; by the time you've finished you'll feel like one of Lewis and Clark's team. The river drops 3000ft during its 105-mile journey through the isolated and spectacular River of No Return Wilderness. Trips usually begin in Stanley and end in Salmon, Idaho (June–Sept only). See ⓦrowadventures.com.

ⓦsawtoothclub.com. Venerable restaurant that was a favourite Hemingway watering hole, now known for American steakhouse classics, fresh seafood, wild game and unique pasta dishes like butternut squash ravioli. $\overline{\underline{\$\$\$}}$

Whiskey Jacques 251 N Main St, Ketchum, ⓦwhiskeyjacques.com. Fun local bar, with live music by mid-level national acts, and a solid range of pizzas and burgers. $\overline{\underline{\$\$}}$

The Sawtooth Mountains

North of Ketchum and Sun Valley, Hwy-75 climbs through rising tracts of forests and mountains to top out after twenty miles at the spectacular panorama of **Galena Summit** (8701ft). Spreading out far below, the meadows of the Sawtooth Valley stretch northward. The winding road – dubbed the **Sawtooth Scenic Byway** – meanders beside the young **Salmon River**, whose headwaters rise in the forbidding icy peaks to the south, as the serrated ridge of the **Sawtooth Mountains** forms an impenetrable barrier along the western horizon. The main highlight along this stretch is **Red Fish Lake** (just off the highway, sixty miles north of Ketchum), beautifully framed by Mount Heyburn and Grand Mogul peaks, home to sockeye salmon and plenty of hiking and camping opportunities in the area of alpine lakes known as Shangri-La. Visit **Redfish Center & Gallery** (June to mid-Sept daily 9.30am–5pm; free; ⓦdiscoversawtooth.org/redfish-center-gallery) by the lake for information, wildlife talks and **boat trips** (summer daily 10am, 1pm, & 3.30pm; charge; 1hr).

A tiny collection of attractive timber buildings, **STANLEY** lies seven miles north of the lake – the main activity here in summer is organizing **rafting trips** (May–Sept). Operators include the River Company (ⓦtherivercompany.com), which offers three- to four-hour trips.

Salmon River Scenic Byway

East of Stanley, the **Salmon River Scenic Byway** (still Hwy-75) follows the Salmon River through the Salmon-Challis National Forest, a gorgeous route that snakes through wooded gorges and soaring mountains. At the town of **Sunbeam** (thirteen miles from Stanley), it's worth branching left onto the **Custer Motorway** (also known as Forest Road 070), a mostly gravel road that curves northwest up the Yankee Fork creek. You'll pass the **Yankee Fork Gold Dredge** (eight miles from Sunbeam) a 112ft, nearly thousand-ton barge that once mined gold from the stream (summer daily 10am–4.30pm; charge; ⓦyankeeforkdredge.com), and a few miles further on, the preserved ghost town of **Custer**, a gold-mining camp that flourished from 1879 to 1910 (you can also visit the less developed site of **Bonanza**). The old school house operates as a small **museum** (summer daily 10am–4pm; free).

Beyond Custer the road is much rougher – unless you have a 4WD it's best to head back to Sunbeam. The two routes come together near **Challis**, where the landscape becomes much more arid and treeless. **Land of the Yankee Fork Interpretive Center** (summer daily 9am–5pm; rest of year Tues–Fri 10am–4pm; charge; ⓦparksandrecreation.idaho.gov/parks/land-yankee-fork) near Challis at the intersection of highways 75 and 93, chronicles the history of the region's Gold Rush from 1870. From Challis Hwy-93 runs sixty miles north through a series of stunning gorges to **Salmon**, where the **Sacajawea Center**, 2700 Main St, Hwy-28 (summer Mon–Sat 9am–5pm, Sun 12.30–

THE BARD IN BOISE

Just outside town in a specially built outdoor theatre, at 5657 Warm Springs Ave, the **Idaho Shakespeare Festival** (June–Sept; idahoshakespeare.org) offers inspired performances, and tickets are usually cheap and available. Around five plays are presented per season, with two or three of them penned by the Bard. A small restaurant provides food and booze, but you can also bring your own.

5pm; charge; sacajaweacenter.org) contains a small exhibit on the Lewis and Clark expedition in Idaho as seen through the eyes of their Shoshone translator.

INFORMATION

THE SAWTOOTH MOUNTAINS

Visitor centre Pick up details of camping sites and hiking trails at the Sawtooth National Recreation Area headquarters, 8 miles north of Ketchum at 5 North Fork Canyon Rd (Mon–Fri 8.30am–5pm; 208 727 5000, fs.usda.gov/sawtooth).

ACCOMMODATION AND EATING

★ **Sawtooth Hotel** 755 Ace of Diamonds St, Stanley, sawtoothhotel.com. Iconic log cabin hotel since 1931, with nine old-country style rooms (five with private bathrooms) and world-class dining (Thurs–Mon 5–9.30pm). Open late May to late Oct. Shared bathrooms $$, private bathrooms $$

Stanley Baking Co & Café 250 Wall St, Stanley, stanleybakingco.com. Simple wooden lodge serving hearty breakfasts and lunches, both featuring delectable home-baked goods (cinnamon rolls, sticky buns, croissants, muffins and coffee cake). $

Stanley High Country Inn 21 Ace of Diamonds St, Stanley, stanleyinn.com. Rustic lodge, with spacious rooms and suites with kitchenettes, satellite TV and a free continental breakfast (computer with internet access available). $$$

Boise

The verdant, likeable capital of Idaho, **BOISE** (pronounced *BOY-see*; never *zee*) straddles I-84, just fifty miles east of the Oregon border, and was established in 1862 for the benefit of pioneers using the Oregon Trail. After adapting (or misspelling) the name originally given to the area by French trappers – *les bois* (the woods) – the earliest residents boosted the town's appearance by planting hundreds more trees.

Today Boise is a friendly, cosmopolitan and outdoorsy city of some 215,000, with great skiing, biking and floating along the Boise River (the favourite way for locals to cool off in the summer), all within paddling distance of a host of excellent independent stores, restaurants and bars. Downtown is centred on the fountains at **Grove Plaza**, where the annual "**Alive after Five**" concert series sees different food and drink vendors take over the square (June–Sept every Wed 5–8pm).

Boise is also unique in having the largest **Basque** population in the world outside of the Basque heartland (in Spain and France), and is the home of **Boise State University** (BSU), whose football team the **Broncos** (with its famed all-blue field, lined with blue-painted turf) receives fanatical support from locals – their rivalry with snooty University of Idaho in Moscow (who are reputed to consider the Broncos uncouth drunks) goes back a long way, though the two teams rarely meet these days. But perhaps Boise's best feature is the **Greenbelt**, a 25-mile bike path and hiking trail that crisscrosses the tranquil **Boise River**, linking various parks right in the heart of the city.

Idaho State Capitol

700 W Jefferson St • Mon–Fri 6.30am–7pm, Sat & Sun 9am–5pm • Free • capitolcommission.idaho.gov

The centrepiece of downtown Boise is the **Idaho State Capitol**, with a fairly typical grand Neoclassical domed exterior completed in 1912, but an unusual, striking interior

1

clad in white marble with green veining (the Corinthian columns are actually scagliola, fake marble, but almost everything else is the real deal). Get maps for a self-guided tour in the basement, where exhibits on the potentially dry subject of the history and structure of Idaho state government are surprisingly entertaining. Nearby, the **Old Boise Historic District** (ⓦoldboise.com) is an elegant area of stone-trimmed brick restaurants and shops (built mostly 1903–10).

Basque Museum and Cultural Center

611 Grove St • Tues–Fri 10am–4pm, Sat 11am–3pm • Charge • ⓦ basquemuseum.com

The **Basque Museum and Cultural Center**, on the "Basque Block" of Grove Street, traces the heritage of the Basque shepherds of mountainous central Idaho through illuminating antiques, relics, photographs and key manuscripts.

The site includes the charming Cyrus Jacobs-Uberuaga boarding house, built in 1864. The international Basque **Jaialdi Festival** attracts people from all over the world, and has been held here several times (most recently in 2020; ⓦjaialdi.com).

Idaho State Museum

610 N Julia Davis Drive • Mon–Sat 10am–5pm, Sun noon–5pm • Charge • ⓦ history.idaho.gov

The interactive **Idaho State Museum** displays artefacts from Native American and Basque peoples, details the difficult experience of the Chinese miners of the 1870s and 1880s, and describes the lives of Idahoans from furriers to gold miners and ranchers. "Stories from Idaho" focuses on individuals who have made an impact on Idaho's history, while the Boomtown Gallery is designed especially for kids.

THE NEZ PERCÉ

The first whites to encounter the **Nez Percé** people (so called by French-Canadian trappers because of their shell-pierced noses – today they call themselves **Niimíipu**) were the weak, hungry and disease-ridden Lewis and Clark expedition in 1805. The natives gave them food and shelter, and cared for their animals until the party was ready to carry on westward.

Relations between the Nez Percé and whites remained agreeable for more than fifty years – until the discovery of gold, and pressure for property ownership led the US government to persuade some renegade Nez Percé to sign a treaty in 1863 that took away three-quarters of tribal land. As settlers started to move into the hunting grounds of the Wallowa Valley in the early 1870s, the majority of the Nez Percé, under **Chief Joseph**, refused to recognize the agreement. In 1877, after much vacillation, the government decided to enact its terms and gave the tribe thirty days to leave.

Ensuing skirmishes resulted in the deaths of a handful of settlers, and a large army force began to gather to round up the tribe. Chief Joseph then embarked upon the famous **Retreat of the Nez Percé**. Around 250 warriors (protecting twice as many women, children and elderly) outmanoeuvred army columns many times their size, launching frequent guerrilla attacks in a series of narrow escapes. After four months and 1700 miles, the Nez Percé were cornered just thirty miles from the safety of the Canadian border. Chief Joseph then (reportedly) made his legendary speech of surrender, "From where the sun now stands I will fight no more forever". Today some 1500 live in a reservation between Lewiston and Grangeville – a minute fraction of their original territory.

Nez Percé National Historic Park, with 38 separate sites, is spread over a huge range of north-central Idaho, eastern Oregon and western Montana. At the visitor centre in Spalding, ten miles east of Lewiston (April–Dec daily 8.30am–4pm; Jan–March Tues–Sat 8.30am–4pm; free; ⓦnps.gov/nepe), the **Museum of Nez Percé Culture** focuses on tribal arts and crafts, while the White Bird Battlefield, seventy miles further south on US-95, was where the tribe inflicted 34 deaths on the US Army, in the first major battle of the Retreat.

JET-BOATING HELLS CANYON

The most exhilarating way to experience Hells Canyon is via a **jet-boat** ride – you won't easily forget the soaring cliffs, whitewater rapids, bald eagles, black bears and gorgeous scenery. On the Idaho side, Killgore Adventures is a reputable outfit, based in the small town of White Bird, thirty miles north of Riggins (ⓦ killgoreadventures.com). Stops include Kirkwood Historical Ranch Museum, Sheep Creek Cabin and the Indian Petroglyph writings, with lunch at the Dam Visitor Center.

Old Idaho Penitentiary

2445 Old Penitentiary Rd, off Warm Springs Ave • Daily: summer 10am–5pm; rest of year noon–5pm • Charge • ⓦ history.idaho.gov

On the edge of town, the grim **Old Idaho Penitentiary** is an imposing sandstone citadel that remained open from 1870 until a major riot in 1973 finally persuaded the authorities to build modern facilities – some shared cells still had slop buckets instead of toilets. Exhibits include confiscated weapons and mugshots of former inmates, including one Harry Orchard, who murdered the state governor in 1905. You can also wander the prison yard and explore the old buildings. There's also the **J.C. Earl Weapons Exhibit**, with a comprehensive if equally macabre collection of knives, swords and guns from rare Iranian Bronze Age arrowheads to modern M16s.

ARRIVAL AND INFORMATION   BOISE

By plane Boise Airport (ⓦ iflyboise.com) is 3 miles south of downtown, just off I-84; get into town by taxi or Valley Regional Transit bus (Mon–Fri 6.15am–9.15pm; every 15–30min, Sat every hour; ⓦ valleyregionaltransit.org).
By bus Greyhound buses stop at 1212 W Bannock St, just west of downtown.

Destinations Moscow (1 daily; 6hr 45min); Portland, OR (1 daily; 9hr 35min); Salt Lake City (1 daily; 6hr 50min); Spokane (1 daily; 8hr 30min).
Visitor centre Concierge Corner on Grove Plaza (850 Front St at 9th St; Mon–Sat 9am–6pm; ☎ 208 344 5338, ⓦ boise. org).

ACCOMMODATION

Grove Hotel 245 S Capitol Blvd, ⓦ grovehotelboise. com. Solid-value, elegant rooms, many offering great views of the city and mountains, with 32-inch flatscreens. Indoor pool. ⑤⑤⑤⑤
Hotel 43 981 Grove St, ⓦ hotel43.com. This is Boise's celebrity boutique, the kind of place that visiting superstars spend the night; rooms offer chic, contemporary style with all the extras. ⑤⑤⑤⑤

★ **The Modern** 1314 W Grove St, ⓦ themodernhotel. com. Revamped *Travelodge* turned boutique motel, which has a smart 1950s themed design and rooms with minimalist designer decor and HDTVs. ⑤⑤⑤
Red Lion Downtowner 1800 Fairview Ave, ⓦ redlion. com/boise. Huge hotel with pool, a handy shuttle that will take you anywhere in town and pick you up and spacious, comfy business-style rooms. ⑤⑤

EATING

Boise claims to have invented "fry sauce" (though Utah also makes a good case), a delicious combo of mayonnaise, ketchup and spices; almost every restaurant has its own version. Less prosaically, Boise is close to Idaho's southwest wine country – try some of the very decent local Pinot Gris vintages before you leave (see ⓦ idahowines.org).
★ **Bar Gernika** 202 S Capitol Blvd, ⓦ bargernika.com. Old Basque-style pub, excellent for its authentic Basque specialities – particularly the range of stews and lamb dishes, and its famous beef tongue. ⑤⑤
★ **Barbacoa** 276 Bobwhite Court, ⓦ barbacoa-boise.com. This whimsical place on Parkcenter Lake blends a mad eclectic interior with giant wire sculptures, crazy chandeliers and a Spanish theme, though the cuisine is mostly contemporary

American; steak sandwich, paella and Idaho trout. ⑤⑤⑤
Bittercreek Alehouse 246 N 8th St, ⓦ bittercreek alehouse.com. With 39 drafts from craft brewers all over the West and decent burgers, this is a fun place to spend an evening. ⑤
★ **Boise Fry Co** 204 N Capitol Blvd, ⓦ boisefrycompany. com. Fittingly for a state so associated with potatoes, this local mini-chain knocks out some of the best burgers and fries anywhere; you choose from six types of potatoes, then the size, and then the style (curly, home-style, shoestring and so on). ⑤
Chandlers 981 W Grove St, ⓦ chandlersboise.com. Try this posh steakhouse for great, expertly grilled cuts of beef, but also the "ten-minute martinis" (it takes that long to freeze the glass with water, chip away at the ice and make

1

ROUTE OF THE HIAWATHA

One of the highlights of the Idaho Panhandle is hiking or biking the **Route of the Hiawatha Bike Trail** (open late May to late Sept; ⓦ ridethehiawatha.com), the former fifteen-mile stretch of rail line between Roland and Pearson that runs through ten tunnels and travels over seven high trestles; the 1.7 mile-long St. Paul Pass tunnel is the highlight. There's a charge for trail passes, and an additional charge for the shuttle between Pearson and Roland. The equally spectacular **Trail of the Coeur d'Alenes** runs 72 miles from Mullan to Plummer (see ⓦ parksandrecreation.idaho.gov/parks/trail-coeur-d-alenes).

the cocktail). \$\$\$\$
Fork 199 N 8th St, ⓦ boisefork.com. Farm-to-table hotspot, with the menu listing where all the produce is sourced; highlights include the addictive asparagus fries, and the "grown-up grilled ham and cheese" (with onion jam). \$\$

Goldy's 108 S Capitol Blvd, ⓦ goldysbreakfastbistro. com. Modern diner serving up a range of savoury items from salmon cakes to biscuits 'n' gravy and the celebrated sweet potato hash browns, and where you can create your own excellent breakfast combos. \$

Hells Canyon

From the busy little watersports and ski resort of **McCALL**, 110 miles north of Boise, Hwy-55 climbs steadily to merge with US-95 and follow the turbulent **Little Salmon River**. Just south of the outdoorsy town of **Riggins**, thirty miles on, comes a good opportunity to see **Hells Canyon** from Idaho. With an average depth of 5500ft this is the deepest river gorge in the US, though you wouldn't guess so due to its broad expanse and lack of sheer walls. Nevertheless, it is impressive, with Oregon's Wallowa and Eagle Cap ranges rising behind it and the river glimmering far down below. **Heaven's Gate Overlook** is the best viewpoint into the canyon from Idaho; from the south end of Riggins, allow a half-day to reach the overlook on a very steep and winding gravel road (Forest Road 517), best tackled in a 4WD. The canyon is also accessible by road from Oregon and by jet-boat trip.

Moscow

The thirty miles of US-95 between Lewiston, at the north end of Hells Canyon, and **MOSCOW**, wind through the beautiful rolling hillsides of the fertile Palouse Valley. Moscow itself is a fun, friendly town that makes a good overnight stop, and is the site of the **University of Idaho** (ⓦ uidaho.edu) Bookstores, galleries, bars and cafés line the tree-shaded **Main Street**, while theatre, music and independent cinema are on offer throughout the year, along with a sprinkling of arts festivals: the **Moscow Artwalk** (☎ 208 883 7036) brings together dozens of artists, galleries and the public for diverting summertime exhibits, and the **Lionel Hampton Jazz Festival** (ⓦ uidaho.edu/class/jazzfest) showcases big names new and old every February.

Idaho Panhandle

The narrow, rugged, northern section of Idaho is known as the **Idaho Panhandle**, more easily accessed from Washington and Montana on I-90 – which follows the Coeur d'Alene River and its South Fork – than the southern part of the state. Though **Wallace** makes for an enticing historical attraction, this region really is all about the outdoors. Note that the Panhandle observes Pacific Time (1hr behind the rest of the state, on Mountain Time).

Coeur d'Alene

Now a major resort and the capital of the Panhandle, **COEUR D'ALENE** ("core da lane") lies fifty miles north of Moscow on the shores of lovely 25-mile-long **Lake Coeur** d'Alene, which stretches into the mountains. Poised on the lake is the expensive **Coeur d'Alene Resort** which dominates the unremarkable downtown, where **cruises** (late April to mid-Nov 1–3 daily; Ⓦcdacruises.com) give you a closer view.

ACCOMMODATION AND EATING   COEUR D'ALENE

★ **Beverly's** Coeur d'Alene Resort 115 S 2nd St, Ⓦ beverlyscda.com. Chic choice with amazing lake views, with fine seafood and beef, king crab and bison carpaccio. $$$
Flamingo Motel 718 E Sherman Ave, Ⓦflamingomotel idaho.com. Aside from the *Coeur d'Alene Resort*, you can stay at this cheap and clean option, which offers kitschy themed rooms kitted out in classic cowboy, tropical cabana

and ultra-patriotic stylings. $$
Roger's Ice Cream & Burgers 1224 E Sherman Ave, Ⓦ rogersicecreamburgers.com. Addictive, home-made flavours such as "huckleberry heaven" and "moose tracks", as well as French fries hand-cut from Idaho potatoes and juicy burgers. $

Wallace

Some 48 miles southeast of Coeur d'Alene lies the authentic Old West mining town of **WALLACE**, established by one Colonel Wallace in 1884 and briefly the silver mining capital of the world. Those days are long gone, and the town has struggled to survive in recent years, despite being extremely picturesque (the 1997 movie *Dante's Peak* was filmed here) – its shabby, historic streets are some of the most memorable in the Rockies. Get acquainted with the town's turbulent history on the **Sierra Silver Mine Tour**, a 75-minute trolley-car ride departing 420 N 5th St (daily: June–Aug every 30min 10am–4pm, May, Sept & Oct 10am–2pm; charge; Ⓦsilverminetour.org), which lets you descend 1000ft to appreciate the hard labour endured by miners a century ago.

To find out more, drop by the **Wallace District Mining Museum** at 509 Bank St (Mon & Thurs–Sun 9am–3pm; donation requested; Ⓦwallaceminingmuseum.com), which has replicas, photos and artefacts from the gold and silver heydays from the 1880s to the 1940s. To see what miners did on their days off, visit the **Oasis Bordello Museum** at 605 Cedar St (May–Oct Mon–Sat 10am–3pm, Sun 11am–3pm; charge; ☎208 753 0801), chronicling the colourful hundred-year history of a certain local "institution".

ACCOMMODATION AND EATING   WALLACE

Red Light Garage 302 5th St, Ⓦ redlightgarage.com. This diner drips with character, smothered with old signs; it's best known for its amazing huckleberry shakes, but also serves up a mean burger. $
Wallace Brewing Co 610 Bank St, Ⓦ wallacebrewing.com.

Local brewpub located in another 1890 building, purveyors of such gems as JackLeg Stout and Huckleberry Lager. $
Wallace Inn 100 Front St, Ⓦ thewallaceinn.com. Best place to stay in town, with a pool, hot tub, sauna and gym, with the comfy, spacious rooms featuring a modern, neat style. $$

Sandpoint

Forty-four miles north of Coeur d'Alene, the pretty little town of **SANDPOINT** lies at the northwestern end of 43-mile long **Lake Pend Oreille** (pronounced "PON-duh-ray"), with its downtown overlooking placid Sandy Creek but its main attractions somewhat further out. At the south end of the lake, **Farragut State Park**, 13400 Ranger Rd (Ⓦparksandrecreation.idaho.gov/parks/farragut), has four thousand acres for boating, hiking, camping and the like. To the northeast, the spiky Selkirk Mountains hold the **Schweitzer Mountain Resort** (Ⓦschweitzer.com), northern Idaho's best ski resort, with plenty of spacious, comfortable lodging. In summer you can use one of the lifts for hiking and mountain biking.

SQUARE TOWER HOUSE AT MESA VERDE NATIONAL PARK

Contexts

History

The history of the Rockies is indeliably linked to the history of North America and the development of the United States. These few pages survey the peopling and political development of the disparate regions that now form the USA.

First peoples

The true pioneers of North America, nomadic hunter-gatherers from Siberia, are thought to have reached what's now **Alaska** around seventeen thousand years ago. Thanks to the last ice age, when sea levels were 300ft lower, a "**land-bridge**" – actually a vast plain, measuring six hundred miles north to south – connected Eurasia to America.

Alaska was at that time separated by glacier fields from what is now Canada, and thus effectively part of Asia rather than North America. Like an air lock, the region has "opened" in different directions at different times; migrants reaching it from the west, unaware that they were leaving Asia, would at first have found their way blocked to the east. Several generations might pass, and the connection back towards Asia be severed, before an eastward passage appeared. When thawing ice did clear a route into North America, it was not along the Pacific coast but via a corridor that led east of the Rockies and out onto the Great Plains.

This migration may well have been spurred by the pursuit of large mammal species, and especially **mammoth**, which had already been harried to extinction throughout almost all of Eurasia. A huge bonanza awaited the hunters when they finally encountered America's own indigenous "**megafauna**", such as mammoths, mastodons, giant ground sloths and enormous long-horned bison, all of which had evolved with no protection against human predation.

Filling the New World

Within a thousand years, ten million people were living throughout both North and South America. Although that sounds like a phenomenally rapid spread, it would only have required a band of just one hundred individuals to enter the continent, and advance a mere eight miles per year, with an annual population growth of 1.1 percent, to achieve that impact. The mass **extinction** of the American megafauna was so precisely simultaneous that humans must surely have been responsible, eliminating the giant beasts in each locality in one fell swoop, before pressing on in search of the next kill.

The elimination of large land mammals precluded future American civilizations from domesticating any of the animal species that were crucial to Old World economies. Without cattle, horses, sheep or goats, or significant equivalents, they lacked the resources to supply food and clothing to large settlements, provide draught power to haul ploughs or wheeled vehicles, or increase mobility and the potential for conquest. What's more, most of the human diseases that were later introduced from the rest of the world had originally evolved in association with domesticated animals; the first Americans developed neither immunity to such diseases, nor any indigenous diseases of their own that might have attacked the invaders.

c.60 million BC	15,000 BC	11,000 BC
Two mighty islands collide, creating North America as a single landmass, and throwing up the Rocky Mountains	First nomadic peoples from Asia reach Alaska	Almost all North America's large mammals become extinct, possibly due to over-hunting

At least three distinct waves of **migrants** arrived via Alaska, each of whom settled in, and adapted to, a more marginal environment than its predecessors. The second, five thousand years on from the first, were the "**Nadene**" or Athapascans – the ancestors of the Haida of the Northwest, and the Navajo and Apache of the Southwest – while the third, another two thousand years later, found their niche in the frozen Arctic and became the **Aleuts** and the **Inuits**.

Early settlements

The earliest known settlement site in the modern United States, dating back 12,000 years, has been uncovered at Meadowcroft in southwest Pennsylvania. Five centuries later, the Southwest was dominated by the so-called **Clovis** culture, while subsequent subgroups ranged from the Algonquin farmers of what's now New England to peoples such as the Chumash and Macah, who lived by catching fish, otters and even whales along the coasts of the Pacific Northwest.

Nowhere did a civilization emerge to rival the wealth and sophistication of the great cities of ancient Mexico. However, the influence of those far-off cultures did filter north; the cultivation of crops such as beans, squash and maize facilitated the development of large communities, while northern religious cults, some of which performed human sacrifice, owed much to Central American beliefs. The **Moundbuilders** of the **Ohio** and **Mississippi** valleys developed sites such as the Great Serpent Mound in modern Ohio and Poverty Point in Louisiana. The most prominent of these early societies, now known as the **Hopewell** culture, flourished during the first four centuries AD. Later on, **Cahokia**, just outside present-day St Louis, became the largest pre-Columbian city in North America, centred on a huge temple-topped mound, and peaking between 1050 and 1250 AD.

In the deserts of the **Southwest**, the **Hohokam** settlement of Snaketown, near what's now Phoenix, grappled with the same problems of water management that plague the region today. Nearby, the **Ancestral Puebloan** "Basketmakers" developed pottery around 200 AD, and began to gather into the walled villages later known as pueblos, possibly for protection against Athapascan invaders, such as the Apache, who were arriving from the north. Ancestral Puebloan "cities", such as Pueblo Bonito in New Mexico's Chaco Canyon – a centre for the turquoise trade with the mighty Aztec – and the "Cliff Palace" at Mesa Verde (see page 74) in Colorado, are the most impressive monuments to survive from ancient North America. Although the Ancestral Puebloans dispersed after a devastating drought in the twelfth century, many of the settlements created by their immediate descendants have remained in use ever since. Despite centuries of migration and war, the desert farmers of the **Hopi Mesas** in Arizona and the pueblos of **Taos** and **Ácoma** in New Mexico, have never been dispossessed of their homes.

Estimates of the total indigenous population before the arrival of the Europeans vary widely, but an acceptable median figure suggests around fifty million people in the Americas as a whole. Perhaps five million of those were in North America, speaking around four hundred different languages.

Christopher Columbus

The crucial moment of contact with the rest of the world came on October 12, 1492, when **Christopher Columbus**, sailing on behalf of the Spanish, reached the Bahamas.

c.2500 BC	900 AD	1050
Agriculture reaches North America from Mexico	Mississippian settlements – city-like conglomerations of earthen mounds – appear throughout the Southeast	Ancestral Puebloan culture reaches its peak at Chaco Canyon in the Southwest

A mere four years later the English navigator John Cabot officially "discovered" Newfoundland, and soon British fishermen were setting up makeshift encampments in what became **New England**, to spend the winter curing their catch.

Over the next few years various expeditions mapped the eastern seaboard. In 1524, the Italian **Giovanni da Verrazano** sailed past Maine, which he characterized as the "Land of Bad People" thanks to the inhospitable and contemptuous behaviour of its natives, and reached the mouth of the Hudson River. The great hope was to find a sea route in the Northeast that would lead to China – the fabled **Northwest Passage**. To the French **Jacques Cartier**, the St Lawrence Seaway seemed a promising avenue, and unsuccessful attempts were made to settle the northern areas of the Great Lakes from the 1530s onwards. Intrepid trappers and traders ventured ever further west.

Spanish explorations

To the south, the Spaniards started to nose their way up from the Caribbean in 1513, when **Ponce de León**'s expedition in search of the Fountain of Youth landed at what's now Palm Beach, and named **Florida**. Following the lucrative conquest of Mexico, the Spanish returned in 1528 under Panfilo de Narvaez, who was shipwrecked somewhere in the Gulf. A junior officer, **Cabeza de Vaca**, survived, and with three shipmates spent the next six years on an extraordinary odyssey across Texas into the Southwest. At times held as slaves, at times revered as seers, they finally got back to Mexico in 1534, bringing tales of golden cities deep in the desert, known as the **Seven Cities of Cibola**.

One of Cabeza de Vaca's companions was a black African slave called **Estevanico the Moor**. Rather than re-submit to slavery, he volunteered to map the route for a new venture; racing alone into the interior, with two colossal greyhounds at his side, he was killed in Zuni Pueblo in 1539. The following year, **Francisco Vázquez de Coronado**'s larger expedition proved to everyone's intense dissatisfaction that the Seven Cities of Cibola did not exist. They reached as far as the Grand Canyon, encountering the Hopi along the way. Hernán Cortés, the conqueror of the Aztec, had meanwhile traced the outline of Baja California, and in 1542 Juan Cabrillo sailed up the coast of California, failing to spot San Francisco Bay in the usual mists.

Although no treasures were found to match the vast riches plundered from the Aztec and Inca empires, a steady stream of less spectacular discoveries – whether new foodstuffs such as potatoes, or access to the cod fisheries of the northern Atlantic – boosted economies throughout Europe. The Spanish established the first permanent settlement in the present United States when they founded **St Augustine** on the coast of Florida in 1565, only for Sir Francis Drake to burn it to the ground in 1586. In 1598 the Spanish also succeeded in subjugating the Pueblo peoples, and founded **New Mexico** along the Rio Grande. More of a missionary than a military enterprise, the colony's survival was always precarious due to the vast tracts of empty desert that separated it from the rest of Mexico. Nonetheless, the construction of a new capital, **Santa Fe**, began in 1610.

The growth of the colonies

The sixteenth-century rivalry between the English and the Spanish extended right around the world. Freebooting English adventurers-cum-pirates contested Spanish hegemony along both coasts of North America. Sir Francis Drake staked a claim to California in

1492	1528	1565
Christopher Columbus makes landfall in the Bahamas	A Spanish expedition is ship-wrecked in Florida; Cabeza de Vaca and three survivors take eight years to walk to Mexico City	Pedro Menéndez de Avilés founds St Augustine in Florida

1579, five years before **Sir Walter Raleigh** claimed **Virginia** in the east, in the name of his Virgin Queen, Elizabeth I. The party of colonists he sent out in 1585 established the short-lived settlement of **Roanoke**, now remembered as the mysterious "Lost Colony".

The Native Americans were seldom hostile at first encounter. To some extent the European newcomers were obliged to make friends with the locals; most had crossed the Atlantic to find religious freedom or to make their fortunes, and lacked the skills to make a success of subsistence farming. Virginia's first enduring colony, **Jamestown**, was founded by Captain John Smith on May 24, 1607. He bemoaned "though there be Fish in the Sea, and Foules in the ayre, and Beasts in the woods, their bounds are so large, they are so wilde, and we so weake and ignorant, we cannot much trouble them"; six in every seven colonists died within a year of reaching the New World.

Gradually, however, the settlers learned to cultivate the strange crops of this unfamiliar terrain. As far as the English government was concerned, the colonies were commercial ventures, to produce crops that could not be grown at home, and the colonists were not supposed to have goals of their own. Following failures with sugar and rice, Virginia finally found its feet with its first **tobacco** harvest in 1615 (the man responsible, John Rolfe, is better known as the husband of Pocahontas). A successful tobacco plantation requires two things in abundance: land and labour. No self-respecting Englishman came to America to work for others; when the first **slave** ship called at Jamestown in 1619, the captain found an eager market for his cargo of twenty African slaves. By that time there were already a million slaves in South America.

New England

The 102 **Puritans** remembered as the "**Pilgrim Fathers**" were deposited on Cape Cod by the *Mayflower* in late 1620, and soon moved on to set up their own colony at Plymouth. Fifty died that winter, and the whole party might have perished but for their fortuitous encounter with the extraordinary **Squanto**. This Native American had twice been kidnapped and taken to Europe, only to make his way home; he had spent four years working as a merchant in the City of London, and had also lived in Spain. Having recently come home to find his entire tribe exterminated by smallpox, he threw in his lot with the English. With his guidance, they finally managed to reap their first harvest, celebrated with a mighty feast of **Thanksgiving**.

Of greater significance to New England was the founding in 1630 of a new colony, further up the coast at Naumkeag (later Salem), by the Massachusetts Bay Company. Its governor, **John Winthrop**, soon moved to establish a new capital on the Shawmut peninsula – the city of **Boston**, complete with its own university of Harvard. His vision of a Utopian "City on a Hill" did not extend to sharing Paradise with the Native Americans; he argued that they had not "subdued" the land, which was therefore a "vacuum" for the Puritans to use as they saw fit. While their faith helped individual colonists to endure the early hardships, the colony as a whole failed to maintain a strong religious identity (the Salem witch trials of 1692 did much to discredit the notion that the New World had any moral superiority to the Old), and breakaway groups left to create the rival settlements of Providence and Connecticut.

Between 1620 and 1642, sixty thousand migrants – 1.5 percent of the population – left England for America. Those in pursuit of economic opportunities often joined the longer-established colonies, thereby serving to dilute the religious zeal of the

1607	1610	1619	1620
English colonists establish Jamestown in Virginia	Santa Fe is founded as capital of New Mexico; horses begin to spread across the Southwest	Twenty African slaves arrive in Virginia on a Dutch ship	A hundred Puritan colonists reach New England aboard the Mayflower, and settle at Plymouth

Puritans. Groups hoping to find spiritual freedom were more inclined to start afresh; thus **Maryland** was created as a haven for Catholics in 1632, and fifty years later **Pennsylvania** was founded by the Quakers.

The English were not alone, however. After Sir Henry Hudson rediscovered Manhattan in 1609, it was "bought" by the **Dutch** in 1624 – though the Native Americans who took their money were passing nomads who had no claim to it either. The Dutch colony of New Amsterdam, founded in 1625, lasted less than forty years before being captured by the English and renamed **New York**; by that time, a strong Dutch presence dominated the lower reaches of the Hudson River.

Venturing west

From their foothold in the Great Lakes region, meanwhile, the **French** sent the explorers Joliet and Marquette to map the Mississippi in 1673. Upon establishing that the river did indeed flow into the Gulf of Mexico, they turned back, having cleared the way for the foundation of the huge and ill-defined colony of **Louisiana** in 1699. The city of **New Orleans**, at the mouth of the Mississippi, was created in 1718.

While the Spanish remained ensconced in Florida, things went less smoothly in the Southwest. The **Pueblo Revolt** of 1680 drove the Spanish out of New Mexico altogether, though they returned in force a dozen years later. Thereafter, a curious synthesis of traditional and Hispanic religion and culture evolved, and the Spanish presence was not seriously challenged.

Things were also changing in the unknown hinterland. The frontier was pushing steadily westwards, as colonists seized Native American land, with or without the excuse of an "uprising" or "rebellion" to provoke them into bloodshed. The major killer of indigenous peoples, however, was **smallpox**, which worked its way deep into the interior of the continent long before the Europeans. As populations were decimated, great migrations took place. The original inhabitants of the region had been sedentary farmers, who also hunted buffalo by driving them over rocky bluffs. With the arrival of **horses** on the Great Plains (probably captured from the Spanish, and known at first as "mystery dogs"), an entirely new, nomadic lifestyle emerged. Groups such as the Cheyenne and the Apache swept their rivals aside to dominate vast territories, and eagerly seized the potential offered by the later introduction of firearms. Increasing dependence on trade with Europeans created a dynamic but fundamentally unstable culture.

The American Revolution

The American colonies prospered during the **eighteenth century**. Boston, New York and Philadelphia in particular became home to a wealthy, well-educated and highly articulate middle class. Frustration mounted at the inequities of the colonies' relationship with Britain, however. The Americans could only sell their produce to the British, and all transatlantic commerce had to be undertaken in British ships.

Full-scale independence was not an explicit goal until late in the century, but the main factor that made it possible was the economic impact of the pan-European **Seven Years War**. Officially, war in Europe lasted from 1756 to 1763, but fighting in North America broke out a little earlier. Beginning in 1755 with the mass expulsion of French settlers from Acadia in eastern Canada (triggering their epic

1759	1773	1775
British General James Wolfe forces the surrender of Québec, ending the French and Indian War	In the Boston Tea Party, two hundred colonists respond to British duties by tipping tea into the sea	The Revolutionary War begins with the "shot heard 'round the world"; George Washington assumes command of the Continental Army

migration to Louisiana, where the **Cajuns** remain to this day), the British went on to conquer all of Canada. In forcing the **surrender of Québec** in 1759, General Wolfe brought the war to a close; the French ceded Louisiana to the Spanish rather than let it fall to the British, while Florida passed briefly into British control before reverting to the Spanish. All the European monarchs were left hamstrung by debts, and the British realized that colonialism in America was not as profitable as in those parts of the world where the native populations could be coerced into working for their overseas masters.

There was also another major player – the **Iroquois Confederacy**. Iroquois culture in the Great Lakes region, characterized by military expansionism and even human sacrifice, dates back around a thousand years. Forever in competition with the Algonquin and the Huron, the southern Iroquois had by the eighteenth century formed a League of Five Nations – the Seneca, Cayuga, Onondaga, Oneida and Mohawk, all in what's now upstate New York. Wooed by both the French and British, the Iroquois charted an independent course. Impressed by witnessing negotiations between the Iroquois and the squabbling representatives of Pennsylvania, Virginia and Maryland, Benjamin Franklin wrote in 1751 that "It would be a very strange thing if…ignorant savages should be capable of forming a scheme for such a union… that has subsisted ages and appears indissoluble; and yet that a like union should be impracticable for ten or a dozen English colonies".

An unsuccessful insurrection by the Ottawa in 1763, spearheaded by their chief **Pontiac**, led the cash-strapped British to conclude that, while America needed its own standing army, it was reasonable to expect the colonists to pay for it. In 1765, they introduced the **Stamp Act**, requiring duty on all legal transactions and printed matter in the colonies to be paid to the British Crown. Arguing for "no taxation without representation", delegates from nine colonies met in the Stamp Act Congress that October. By then, however, the British prime minister responsible had already been dismissed by King George III, and the Act was repealed in 1766.

However, in 1767, Chancellor Townshend made political capital at home by proclaiming "I dare tax America", as he introduced legislation including the broadly similar Revenue Act. That led Massachusetts merchants, inspired by **Samuel Adams**, to vote to boycott English goods; they were joined by all the other colonies except New Hampshire. Townshend's Acts were repealed in turn by a new prime minister, Lord North, on March 5, 1770. By chance, on that same day a stone-throwing mob surrounded the Customs House in Boston; five people were shot in what became known as the **Boston Massacre**. Even so, most of the colonies resumed trading with Britain, and the crisis was postponed for a few more years.

In May 1773, Lord North's **Tea Act** relieved the debt-ridden East India Company of the need to pay duties on exports to America, while still requiring the Americans to pay duty on tea. Massachusetts called the colonies to action, and its citizens took the lead on December 16 in the **Boston Tea Party**, when three tea ships were boarded and 342 chests thrown into the sea.

The infuriated British Parliament thereupon began to pass legislation collectively known as both the "Coercive" and the "Intolerable" Acts, which included closing the port of Boston and disbanding the government of Massachusetts. Thomas Jefferson argued that the acts amounted to "a deliberate and systematical plan of reducing us to

1776	1781	1787	1789
The Declaration of Independence is signed on July 4	Surrounded by land and sea, British commander Lord Cornwallis surrenders at Yorktown	The Constitution is signed in Philadelphia	George Washington is inaugurated as the first president of the United States

THE US CONSTITUTION

As signed in 1787 and ratified in 1788, the **Constitution** stipulated the following form of government:

All **legislative** powers were granted to the **Congress of the United States**. The lower of its two distinct houses, the **House of Representatives**, was to be elected every two years, with its members in proportion to the number of each state's "free Persons" plus "three fifths of all other persons" (meaning slaves). The upper house, the **Senate**, would hold two Senators from each state, chosen by state legislatures rather than by direct elections. Each Senator was to serve for six years, with a third of them to be elected every two years.

Executive power was vested in the **President**, who was also Commander in Chief of the Army and Navy. He would be chosen every four years, by as many "**Electors**" from each individual state as it had Senators and Representatives. Each state could decide how to appoint those Electors; almost all chose to have direct popular elections. Nonetheless, the distinction has remained ever since between the number of popular votes, across the whole country, received by a presidential candidate, and the number of state-by-state "electoral votes", which determines the actual result. Originally, whoever came second in the voting automatically became **vice president**.

The President could **veto** acts of Congress, but that veto could be overruled by a two-thirds vote in both houses. The House of Representatives could **impeach** the President for treason, bribery or "other high crimes and misdemeanors", in which instance the Senate could remove him from office with a two-thirds majority.

Judicial power was invested in a **Supreme Court**, and as many "inferior Courts" as Congress should decide.

The Constitution has so far been altered by 27 **Amendments**. Numbers **14** and **15** extended the vote to black males in 1868 and 1870; **17** made Senators subject to election by direct popular vote in 1913; **19** introduced women's suffrage in 1920; **22** restricted the President to two terms in 1951; **24** stopped states using poll taxes to disenfranchise black voters in 1964; and **26** reduced the minimum voting age to 18 in 1971.

slavery". To discuss a response, the first **Continental Congress** was held in Philadelphia on May 5, 1774, and attended by representatives of all the colonies except Georgia.

The Revolutionary War

War finally broke out on April 18, 1775, when General Gage, the governor of Massachusetts, dispatched four hundred British soldiers to destroy the arms depot at **Concord**, and prevent weapons from falling into rebel hands. Silversmith **Paul Revere** was dispatched on his legendary ride to warn the rebels, and the British were confronted en route at Lexington by 77 American "Minutemen". The resulting skirmish led to the "shot heard 'round the world".

Congress set about forming an army at Boston, and decided for the sake of unity to appoint a Southern commander, **George Washington**. One by one, as the war raged, the colonies set up their own governments and declared themselves to be states, and the politicians set about defining the society they wished to create. The writings of pamphleteer Thomas Paine – especially *Common Sense* – were, together with the

1803	1804	1812	1824
President Thomas Jefferson buys Louisiana west of the Mississippi for $15 million	The Lewis and Clark Expedition explores the Rockies through to 1806	South Pass in Wyoming is discovered – the Oregon Trail subsequently follows this route	The first mountain man rendezvous held in Wyoming

Confederacy of the Iroquois, a great influence on the **Declaration of Independence**. Drafted by Thomas Jefferson, this was adopted by the Continental Congress in Philadelphia on July 4, 1776. Anti-slavery clauses originally included by Jefferson – himself a slave-owner – were omitted to spare the feelings of the Southern states, though the section that denounced the King's dealings with "merciless Indian Savages" was left in.

At first, the Revolutionary War went well for the British. General Howe crossed the Atlantic with twenty thousand men, took New York and New Jersey, and ensconced himself in Philadelphia for the winter of 1777–78. Washington's army was encamped not far away at Valley Forge, freezing cold and all but starving to death. It soon became clear, however, that the longer the Americans could avoid losing an all-out battle, the more likely the British were to over-extend their lines as they advanced through the vast and unfamiliar continent. Thus, General Burgoyne's expedition, which set out from Canada to march on New England, was so harried by rebel guerrillas that he had to surrender at Saratoga in October 1777. Other European powers took delight in coming to the aid of the Americans. Benjamin Franklin led a wildly successful delegation to France to request support, and soon the nascent American fleet was being assisted in its bid to cut British naval communications by both the French and the Spanish. The end came when Cornwallis, who had replaced Howe, was instructed to dig in at Yorktown and wait for the Royal Navy to come to his aid, only for the French to seal off Chesapeake Bay and prevent reinforcement. Cornwallis surrendered to Washington on October 17, 1781.

The ensuing **Treaty of Paris** granted the Americans their independence on generous terms – the British abandoned their Native American allies, including the Iroquois, to the vengeance of the victors – and Washington entered New York as the British left in November 1783. The Spanish were confirmed in possession of Florida.

The victorious US Congress met for the first time in 1789, and the tradition of awarding political power to the nation's most successful generals was instigated by the election of George Washington as the first **president**. He was further honoured when his name was given to the new capital city of **Washington DC**, deliberately sited between the North and the South.

The nineteenth century

During its first century, the territories and population of the new **United States of America** expanded at a phenomenal rate. The white population of North America in 1800 stood at around five million, and there were another one million African slaves (of whom thirty thousand were in the North). Of that total, 86 percent lived within fifty miles of the Atlantic, but no US city could rival Mexico City, whose population approached 100,000 inhabitants (both New York and Philadelphia reached that figure within twenty years, however, and New York had passed a million fifty years later).

It had suited the British to discourage settlers from venturing west of the Appalachians, where they would be far beyond the reach of British power. However, adventurers such as **Daniel Boone** started to cross the mountains into Tennessee and Kentucky during the 1770s. Soon makeshift rafts, made from the planks that were zlater assembled to make log cabins, were careering west along the Ohio River (the only westward-flowing river on the continent).

1847	1848	1858	1859
Fort Benton established as a fur trading post in Montana	Mexico cedes California, most of Colorado and New Mexico to the USA for $18.25 million	Pike's Peak Gold Rush in Colorado – Denver founded	Gold is discovered in Montana

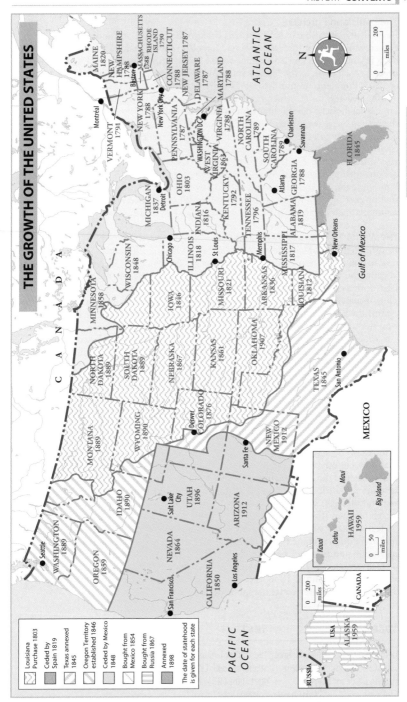

THE GROWTH OF THE UNITED STATES

The Louisiana Purchase

In 1801, the Spanish handed Louisiana back to the French, on condition that the French would keep it forever. However, Napoleon swiftly realized that attempting to hang on to his American possessions would spread his armies too thinly, and chose instead to sell them to the United States for $15 million, in the **Louisiana Purchase** of 1803. President Thomas Jefferson swiftly sent the explorers **Lewis and Clark** to map out the new territories, which extended far beyond the boundaries of present-day Louisiana; modern-day Montana, most of Wyoming and Idaho were all included. With the help of Sacagawea, their female Shoshone guide, they followed the Missouri and Columbia rivers all the way to the Pacific; in their wake, trappers and "mountain men" came to hunt in the wilderness of the Rockies. Founded in 1807 by fur trader Manuel Lisa at the confluence of the Bighorn and the Yellowstone Rivers, Fort Raymond became the first European-American trading post in Montana; Kullyspell House was built on Idaho's Lake Pend Oreille in 1809 by fur trader David Thompson. The first trading post in Wyoming, Fort Bonneville, wasn't established until 1832, though mountain men began annual "rendezvous" trades here in 1824.

The War of 1812 and Andrew Jackson

British attempts to blockade the Atlantic, primarily targeted against Napoleon, gave the new nation a chance to flex its military muscles. British raiders succeeded in capturing Washington DC, and burned the White House, but the **War of 1812** provided the USA with a cover for aggression against the Native American allies of the British. Thus **Tecumseh** of the Shawnee was defeated near Detroit, and **Andrew Jackson** moved against the Creek of the southern Mississippi. Jackson's campaign against the Seminole won the USA possession of Florida from the Spanish; he was rewarded first with the governorship of the new state, and later by his election to the presidency. While in office, in the 1830s, Jackson went even further, and set about clearing all states east of the Mississippi of their native populations. The barren region that later became Oklahoma was designated as "Indian Territory", home to the "Five Civilized Tribes". The Creek and the Seminole, and the Choctaw and Chickasaw of Mississippi were eventually joined by the Cherokee of the lower Appalachians there, after four appalling months on the forced march known as the "**Trail of Tears**".

Manifest Destiny and the Mexican War

It took only a small step for the citizens of the young republic to move from realizing that their country might spread across the whole continent to supposing that it had a quasi-religious duty – a "**Manifest Destiny**" – to do so. At its most basic, that doctrine amounted to little more than a belief that might must be right, but the idea that they were fulfilling the will of God inspired countless pioneers to set off across the plains in search of a new life.

Mexico was by now independent of Spain. The Spanish territories of the Southwest had never quite become fully-fledged colonies, and as American settlers arrived in ever-increasing numbers they began to dominate their Hispanic counterparts. The Anglos of **Texas** rebelled in 1833, under General Sam Houston. Shortly after the legendary setback at the **Alamo** in 1836, they defeated the Mexican army of Santa Anna and Texas became an independent republic in its own right.

1860	**1861**	**1862**
Lincoln's election as president prompts South Carolina and other Southern states to secede and form the Confederacy; gold rush begins in Idaho	The artillery bombardment of Fort Sumter in South Carolina marks the start of the Civil War; Territory of Colorado established	Homestead Act: settlers pour into the Rocky Mountain states in subsequent years

The ensuing **Mexican-American War (1846–1848)** was a bare-faced exercise in American aggression, in which most of the future Civil War generals received their first experience fighting on the same side. The conflict resulted in the acquisition not only of Texas, but also of Arizona, Utah, Colorado, Nevada, New Mexico and finally California, in 1848. A token US payment of $18.25 million to Mexico was designed to match the Louisiana Purchase. Controversy over whether slavery would be legal in the new states was rendered academic by the simultaneous discovery of gold in the Sierra Nevada of California. The resultant **Gold Rush** created California's first significant city, **San Francisco**, and brought a massive influx of free white settlers to a land that was in any case unsuitable for a plantation-based economy.

The Civil War

From its inception, the unity of the United States had been based on shaky foundations. Great care had gone into devising a **Constitution** that balanced the need for a strong federal government with the aspirations for autonomy of its component states. That was achieved by giving Congress two separate chambers – the **House of Representatives**, in which each state was represented in proportion to its population, and the **Senate**, in which each state, regardless of size, had two members. Thus, although in theory the Constitution remained silent on the issue of **slavery**, it allayed the fears of the less populated Southern states that Northern voters might destroy their economy by forcing them to abandon their "peculiar institution".

However, the system only worked so long as there were equal numbers of "Free" and slave-owning states. The only practicable way to keep the balance was to ensure that each time a new state was admitted to the Union, a matching state taking the opposite stance on slavery was also admitted. Thus the admission of every new state became subject to endless intrigue. The 1820 **Missouri Compromise**, under which Missouri joined as a slave-owning state and Maine as a Free one, was straightforward in comparison to the prevarication and chest-beating that surrounded the admission of Texas, while the Mexican War was widely seen in the North as a naked land grab for new slave states.

Matters came to a head in 1854, when the **Kansas-Nebraska Act** sparked guerrilla raids and mini-wars between rival settlers by allowing both prospective states self-determination on the issue. That same year, the **Republican Party** was founded to resist the further expansion of slavery. Escaped former slaves such as Frederick Douglass were by now spurring Northern audiences to moral outrage, and Harriet Beecher Stowe's *Uncle Tom's Cabin* found unprecedented readership.

In October 1859, **John Brown** – a white-bearded, wild-eyed veteran of Kansas's bloodiest infighting – led a dramatic raid on the US Armory at Harpers Ferry, West Virginia, intending to secure arms for a slave insurrection. Swiftly captured by forces under Robert E. Lee, he was hanged within a few weeks, proclaiming that "I am now quite certain that the crimes of this guilty land will never be purged away but with blood".

The Republican presidential candidate in 1860, the little-known **Abraham Lincoln** from Kentucky, won no Southern states, but with the Democrats split into Northern and Southern factions he was elected with 39 percent of the popular vote. Within weeks, on December 20, South Carolina became the first state to secede from the Union; the **Confederacy** was declared on February 4, 1861, when it was joined by Mississippi, Florida,

1863	1864	1865
Creation of Idaho Territory	Montana Territory is created; John Bozeman helps found the town named after him	General Robert E. Lee of the Confederacy surrenders to Union General Ulysses Grant on April 9; five days later, Lincoln is assassinated

Alabama, Georgia, Louisiana and Texas. Its first (and only) president was **Jefferson Davis**, also from Kentucky; his new vice president remarked at their joint inauguration that their government was "the first in the history of the world based upon the great physical and moral truth that the negro is not equal to the white man". Lincoln was inaugurated in turn in March 1861, proclaiming that "I have no purpose, directly or indirectly, to interfere with the institution of slavery in the States where it exists. I believe I have no lawful right to do so, and I have no inclination to do so". He was completely inflexible, however, on one paramount issue: the survival of the Union.

The coming of war

The **Civil War** began just a few weeks later. The first shots were fired on April 12, when a federal attempt to resupply Fort Sumter, off Charleston, South Carolina, was greeted by a Confederate bombardment that forced its surrender. Lincoln's immediate call to raise an army against the South was greeted by the further secession of Virginia, Arkansas, Tennessee and North Carolina. Within a year, both armies had amassed 600,000 men. Robert E. Lee was offered command of both and opted for the Confederacy, while George McLellan became the first leader of the Union forces. Although the rival capitals of Washington DC, and Richmond, Virginia, were a mere one hundred miles apart, over the next four years operations reached almost everywhere south of Washington and east of the Mississippi.

Tracing the ebb and flow of the military campaigns – from the early Confederate victories, via Grant's successful siege of Vicksburg in 1863 and Sherman's devastating March to the Sea in 1864, to Lee's eventual surrender at Appomattox in April 1865 – it's easy to forget that it was not so much generalship as sheer economic (and man-) power that won the war. The **Union** of 23 Northern states, holding more than 22 million people, wore down the **Confederacy** of eleven Southern states, with nine million. As for potential combatants, the North initially drew upon 3.5 million white males aged between 18 and 45 – and later recruited black males as well – whereas the South had more like one million. In the end, around 2.1 million men fought for the Union, and 900,000 for the Confederacy. Of the 620,000 soldiers who died, a disproportionate 258,000 came from the South – one quarter of its white men of military age. Meanwhile, not only did the North continue trading with the rest of the world while maintaining its industrial and agricultural output, it also stifled the Confederacy with a devastating **naval blockade**. The Southern war effort was primarily financed by printing $1.5 billion of paper currency, which was so eroded by inflation that it became worthless.

Even so, the Confederacy came much closer to victory than is usually appreciated. The repeated out-manoeuvring of federal forces by General **Robert E. Lee**, and his incursions into Union territory, meant that in each of three successive years, from 1862 to 1864, there was a genuine possibility that Northern morale would collapse, allowing opponents of the war to be elected to power and agree to peace. After all, the Revolutionary War had shown how such a war could be won: for the Union to triumph, it had to invade and occupy the South, and destroy its armies, but for the South to win it had only to survive until the North wearied of the struggle.

The dashing tactics of Confederate generals Lee and Jackson, forever counter-attacking and carrying the fight to the enemy, arguably contributed to the Southern defeat. The grim, relentless total-war campaigning of Grant and Sherman eventually ground the South

1866	1868	1869
Red Cloud's War between the Lakota, Northern Cheyenne, and Northern Arapaho and the United States rages until 1868	Territory of Wyoming is organized	Wyoming becomes first US territory to grant women the right to vote

down. Ironically, had the Confederacy sued for peace before Lee gave it fresh hope, a negotiated settlement might not have included the abolition of slavery. In the event, as the war went on, with Southern slaves flocking to the Union flag and black soldiers fighting on the front line, emancipation did indeed become inevitable. Lincoln took the political decision to match his moral conviction by issuing his **Emancipation Proclamation** in 1862, though the **Thirteenth Amendment** outlawing slavery only took effect in 1865.

Reconstruction
Lincoln himself was assassinated within a few days of the end of the war, a mark of the deep bitterness that would almost certainly have precluded successful **Reconstruction** even if he had lived. For a brief period, after black men were granted the vote in 1870, Southern states elected black political representatives, but without a sustained effort to enable former slaves to acquire land, racial relations in the South swiftly deteriorated. Thanks to white supremacist organizations such as the Ku Klux Klan, nominally clandestine but brazenly public, Southern blacks were soon effectively disenfranchised once more. Anyone working to transform the South came under attack either as a "carpetbagger" (a Northern opportunist heading South for personal profit) or a treacherous "scalawag" (a Southern collaborator).

Opening up the Rockies
The Rockies remained wild, untamed territory until well into the nineteenth century, inhabited primarily by mountain men and Native American tribes. In 1841, the Jesuits established St. Mary's Mission, the first permanent European-American settlement in Montana. Fort Benton on the Missouri River followed in 1847, given a boost by the arrival of steamboats in 1860. The discovery of gold in 1859 prompted the creation of Montana Territory by 1864 – it became a state in 1889. Wyoming was criss-crossed by pioneers heading west on the Oregon Trail in the 1830s, but permanent settlement remained rare. Fort Laramie (initially Fort William) was set up to service the trails in 1834, but after the Civil War conflict between growing numbers of settlers and Native American tribes flaired into the Indian Wars. Wyoming Territory was established in 1868, but remained thinly populated. Mormon pioneers set up communites in Idaho in the 1860s, and it became Idaho Territory in 1863 – the gold rush town of Lewiston (founded two years earlier) became the capital, though a rival gold camp, Boise, replaced it in 1864. Wyoming and Idaho both became states in 1890, though Wyoming Territory had granted women the right to vote back in 1869, the first US territory to do so.

Colorado's first permanent European settlement was San Luis, in 1851, but the initial development of the state, like Idaho and Montana, was largely due to gold mining. The Pike's Peak Gold Rush of 1858 boosted settlement of Denver, and led to a spate of mining towns being established across the mountains (the Colorado Silver Boom was initiated by the discovery of silver in Leadville in 1879). The Territory of Colorado was created in 1861, and Colorado became a state in 1876.

The Indian Wars
With the completion of the transcontinental railroad in 1867, Manifest Destiny became an undeniable reality. Among the first to head west were the troops of the federal army, with

1870	1872	1876	1877
Colorado becomes the 38th US state	Yellowstone becomes the world's first National Park	Sioux warriors defeat the Seventh Cavalry, and kill General George Custer, at Little Bighorn	The flight of the Nez Percé from the Pacific Northwest to Montana

Union and Confederate veterans marching under the same flag to battle the remaining Native Americans. Treaty after treaty was signed, only to be broken as soon as expedient (usually upon the discovery of gold or precious metals). When the whites overreached themselves, or when driven to desperation, the Native Americans fought back. The defeat of **General George Custer** at Little Bighorn in 1876 in Montana, by **Sitting Bull** and his Sioux and Cheyenne warriors (see page 92), provoked the full wrath of the government. Within a few years, leaders such as **Crazy Horse** of the Oglala Sioux and **Geronimo** of the Apache had been forced to surrender, and their people confined to reservations. The flight of the Nez Percé, led by Chief Joseph, took place largely in Idaho, Yellowstone National Park, and Montana – they surrendered in Montana in 1877. One final act of resistance was the visionary, messianic cult of the **Ghost Dance**, whose practitioners hoped that by ritual observance they could win back their lost way of life, in a land miraculously cleared of white intruders. Such aspirations were regarded as hostile, and military harassment of the movement culminated in the massacre at **Wounded Knee** in South Dakota in 1890.

A major tactic in the campaign against the Plains Indians was to starve them into submission, by eliminating the vast herds of **bison** that were their primary source of food. As General Philip Sheridan put it, "For the sake of a lasting peace…kill, skin and sell until the buffalo are exterminated. Then your prairies can be covered by the speckled cow and the festive cowboy". More significant than the activities of the much-mythologized cowboys, however, was the back-breaking toil of the miners up in the mountains, and the homesteading families out on the plains.

Industry and immigration

The late nineteenth century saw massive **immigration** to North America, with influxes from Europe to the East Coast paralleled by those from Asia to the West. As in colonial times, national groups tended to form enclaves in specific areas – from the Scandinavian farmers of Minnesota and the northern Plains to the Basque shepherds of Idaho and the Cornish miners of Colorado. In the Southwest, where individual hard work counted for less than shared communal effort, the **Mormons** of Utah had fled persecution to become the first white settlers to eke a living from the unforgiving desert.

Stretching "from sea to shining sea", the territorial boundaries of the USA had almost reached their current limits. In 1867, however, Secretary of State William Seward agreed to buy **Alaska** from the crisis-torn Russian government for $7.2 million. The purchase was at first derided as "Seward's Folly", but soon gold was discovered there as well.

The various presidents of the day, from the victorious General Grant onwards, now seem anonymous figures compared to the industrialists and financiers who manipulated the national economy. These "**robber barons**" included such men as John D. Rockefeller, who controlled seventy percent of the world's oil almost before anyone else had realized it was worth controlling; Andrew Carnegie, who made his fortune introducing the Bessemer process of steel manufacture; and J.P. Morgan, who went for the most basic commodity of all – money. Their success was predicated on the willingness of the government to cooperate in resisting the development of a strong labour movement. Strikes on the railroads in 1877, in the mines of Tennessee in 1891 and in the steel mills of Pittsburgh in 1892 were forcibly crushed.

In the Rockies, Montana was dominated by "Copper Kings" such Irish-born Marcus Daly (who founded Anaconda, Montana), and Butte's W.A. Clark. Mining was also

1879	1889	1890	1892
Colorado Silver Boom begins in Leadville	Montana becomes the 41st state	Idaho becomes 43rd US state; Wyoming becomes the 44th state	Johnson County War in Wyoming; small ranches and settlers fight large cattle companies and ranch-es

the primary economic driver in Idaho, though here unions fought back against low pay and poor conditions throughout the 1890s. Mining strikes were also common in Colorado, many resulting in bloody confrontations (the Ludlow Massacre of 1914 was the most notorious incident). In Wyoming it was the extension of the Union Pacific Railroad that led to the creation of settlements across the region, with cattle ranching the dominant industry. Tourism also became an early money spinner here after Yellowstone became the world's first National Park in 1872.

The nineteenth century had also seen the development of a distinctive American voice in **literature**, which rendered increasingly superfluous the efforts of passing English visitors to "explain" the United States. From the 1830s onwards, writers explored new ways to describe their new world, with results as varied as the introspective essays of Henry Thoreau, the morbid visions of Edgar Allan Poe, the all-embracing novels of Herman Melville and the irrepressible poetry of Walt Whitman, whose endlessly revised *Leaves of Grass* was an exultant hymn to the young republic. Virtually every leading participant in the Civil War wrote at least one highly readable volume of memoirs, while public figures as disparate as Buffalo Bill Cody and the showman P. T. Barnum produced lively autobiographies. The boundless national self-confidence found its greatest expression in the vigorous vernacular style of **Mark Twain**, whose depictions of frontier life, fictionalized for example in *Huckleberry Finn*, gave the rest of the world an abiding impression of the American character.

Many Americans saw the official "closure" of the Western frontier, announced by the Census Bureau in 1890, as tantamount to depriving the country of the Manifest Destiny that was its *raison d'être*, and sought new frontiers further afield. Such **imperialist ventures** reached a crescendo in 1898, with the annexation of the Kingdom of **Hawaii** – which even then-President Cleveland condemned as "wholly without justification…not merely wrong but a disgrace" – and the double seizure of Cuba and the Philippines in the **Spanish-American War**, which catapulted **Theodore Roosevelt** to the presidency. Though he took the African proverb "speak softly and carry a big stick" as his motto – and was hardly, if truth be told, noted for being soft-spoken – Roosevelt in office did much to heal the divisions within the nation. While new legislation reined in the worst excesses of the robber barons, and of rampant capitalism in general, it alleviated popular discontent without substantially threatening the business community or empowering the labour movement. A decade into the twentieth century, the United States had advanced to the point that it knew, even if the rest of the world wasn't yet altogether sure, that it was the strongest, wealthiest country on earth.

The twentieth century

The first years of the twentieth century witnessed the emergence of many features that came to characterize modern America. In 1903 alone, Wilbur and Orville Wright achieved the first successful powered **flight** and Henry Ford established his Ford Motor Company. Ford's enthusiastic adoption of the latest technology in mass production – the assembly line – gave Detroit a head start in the new **automobile** industry, which swiftly became the most important business in America. Both **jazz** and **blues** music first reached a national audience during that same period, while Hollywood acquired

1893	1895	1914
Women win the right to vote in Colorado	Buffalo Bill helps found the town of Cody, Wyoming	Ludlow Massacre: 21 people (striking coal miners and family members) killed during the Colorado Coalfield War

its first **movie** studio in 1911, and its first major hit in 1915 with D.W. Griffith's unabashed glorification of the Ku Klux Klan in *Birth of a Nation*.

This was also a time of growing **radicalism**. Both the NAACP (National Association for the Advancement of Colored People) and the socialist International Workers of the World ("the Wobblies") were founded in the early 1900s, while the campaign for women's suffrage also came to the forefront. Writers such as Jack London and Upton Sinclair, who exposed conditions in Chicago's stockyards in *The Jungle*, proselytized to the masses.

Though President Wilson kept the USA out of the **First World War** for several years, American intervention was, when it came, decisive. With the Russian Revolution illustrating the dangers of anarchy, the USA also took charge of supervising the peace. However, even as Wilson presided over the negotiations that produced the Treaty of Versailles in 1919, isolationist sentiment at home prevented the USA from joining his pet scheme to preserve future world peace, the League of Nations.

Back home, the 18th Amendment forbade the sale and distribution of alcohol, while the 19th finally gave all American women the vote. Quite how **Prohibition** ever became the law of the land remains a mystery; certainly, in the buzzing metropolises of the Roaring Twenties, it enjoyed little conspicuous support. There was no noticeable elevation in the moral tone of the country, and Chicago in particular became renowned for the street wars between bootlegging gangsters such as Al Capone and his rivals.

The two Republican presidents who followed Wilson did little more than sit back and watch the Roaring Twenties unfold. Until his premature death, **Warren Harding** enjoyed considerable public affection, but he's now remembered as probably the worst US president of all, thanks to the cronyism and corruption of his associates. It's hard to say quite whether **Calvin Coolidge** did anything at all; his laissez-faire attitude extended to working a typical four-hour day, and announcing shortly after his inauguration that "four-fifths of our troubles would disappear if we would sit down and keep still".

The Depression and the New Deal

By the middle of the 1920s, the USA was an industrial powerhouse, responsible for more than half the world's output of manufactured goods. Having led the way into a new era of prosperity, however, it suddenly dragged the rest of the world down into economic collapse. The consequences of the **Great Depression** were out of all proportion to any one specific cause. Possible factors include American over-investment in the floundering economy of postwar Europe, combined with high tariffs on imports that effectively precluded European recovery. Conservative commentators at the time chose to interpret the calamitous **Wall Street Crash** of October 1929 as a symptom of impending depression rather than a contributory cause, but the quasi-superstitious faith in the stock market that preceded it showed all the characteristics of classic speculative booms. On "Black Tuesday" alone, enough stocks were sold to produce a total loss of ten thousand million dollars – more than twice the total amount of money in circulation in the USA. Within the next three years, industrial production was cut by half, the national income dropped by 38 percent, and, above all, unemployment rose from 1.5 million to 13 million.

National self-confidence, however shaky its foundations, has always played a crucial role in US history, and President Hoover was not the man to restore it. Matters only began to improve in 1932, when the patrician **Franklin Delano Roosevelt** accepted the Democratic

1919	1929	1932
The 18th Amendment heralds the introduction of Prohibition; the 19th Amendment gives women the vote	The Wall Street Crash plunges the USA into economic turmoil	Franklin D. Roosevelt pledges "a new deal for the American people"

nomination for president with the words "I pledge myself to a new deal for America", and went on to win a landslide victory. At the time of his inauguration, early in 1933, the banking system had all but closed down; it took Roosevelt the now-proverbial "Hundred Days" of vigorous legislation to turn around the mood of the country.

Taking advantage of the new medium of radio, Roosevelt used "Fireside Chats" to cajole America out of crisis; among his earliest observations was that it was a good time for a beer, and that the experiment of Prohibition was therefore over. The **New Deal** took many forms, but was marked throughout by a massive growth in the power of the federal government. Among its accomplishments were the National Recovery Administration, which created two million jobs; the Social Security Act, of which Roosevelt declared "no damn politician can ever scrap my social security program"; the Public Works Administration, which built dams and highways the length and breadth of the country; the Tennessee Valley Authority, which by generating electricity under public ownership for the common good was probably the closest the USA has ever come to institutionalized socialism; and measures to legitimize the role of the unions and revitalize the "Dust Bowl" farmers out on the plains.

After the work-creation programmes of the New Deal had put America back on its feet, the deadly pressure to achieve victory in **World War II** spurred industrial production and know-how to new heights. Once again the USA stayed out of the war at first, until it was finally forced in when the Japanese launched a pre-emptive strike on Hawaii's Pearl Harbor in 1941. In both the Pacific and in Europe, American manpower and economic muscle eventually carried all before it. By dying early in 1945, having laid the foundations for the postwar carve-up with Stalin and Churchill at Yalta, Roosevelt was spared the fateful decision, made by his successor Harry Truman, to use the newly developed atomic bomb on Hiroshima and Nagasaki.

The coming of the Cold War

With the war won, Americans were in no mood to revert back to the isolationism of the 1930s. Amid much hopeful rhetoric, Truman enthusiastically participated in the creation of the **United Nations**, and set up the **Marshall Plan** to speed the recovery of Europe. However, as Winston Churchill announced in Missouri in 1946, an "**Iron Curtain**" had descended upon Europe, and Joseph Stalin was transformed from ally to enemy almost overnight.

The ensuing **Cold War** lasted for more than four decades, at times fought in ferocious combat (albeit often by proxy) in scattered corners of the globe, and during the intervals diverting colossal resources towards the stockpiling of ever more destructive arsenals. Some of its ugliest moments came in its earliest years; Truman was still in office in 1950 when war broke out in **Korea**. A dispute over the arbitrary division of the Korean peninsula into two separate nations, North and South, soon turned into a standoff between the USA and China (with Russia lurking in the shadows). Two vyears of bloody stalemate ended with little to show for it, except that Truman had by now been replaced by the genial **Dwight D. Eisenhower**, the latest war hero to become president.

The Eisenhower years are often seen as characterized by bland complacency. Once Senator **Joseph McCarthy**, the "witch-hunting" anti-Communist scourge of the State Department and Hollywood, had finally discredited himself by attacking the army as well, middle-class America seemed to lapse into a wilful suburban stupor. Great social changes

1941	1945	1954
A surprise Japanese attack on Pearl Harbor precipitates US entry into World War II	President Truman's decision to drop atomic bombs on Hiroshima and Nagasaki marks the end of World War II	The Supreme Court declares racial segregation in schools to be unconstitutional

were taking shape, however. World War II had introduced vast numbers of women and members of ethnic minorities to the rewards of factory work, and shown many Americans from less prosperous regions the lifestyle attainable elsewhere in their own country. The development of a **national highway system**, and a huge increase in automobile ownership, encouraged people to pursue the American Dream wherever they chose. Combined with increasing mechanization on the cotton plantations of the South, this led to another **mass exodus** of blacks from the rural South to the cities of the North, and to a lesser extent the West. **California** entered a period of rapid growth, with the aeronautical industries of Los Angeles in particular attracting thousands of prospective workers.

Also during the 1950s, **television** reached almost every home in the country. Together with the LP record, it created an entertainment industry that addressed the needs of consumers who had previously been barely identified. **Youth culture** burst into prominence from 1954 onwards, with Elvis Presley's recording of *That's All Right Mama* appearing within a few months of Marlon Brando's moody starring role in *On the Waterfront* and James Dean's in *Rebel Without a Cause*.

The civil rights years

Racial segregation of public facilities, which had remained the norm in the South ever since Reconstruction, was finally declared illegal in 1954 by the Supreme Court ruling on *Brown v. Topeka Board of Education*. Just as a century before, however, the Southern states saw the issue more in terms of states' rights than of human rights, and attempting to implement the law, or even to challenge the failure to implement it, required immense courage. The action of Rosa Parks in refusing to give up her seat on a bus in Montgomery, Alabama, in 1955, triggered a successful mass boycott, and pushed the 27-year-old **Rev Dr Martin Luther King, Jr.** to the forefront of the civil rights campaign. Further confrontation took place at the Central High School in Little Rock, Arkansas, in 1957, when the reluctant Eisenhower had to call in federal troops to counter the state's unwillingness to integrate its education system.

The election of **John F. Kennedy** to the presidency in 1960, by the narrowest of margins, marked a sea-change in American politics, even if in retrospect his policies do not seem exactly radical. At 43 the youngest man ever to be elected president, and the first Catholic, he was prepared literally to reach for the moon, urging the USA to victory in the Space Race in which it had thus far lagged humiliatingly behind the Soviet Union. The two decades that lay ahead, however, were to be characterized by disillusion, defeat and despair. If the Eisenhower years had been dull, the 1960s in particular were far too interesting for almost everybody's liking.

Kennedy's sheer glamour made him a popular president during his lifetime, while his assassination suffused his administration with the romantic glow of "Camelot". His one undisputed triumph, however, came with the **Cuban missile crisis** of 1962, when the US military fortunately spotted Russian bases in Cuba before any actual missiles were ready for use, and Kennedy faced down premier Khrushchev to insist they be withdrawn. On the other hand, he'd had rather less success the previous year in launching the abortive **Bay of Pigs** invasion of Cuba, and he also managed to embroil America deeper in the ongoing war against Communism in Vietnam by sending more "advisers" to Saigon.

Although a much-publicized call to the wife of Rev Martin Luther King, Jr. during one of King's many sojourns in Southern jails was a factor in his election success,

1955	**1961**	**1963**
Black seamstress Rosa Parks refuses to change her seat on a bus in Montgomery, Alabama	Author Ernest Hemingway commits suicide at his house in Ketchum, Idaho	Rev Martin Luther King, Jr. delivers "I Have a Dream" speech; President Kennedy is assassinated

Kennedy was rarely identified himself with the **civil rights** movement. The campaign nonetheless made headway, lent momentum by television coverage of such horrific confrontations as the onslaught by Birmingham police on peaceful demonstrators in 1963. The movement's defining moment came when Rev King delivered his electrifying "I Have a Dream" speech later that summer. King was subsequently awarded the Nobel Peace Prize for his unwavering espousal of Gandhian principles of nonviolence. Perhaps an equally powerful factor in middle America's recognition that the time had come to address racial inequalities, however, was the not-so-implicit threat in the rhetoric of **Malcolm X**, who argued that black people had the right to defend themselves against aggression.

After Kennedy's assassination in November 1963, his successor, **Lyndon B. Johnson**, pushed through legislation that enacted most of the civil rights campaigners' key demands. Even then, violent white resistance in the South continued, and only the long, painstaking and dangerous work of registering Southern black voters en masse eventually forced Southern politicians to mend their ways.

Johnson won election by a landslide in 1964, but his vision of a "**Great Society**" soon foundered. He was brought low by the war in **Vietnam**, where US involvement escalated beyond all reason or apparent control. Broad-based popular opposition to the conflict grew in proportion to the American death toll, and the threat of the draft heightened youthful rebellion. San Francisco in particular responded to psychedelic prophet Timothy Leary's call to "turn on, tune in, drop out"; 1967's "Summer of Love" saw the lone beatniks of the 1950s transmogrify into an entire generation of hippies.

Dr King's long-standing message that social justice could only be achieved through economic equality was given a new urgency by riots in the ghettoes of Los Angeles in 1965 and Detroit in 1967, and the emergence of the Black Panthers, an armed defence force in the tradition of the now-dead Malcolm X. King also began to denounce the Vietnam War; meanwhile, after refusing the draft with the words "No Vietcong ever called me nigger", **Muhammad Ali** was stripped of his title as world heavyweight boxing champion.

In 1968, the social fabric of the USA reached the brink of collapse. Shortly after Johnson was forced by his plummeting popularity to withdraw from the year-end elections, Martin Luther King was gunned down in a Memphis motel. Next, JFK's brother **Robert Kennedy**, now redefined as spokesman for the dispossessed, was fatally shot just as he emerged as Democratic front-runner. It didn't take a conspiracy theorist to see that the spate of deaths reflected a malaise in the soul of America.

Richard Nixon to Jimmy Carter

Somehow – perhaps because the brutally suppressed riots at the Chicago Democratic Convention raised the spectre of anarchy – the misery of 1968 resulted in the election of Republican **Richard Nixon** as president. Nixon's conservative credentials enabled him to bring the USA to a rapport with China, but the war in Vietnam dragged on to claim a total of 57,000 American lives. Attempts to win it included the secret and illegal bombing of Cambodia, which raised opposition at home to a new peak, but ultimately it was simpler to abandon the original goals in the name of "peace with honor". Perceptions differ as to whether the end came in 1972 – when Henry Kissinger and Le Duc Tho were awarded the Nobel Peace Prize for negotiating a treaty, and Tho at least had the grace to decline – or in 1975, when the Americans finally withdrew from Saigon.

1968	1974	1980
With the nation polarized by war in Vietnam, Rev Martin Luther King, Jr, and Robert Kennedy are assassinated	Embroiled in the Watergate scandal, Richard Nixon resigns	With Iranian students holding the US embassy in Tehran, Ronald Reagan defeats President Jimmy Carter

During Nixon's first term, many of the disparate individuals politicized during the 1960s coalesced into **activist groupings**. Feminists united to campaign for abortion rights and an Equal Rights Amendment; gay men in New York's *Stonewall* bar fought back after one police raid too many; Native Americans formed the American Indian Movement; and even prisoners attempted to organize themselves, resulting in such bloody debacles as the storming of Attica prison in 1971. Nixon directed various federal agencies to monitor the new radicalism, but his real bugbear was the antiwar protesters. Increasingly ludicrous covert operations against real and potential opponents culminated in a botched attempt to burgle Democratic National Headquarters in the **Watergate** complex in 1972. It took two years of investigation for Nixon's role in the subsequent cover-up to be proved, but in 1974 he **resigned**, one step ahead of impeachment by the Senate, to be succeeded by **Gerald Ford**, his own appointee as vice president.

With the Republicans momentarily discredited, former Georgia governor **Jimmy Carter** was elected president as a clean-handed outsider in the bicentennial year of 1976. However, Carter's enthusiastic attempts to put his Baptist principles into practice on such issues as global human rights were soon perceived as naive, if not un-American. Misfortune followed misfortune. He had to break the news that the nation was facing an **energy crisis**, while after the Shah of Iran was overthrown, staff at the US embassy in Tehran were taken hostage by Islamic revolutionaries. Carter's failed attempts to arrange their release all but destroyed his hopes of winning re-election in 1980. Instead he was replaced by a very different figure, the former movie actor **Ronald Reagan**.

From Reagan to Clinton

Reagan was a new kind of president. Unlike his workaholic predecessor, he made a virtue of his hands-off approach to the job, joking that "they say hard work never killed anybody, but I figured why take the risk?" That laissez-faire attitude was especially apparent in his domestic economic policies, under which the rich were left to get as rich as they could. The common perception that Reagan was barely aware of what went on around him allowed his popularity to remain undented by scandals that included the labyrinthine **Iran-Contra** affair.

Reagan's most enduring achievement came during his second term, when his impeccable credentials as a Cold Warrior enabled him to negotiate **arms-control** agreements with **Mikhail Gorbachev**, the new leader of what he had previously called the "Evil Empire".

In 1988, **George H.W. Bush** became the first vice president in 150 years to be immediately elected to the presidency. Despite his unusually broad experience in foreign policy, Bush did little more than sit back and watch in amazement as the domino theory suddenly went into reverse. One by one, the Communist regimes of eastern Europe collapsed, until finally even the Soviet Union crumbled away. Bush was also president when **Operation Desert Storm** drove the Iraqis out of Kuwait in 1991, an undertaking that lasted one hundred hours and in which virtually no American lives were lost.

However, the much-anticipated "**peace dividend**" – the dramatic injection of cash into the economy that voters expected to follow the end of the arms race – never

1991	1993	1996	1999
Following the Iraqi invasion of Kuwait, the Gulf War begins	Seven people are killed, and a thousand injured, in a bombing of the World Trade Center	Ted Kaczynski, aka the Unabomber, is arrested at his cabin in Lincoln, Montana	The Columbine High School massacre in Colorado; 12 students and one teacher murdered

materialized. With the 1992 campaign focusing on domestic affairs rather than what was happening overseas, twelve years of Republican government were ended by the election of Arkansas Governor **Bill Clinton**.

Although Clinton's initial failure to deliver on specific promises – most obviously, the attempt, spearheaded by his wife Hillary, to reform the healthcare system – enabled the Republicans to capture control of Congress in 1994, the "Comeback Kid" was nonetheless elected to a second term. Holding on to office proved more of a challenge in the face of humiliating sexual indiscretions, but the Senate ultimately failed to convict him in **impeachment** proceedings.

The twenty-first century

When Clinton left the presidency, the economy was **booming**. His former vice president, however, **Al Gore**, contrived to throw away the 2000 presidential election, a tussle for the centre ground that ended in a **tie** with his Republican opponent, **George W. Bush**. With the final conclusion depending on a mandatory re-count in Florida, the impasse was decided in Bush's favour by the conservative **Supreme Court**. At the time, the charge that he had "stolen" the election was expected to overshadow his presidency, while the authority of the Supreme Court was also threatened by the perception of its ruling as partisan.

Within a year, however, the atrocity of **September 11, 2001** drove such concerns into the background, inflicting a devastating blow to both the nation's economy and its pride. More than three thousand people were killed in the worst terrorist attack in US history, when hijacked planes were flown into the World Trade Center in New York City and the Pentagon. The attacks were quickly linked to the al-Qaeda network of Osama bin Laden, and within weeks President Bush declared an open-ended "War on Terror".

A US-led invasion of **Afghanistan** in 2001 was followed by a similar incursion into **Iraq** in 2003, ostensibly on the grounds that Iraqi dictator Saddam Hussein was developing "weapons of mass destruction". Although Saddam was deposed, and executed, no such weapons proved to exist, and Iraq degenerated into civil war.

Despite a wave of financial scandals, spearheaded by the collapse of the mighty energy firm Enron, Bush was elected to a second term in 2004. The country remained polarized, however, and the Bush administration was lambasted for its appallingly inadequate response when **Hurricane Katrina** devastated New Orleans and the Gulf Coast in 2005.

President Obama

That the Democrats regained control of both Senate and House in 2006 was due largely to the deteriorating situation in Iraq. Similarly, the meteoric rise of Illinois Senator **Barack Obama** owed much to his being almost unique among national politicians in his consistent opposition to the Iraq war. However, while Obama's message of change and optimism, coupled with his oratorical gifts and embrace of new technologies, resonated with young and minority voters, his ultimate triumph over John McCain in that year's presidential election was triggered by a new **recession**. After bankers Lehman Brothers filed for bankruptcy in 2008 – the largest bankruptcy in US

2000	2001	2008
The Supreme Court rules George W. Bush to have been elected president; Wyoming's Dick Cheney becomes VP	On September 11, more than three thousand people die in the worst terrorist attack in US history	Barack Obama wins election as the first black president

history – no element of the economy appeared safe from the consequences of reckless "subprime" mortgage lending.

The exhilaration over Obama's becoming the first black US president soon faded. Despite managing to introduce a universal system of healthcare, which became known as **Obamacare**, he was seen as failing to deliver on many campaign pledges. In particular, he never closed the detention camp at Guantanamo Bay, while his Middle East initiatives had little impact. Although US forces killed Osama bin Laden in 2011, Obama was wrong-footed when the so-called "Arab Spring" toppled governments in Tunisia, Egypt and Libya that same year, and the death of the US ambassador to Libya when terrorists attacked **Benghazi** in 2012 damaged both his credibility and that of his Secretary of State, Hillary Clinton. Above all, the war in Afghanistan dragged on to become the longest conflict in US history.

President Obama's comfortable re-election in 2012 owed much to the role of the Tea Party in drawing the Republican Party ever further to the right. The Republican majority in the House of Representatives, however, continued to impede his agenda, precipitating a two-week **government shutdown** in 2013, and refusing to confirm any nominee to the Supreme Court. During his second term, Obama attempted to govern without Republican support, launching such initiatives as a rapprochement with Cuba, and a deal with Iran over its nuclear programme. Illusions that his rise to the presidency had marked the start of a new "post-racial" era of reconciliation, however, were punctured when the **Black Lives Matter** movement emerged in response to institutionalized indifference to the deaths of young black men.

The Trump presidency and beyond

For the presidential election of 2016, the Republican Party confounded expectations by selecting real-estate tycoon **Donald Trump** as its candidate. Derided by many as a boorish buffoon, Trump had burnished his image as a business mogul by hosting the TV show *The Apprentice*, and came to political prominence advocating the "birther" smear that Obama had supposedly been born outside the US. Polls and pundits alike confidently predicted that Trump's Democratic opponent, the vastly more experienced **Hillary Clinton**, would become the first woman president of the United States. She however failed to counter allegations of wrongdoing over her use of a private email server while Secretary of State, and in a sensational upset it was Trump who triumphed.

Hopes that **President Trump** might put the demagoguery of the campaign trail behind him on assuming power were dashed at his inauguration, when he claimed to see "record crowds" along the visibly depopulated Mall. His term in office saw the US shift towards an isolationist stance, abandoning its commitment to climate-change programmes and withdrawing from the anti-nuclear proliferation agreement with Iran. Pandering to the hard right, and most at ease addressing rallies of his long-term supporters, Trump survived a first impeachment attempt in 2019 and continued to provoke despair in his opponents as no amount of scandal or blatant "alternative facts" seemed able to bring him down.

However, in early 2020, the worldwide coronavirus (Covid-19) pandemic began to spread across the US. Initially dismissed as a "flu" by Trump that would "miraculously…go away", at the time of writing, the US has suffered the highest Covid-19 death toll in the world, with over 850,000 dead and the figure still climbing.

2012	2016	2017
Aurora, Colorado shooting: 12 people are killed, and 70 more injured	To worldwide astonishment, Donald Trump is elected 45th president of the United States	Liz Cheney elected as Wyoming's single US House member

Unlike in many countries, stay-at-home orders and social distancing and mask-wearing requirements were made on a state or local level, and orders fluctuated as the country went through and recovered from three successive waves of the virus. By spring 2021, infection numbers were still fairly high and there were fears of a fourth wave, but concurrently, the US was making huge strides in its vaccination programme, with 200 million people already vaccinated.

The Covid-19 pandemic was ultimately a major catalyst for Trump's downfall. His lack of empathy for its victims, perception he wasn't taking the outbreak seriously enough and frequent flouting of safety protocols (as well as suggesting people might inject bleach to "clean" themselves at a press conference, to the horror of his scientific advisors) – combined with the inevitable economic downturn – conspired to ultimately lose him many swing voters, whose lives had been so hugely impacted by the pandemic.

But this was not the only major crisis in 2020. The Black Lives Matter movement exploded around the country and the world after African-American George Floyd was killed by a police officer kneeling on his neck to restrain him for over eight minutes. It was one of several killings of Black Americans by the police, but the collective anger and taking to the streets of BLM supporters in protest, despite pandemic restrictions, had a profound impact that raised awareness of ongoing racial injustice.

After a slow start, the Democrat challenger for the Presidency, Joe Biden, energised the African-American vote with his own support and his selection of Kamala Harris as his running mate, casting his campaign as a "battle for the soul of America". By the time Americans went to the polls in November 2020, the expected result was too close to call. However, Biden prevailed, winning more than 81 million votes, the most ever cast for a candidate in a presidential election, and securing 306 of the electoral college votes to Trump's 232.

President Biden and Vice-President Harris – the first female, African-American and Asian-American to hold the office – had made history. But their win wasn't the last twist in the tale. As Congress gathered to count electoral college votes to formalize Biden's win, ahead of his inauguration, the US Capitol building was stormed and occupied by a pro-Trump mob, seeking to overturn the result. Encouraged to gather by Trump himself, who had failed to concede the election and was alleging vast vote fraud that he claimed had stolen millions of votes, the rioters forced terrified politicians to flee and vandalized and looted the building, while the world watched in real time in horror. For Americans, this attack on the heart of their democratic traditions was traumatizing. Trump failed to call in the National Guard or explicitly denounce his supporters' actions, and in the aftermath, he was impeached for a second time for incitement to insurrection, although he was eventually acquitted.

President Biden was inaugurated on January 20 2021, in a ceremony that looked very different to normal, shorn of crowds due to Covid-19 precautions and with the assembled attendees in face masks. His first 100 days have been witness to a huge economic relief package to aid pandemic recovery, as well as the successful vaccine roll-out and re-joining of the Paris Climate Accord. Significantly, the conviction of George Floyd's killer, former officer Derek Chauvin, on April 20, has marked a step forward in police accountability. The US remains a country deeply riven by its racial inequalities

2020	2021
The global Covid-19 crisis hits the US hard; Trump is ousted as president by Joe Biden. Montana legalizes marijuana	Pro-Trump militants storm the US Capitol building; Kamala Harris makes history as first female Vice-President

and entrenched political and cultural perspectives, but with a more centrist President, time will tell if these divides can begin to be bridged.

The Rockies in the 21st Century

Colorado became one of the first states to legalize marijuana in 2012 (Montana followed in 2020), though it's only liberal to a point; parts are still very conservative, and it was here that horrific mass shootings took place in Columbine (1999) and Aurora (2012). In Montana, a series of oil discoveries have led to an economic boom, though the state remains primarily rural and agricultural. Like Wyoming and Idaho, it has a become a bastion of the Republican party in presidential elections, though Steve Bullock served as the Democratic Governor of Montana from 2013 to 2021. Wyoming is so thinly populated it gets just one one member of the House of Representatives (Liz Cheney since 2017), though it gets the mandatory two senators; Montana also gets just one, while Idaho gets two representatives (all reliably conservative Republican). In contrast, Colorado is now considered a fairly safe Democratic state.

Books

An overview of American literature centered on themes relevant to or set in The Rockies. The following list is an idiosyncratic selection of books exploring themes of the Old West or written by authors from the area.

HISTORY AND SOCIETY

Bill Bryson *Made in America*. A compulsively readable history of the American language, packed with bizarre snippets.

Brian Fagan *Ancient North America*. Archeological history of America's native peoples, from the first hunters to cross the Bering Strait up to initial contact with Europeans.

Clyde A. Milner II, Carol A. O'Connor and Martha A. Sandweiss *The Oxford History of the American West*. Fascinating collection of essays on Western history, covering topics ranging from myths and movies to art and religion.

Dee Brown *Bury My Heart at Wounded Knee*. Still the best narrative of the impact of white settlement and expansion on Native Americans across the continent.

James Mooney *The Ghost Dance Religion and The Sioux Outbreak of 1890*. An extraordinary Bureau of Ethnology report, first published in 1890 but still available in paperback. Mooney persuaded his Washington superiors to allow him to roam the West in search of first-hand evidence and even interviewed Wovoka, the Ghost Dance prophet, in person.

Marc Reisner *Cadillac Desert*. Concise, engaging account of the environmental and political impact on the West of the twentieth-century mania for dam-building and huge irrigation projects.

Meriwether Lewis and William Clark *The Original Journals of the Lewis and Clark Expedition, 1804–1806*. Eight volumes of meticulous jottings by the Northwest's first inland explorers, scrupulously following President Jefferson's orders to record every detail of flora, fauna and native inhabitant.

Richard White *It's Your Misfortune And None of My Own*. Dense, authoritative and all-embracing history of the American West, which debunks the notion of the rugged pioneer by stressing the role of the federal government.

Roderick Frazier Nash *Wilderness and the American Mind*. Classic study of the American take on environmental and conservation issues over the past couple of hundred years. Especially good sections on John Muir and his battles to preserve Yosemite.

Tim Flannery *The Eternal Frontier*. "Ecological" history of North America that reveals how the continent's physical environment has shaped the destinies of all its inhabitants, from horses to humans.

BIOGRAPHY AND ORAL HISTORY

Donald A. Barclay, James H. Maguire and Peter Wild (eds) *Into the Wilderness Dream*. Gripping collection of Western exploration narratives written between 1500 and 1800; thanks to any number of little-known gems, the best of many such anthologies.

Joanna L. Stratton *Pioneer Women*. Original memoirs of women – mothers, teachers, homesteaders and circuit riders – who ventured across the plains from 1854 to 1890. Lively, superbly detailed accounts, with chapters on journeys, homebuilding, daily domestic life, the church, the cow-town, temperance and suffrage.

T.J. Stiles *Custer's Trials: A Life on the Frontier of a New America*. No-holds-barred biography of one of the most charismatic figures of the frontier West, at once a genuinely brave general and a self-aggrandizing glamour-puss.

William F. Cody *The Life of Hon. William F. Cody, Known as Buffalo Bill*. Larger-than-life autobiography of one of the Wild West's greatest characters, treasurable for the moment when he refers to himself more formally as "Bison William".

TRAVEL WRITING

Bill Bryson *The Lost Continent*. Using his boyhood home of Des Moines in Iowa as a benchmark, the author travels the length and breadth of America to find the perfect small town. Hilarious, if at times a bit smug.

FICTION

A.B. Guthrie Jr *Big Sky*. When published in the Thirties it shattered the image of the mythical West. Realistic historical fiction at its very best, following desperate mountain man and fugitive Boone Caudill, whose idyllic life in Montana was ended by the arrival of white settlers.

E. Annie Proulx *Close Range: Wyoming Stories*. Proulx's masterly Wyoming-set short stories includes *Brokeback Mountain*. See also *Bad Dirt: Wyoming Stories 2*, though not as good.

Emily M. Danforth *The Miseducation of Cameron Post*. Compelling LGBTQ coming-of-age story set in Miles City, Montana, tackling the controversial issue of "conversion therapy".

James A. Michener *Centennial*. Michener's easy-to-read

saga is based on the fictional town of Centennial, but is set amidst the real history of north-east Colorado, from prehistory to the modern day.

Marilynne Robinson *Housekeeping*. The award-winning author is thought to have based the fictional town of Fingerbone, Idaho in her haunting 1980 novel following the lives of here women on her hometown of Sandpoint.

Norman MacLean *A River Runs Through It.* Unputdownable – the best-ever novel about fly-fishing, set in beautiful Montana lake country.

Owen Wister *The Virginian*. Wister's most famous Western novel, is still a good read, set in 1880s Wyoming.

Peter Heller *Dog Stars*. Enigmatic story set in post-apocalyptic Colorado, part love story, with shades of Mad Max. Heller's subsequent novels also tend feature the Rockies states.

Film

The list below focuses on key films in certain genres that have helped define the Old West and the Rockies – both the light and the dark. Those tagged with the ★ symbol are particularly recommended.

MUSIC/MUSICALS

Calamity Jane (David Butler, 1953). The Western gets a rumbustious musical twist with Doris Day bringing thigh-slapping gusto to the title role and Howard Keel as the rugged hero who (almost) tames her.

WESTERNS

Once Upon a Time in the West (Sergio Leone, 1968). The quintessential spaghetti Western, filmed in Spain by an Italian director, but steeped in mythic American themes.

Red River (Howard Hawks, 1948). Upstart Montgomery Clift battles beef-baron John Wayne on a momentous cattle drive through the Midwest. Prototypical Hawks tale of clashing tough-guy egos and no-nonsense professionals on the range.

★ **The Searchers** (John Ford, 1956). Perhaps Ford's most iconic Western, with vivid cinematography and epic scale; John Wayne relentlessly hunts down the Native American chief who massacred his friends and family.

The Wild Bunch (Sam Peckinpah, 1969). A movie that says as much about the chaotic end of the 1960s as it does about the West, featuring a band of killers who hunt for women and treasure and wind up in a bloodbath unprecedented in film history.

AMERICANA

Badlands (Terrence Malick, 1973). Midwest loner-loser Martin Sheen and girlfriend Sissy Spacek cross the Montana badlands on a random murder spree. Life on the road as a metaphor for existential futility.

There Will Be Blood (Paul Thomas Anderson, 2007). This unsettling epic saga of America's turn-of-the-century oil boom differs from Upton Sinclair's novel, *Oil!* in unexpected ways to become dominated by Daniel Day-Lewis, whose magisterial performance as monstrous prospector Daniel Plainview raises disturbing questions about the American Dream.

ON LOCATION

Although many memorable sights are off-limits to the public or exist only on backlot tours of movie-studio theme parks, countless filmmaking locations are accessible to visitors. This list provides an overview of notable films shot in the Rockies.

A River Runs Through It (Robert Redford, 1992). Bozeman and Livingston, Montana. See page 86.

Butch Cassidy & the Sundance Kid (George Roy Hill, 1969). Silverton, Durango and Telluride, Colorado. See page 86.

Close Encounters of the Third Kind (Steven Spielberg, 1978). Devils Tower, Wyoming. See page 86.

Dante's Peak (Roger Donaldson, 1997). Wallace, Idaho. See page 86.

The Horse Whisperer (Robert Redford, 1998). Livingston, Montana.

The Revenant (Alejandro G. Iñárritu, 2015). Kootenai Falls and Glacier Country in northern Montana.

Shane (George Stevens, 1953). Wyoming: Grand Teton National Park (see page 86); Jackson Hole. See page 90.

The Thing (Christian Nyby/Howard Hawks, 1951). Glacier National Park, Montana. See page 103.

Wind River (Taylor Sheridan, 2017). Wind River Reservation, Wyoming. See page 103.

Small print and index

A ROUGH GUIDE TO ROUGH GUIDES

Published in 1982, the first Rough Guide – to Greece – was a student scheme that became a publishing phenomenon. Mark Ellingham, a recent graduate in English from Bristol University, had been travelling in Greece the previous summer and couldn't find the right guidebook. With a small group of friends he wrote his own guide, combining a contemporary, journalistic style with a thoroughly practical approach to travellers' needs.

The immediate success of the book spawned a series that rapidly covered dozens of destinations. And, in addition to impecunious backpackers, Rough Guides soon acquired a much broader readership that relished the guides' wit and inquisitiveness as much as their enthusiastic, critical approach and value-for-money ethos. These days, Rough Guides include recommendations from budget to luxury and cover more than 120 destinations around the globe, from Amsterdam to Zanzibar, all regularly updated by our team of roaming writers.

Browse all our latest guides, read inspirational features and book your trip at **roughguides.com**.

Rough Guide credits

Editor: Beth Williams
Cartography: Carte
Picture editor: Tom Smyth

Layout: Katie Bennett
Head of DTP and Pre-Press: Katie Bennett
Head of Publishing: Kate Drynan

Publishing information

First edition 2022

Distribution

UK, Ireland and Europe
Apa Publications (UK) Ltd; sales@roughguides.com
United States and Canada
Ingram Publisher Services; ips@ingramcontent.com
Australia and New Zealand
Booktopia; retailer@ booktopia.com.au
Worldwide
Apa Publications (UK) Ltd; sales@roughguides.com

Special Sales, Content Licensing and CoPublishing

Rough Guides can be purchased in bulk quantities
at discounted prices. We can create special editions,
personalised jackets and corporate imprints tailored to
your needs. sales@roughguides.com.
roughguides.com

Printed in Spain

A catalogue record for this book is available from the
British Library

The publishers and authors have done their best to
ensure the accuracy and currency of all the information
in **The Rough Guide to USA: The Rockies**, however,
they can accept no responsibility for any loss, injury, or
inconvenience sustained by any traveller as a result of
information or advice contained in the guide.

Help us update

We've gone to a lot of effort to ensure that this edition
of **The Rough Guide to USA: The Rockies** is accurate
and up-to-date. However, things change – places get
"discovered", opening hours are notoriously fickle,
restaurants and rooms raise prices or lower standards. If
you feel we've got it wrong or left something out, we'd like
to know, and if you can remember the address, the price,
the hours, the phone number, so much the better.

Please send your comments with the subject line
"Rough Guide USA: The Rockies Update" to mail@
uk.roughguides.com. We'll credit all contributions and
send a copy of the next edition (or any other Rough Guide
if you prefer) for the very best emails.

ABOUT THE AUTHOR

Stephen Keeling has lived in New York City since 2006 and has written several titles for
Rough Guides, including the guide to New York City, California, Puerto Rico, New England,
Florida, Canada and the US's national parks.

Photo credits

(Key: T-top; C-centre; B-bottom; L-left; R-right)

Index

Map symbols

The symbols below are used on maps throughout the book

International boundary	International airport	Spring	Boat
State/province boundary	Domestic airport/airfield	National Park	Hindu/Jain temple
Chapter division boundary	Transport stop	Gate/park entrance	Church (regional maps)
Interstate highway	Parking	State capital	Church (town maps)
US highway	Post office	Lighthouse	Cemetery
State highway	Information centre	Statue	Building
Pedestrianized road	Hospital/medical centre	Bridge	Stadium
Path	Cave	Battle site	Park/forest
Railway	Point of interest	Ski	Beach
Funicular	Viewpoint/lookout	Mountain range	Native American reservation
Coastline	Campground	Mountain peak	
Ferry route	Museum	Swamp/marshland	
National Parkway	Monument/memorial	Tree	
Metro/subway	Fountain/garden	Gorge	
Tram/trolleybus	Waterfall	Arch	